# Reforming the Law of Nature

**Edinburgh Studies in Comparative Political Theory & Intellectual History**
Series Editor: Vasileios Syros

*Edinburgh Studies in Comparative Political Theory & Intellectual History* welcomes scholars interested in the comparative study of intellectual history/political ideas in diverse cultural contexts and periods of human history and Comparative Political Theory (CPT).

The series addresses the core concerns of CPT by placing texts from various political, cultural and geographical contexts in conversation. It calls for substantial reflection on the methodological principles of comparative intellectual history in order to rethink some of the conceptual categories and tools used in the comparative exploration of political ideas. The series seeks original, high-quality monographs and edited volumes that challenge and expand the canon of readings used in teaching intellectual history and CPT in Western universities. It will showcase innovative and interdisciplinary work focusing on the comparative examination of sources, political ideas and concepts from diverse traditions.

**Available Titles:**
*Reforming the Law of Nature: The Secularisation of Political Thought, 1532–1689*
Simon P. Kennedy

*Recovering the Political Economy of British Classical Liberalism: Natural Rights and the Harmony of Interests*
Lee Ward

# Reforming the Law of Nature

## The Secularisation of Political Thought, 1532–1689

SIMON P. KENNEDY

EDINBURGH
University Press

Edinburgh University Press is one of the leading university presses in the UK. We publish academic books and journals in our selected subject areas across the humanities and social sciences, combining cutting-edge scholarship with high editorial and production values to produce academic works of lasting importance. For more information visit our website: edinburghuniversitypress.com

© Simon P. Kennedy, 2022

Edinburgh University Press Ltd
The Tun – Holyrood Road
12(2f) Jackson's Entry
Edinburgh EH8 8PJ

Typeset in 11/15 Adobe Sabon by
IDSUK (DataConnection) Ltd

A CIP record for this book is available from the British Library

ISBN 978 1 4744 9398 7 (hardback)
ISBN 978 1 4744 9400 7 (webready PDF)
ISBN 978 1 4744 9401 4 (epub)

The right of Simon P. Kennedy to be identified as the author of this work has been asserted in accordance with the Copyright, Designs and Patents Act 1988, and the Copyright and Related Rights Regulations 2003 (SI No. 2498).

# Contents

# Acknowledgements

I am grateful to a number of organisations for their financial support in the completion of this book. I was the blessed recipient of a Research Training Program Scholarship, supplied by the Australian Federal Government during the earliest stages of writing and research. I was also awarded a Fellowship from the Davenant Institute, which allowed me to build my personal library as I worked on this project. Thanks to Brad Littlejohn, Steven Wedgeworth, Jake Meador and the other fine people at Davenant for their support. My thanks also extend to the Australian Academy of Humanities for providing a publication subsidy for the final stages of the project.

The substance of this book came into being under the watchful eye of Peter Harrison and Leigh T. I. Penman, whilst I was working on my PhD at the Institute for Advanced Studies in the Humanities (IASH) at the University of Queensland. Their mentorship, advice, guidance and scholarship are some of the main reasons I was able to complete the work. I am indebted to Mark Earngey for his careful reading of a draft of the manuscript, and to Stephen Wolfe for his comments on the introduction and conclusion. Cary Nederman and Mark Goldie provided invaluable feedback in their examination reports of my thesis, which I believe I have taken on board, and which was very useful for expanding it into book form. They were model scholars: critical, incisive, generous and fair. I want to make special mention of Cary, who has helped me navigate the often bewildering world of academic publishing.

My first experience working with a press on a book manuscript has been, frankly, quite delightful, thanks to the generous and professional people at Edinburgh University Press. Gillian Leslie, Ersev

Ersoy, Joannah Duncan, Caroline Richards and Sarah Foyle were enthusiastic and supportive at each step. Thanks to Vasileios Syros for giving me the privilege of being an early part of the Edinburgh Studies in Comparative Political Theory and Intellectual History series. There are no doubt others I have neglected to mention who deserve recognition.

Numerous people provided friendship, support, mentorship or guidance at various stages along the way, including (in no particular order) Nicholas Aroney, George Duke, Michelle Pfeffer, James Ungureanu, Brendan Walsh, Ben Saunders, George Duke, Stephen Chavura, Jonathan Cole, Paul Henderson, Bruce Pass, Ian Hunter, Seung-Joo Lee, Brad Littlejohn, Ben Nelson and Peter Hastie. Special mention should go to the Reformed Irenics, who were a stimulating source of ideas, encouragement and discussion.

I have benefited from some wonderful colleagues and opportunities at Christian Heritage College during the final stages of writing. Ben Myers and Aaron Ghiloni were encouraging and wise. They provided ample friendship and advice at various points in the journey. To my colleagues at the University of Queensland, particularly those at IASH, I extend my thanks. I want to make special mention of the UQ Library staff for cheerfully responding to, and fulfilling, my seemingly endless list of requests for chapters, books and articles.

I am grateful and indebted to my parents Paul and Meredith. They have looked on with some bemusement at my pursuit of early modern intellectual history and have nevertheless been supportive in innumerable ways. Thanks for your love and care over decades. This book is dedicated to you. I need to also honour Allan and Daphne (Peg) Kennedy, whose financial prudence provided the means for me to pursue my doctorate full-time.

And last, I must acknowledge my *oikos*. My children, Lydia, Lesla, Judson, Adelaide and Calvin have been a genuine and constant delight. They also provided me with the necessary grounding in true reality when the world of scholarship became an all-consuming alternative reality. My wife, Hayley, has been with me every step towards the publication of this monograph. She has supported me, prayed with me, prayed for me, encouraged me, and, not unimportantly, fed me. Scholars need companions, and she is the most beautiful and best companion one could ask for.

# Abbreviations, Citations and Style

References to Augustine of Hippo, *De civitate Dei*, will be cited as DCD [book]:[section]. Translations of this work are taken from Augustine, *The City of God against the pagans*, ed. and trans. R. W. Dyson (Cambridge: Cambridge University Press, 1998). Reference with quotations will be cited as follows: Augustine, DCD, [book]:[chapter], [page number from Dyson]. So, DCD, 19:15, 942.

References to Thomas Aquinas, *Summa Theologica*, will be in the following form: *ST* [part]-[part], [question number], [answer number]. References to sections as follows: 'Prima' (I), 'Secunda' (II). So, references to the 'Prima Secundae' will be 'Ia-IIae'. Translation from Thomas Aquinas, *The Summa Theologica*, trans. Fathers of the English Dominican Province (Chicago: Encyclopedia Britannica, 1952).

References to John Calvin's *Institutes of the Christian Religion* will be to John Calvin, *Institutio christianae religionis, in libros quatuor nunc primum digesta, certisque distincta capitibus, ad aptissimam methodum: aucta etiam tam magna accessione ut propemodum opus novum haberi possit* (Geneva: Robert I. Estienne, 1559). References to this work will be in the following form: *Institutes*, [book number], [chapter number], [section number]. Translations (unless otherwise noted) from John Calvin, *Institutes of the Christian Religion*, 2 volumes, trans. Ford L. Battles (Louisville, KY: Westminster John Knox Press, 2011).

References to John Calvin's works (other than the *Institutes*) will be from the *Joannis Calvini opera quae supersunt omnia* from the *Corpus Reformatorum*, ed. Guilielmus Baum, Eduardus Cunitz and Eduardus Reuss (Brunsvigae: C.A. Schwetschke, 1863), hereafter 'CO', and any translations used will be cited alongside them. Citations will appear as follows: [Sermon text/Commentary text]; CO [volume]:[page]; [translation volume reference], [page number of translation].

References to John Locke's *Two Treatises of Government* will be from John Locke, *Two Treatises of Government*, ed. Peter Laslett (Cambridge: Cambridge University Press, 1988), and will be cited as TT, [Treatise number]:[chapter number], [page number in Laslett].

References to Martin Luther, *Luther's Works*, ed. Jaroslav Pelikan et al. (St Louis, MO: Concordia Publishing House, 1955–), will be cited *LW*, [volume]:[page].

References to *Leviathan* will be from Thomas Hobbes, *Leviathan*, ed. Richard Tuck (Cambridge: Cambridge University Press, 1991). I will cite as follows: *Lev* [chapter number in Roman numerals], [page number from the 1651 'Head' edition of Leviathan]:[page number from Tuck's edition].

References to the Holy Bible will be in the standard form of [Book] [chapter]:[verse]. E.g. Romans 1:25. Translation will be from the English Standard Version (Wheaton, IL: Crossway, 2007), unless otherwise stated.

For early modern texts in languages other than English I have, where necessary or possible, cited the original primary source and then cited the translation which I am using. I will note if it is my own translation in the corresponding footnote.

When quoting sources, I retain the original spelling from the source, whether primary or secondary sources. References to 'man' as referring to humanity or humankind will be avoided where possible, although where a gendered pronoun is used in a source the original wording will be retained.

# Introduction

In this book, I will address changes over time to Reformed Protestant conceptions of natural law. This exercise is significant because, I contend, these changes contributed to the desacralisation of theories of the origins of political life. This desacralisation contributed to a further phenomenon: the secularisation of political thought during the sixteenth and seventeenth centuries. When early Reformed Protestant figures wrote about natural law, they tended to do so in a way that was reflective of the scholastic and Aristotelian inheritance from medieval theology, philosophy and jurisprudence. God governed the universe, in part through the natural law. Humans were naturally social and political, and therefore human political life was part of God's creation order. It was a theistic foundation for politics. This changed when the emphasis in theories of natural law shifted from a theistic basis to an anthropocentric basis. Certain Reformed thinkers, some of whom were extremely influential on the shaping of western political philosophy, based their understanding of the law of nature upon human self-preservation, rather than on God. At the same time, these thinkers conceived of political existence as an artifice, rather than divinely created. If the law of nature did not issue from God, then any human political disposition reflective of human nature must be artificial. Therefore, political life was also desacralised. Here, we see the emptying of the sacred from politics.

A contemporary application lies fallow in this historical argument. The secularisation of anything, let alone something as important as politics, is likely to have consequences. Readers attuned to questions about the viability and vitality of liberal democracy might have come across certain critiques of the secular roots, and secular horizon, of political liberalism. While this intellectual history does not directly address the religious roots of liberalism, the findings and conclusion do raise a question about whether the roots of liberalism were unstable from the beginning. Perhaps something could be amiss in the dominant western political ideology of the nineteenth, twentieth and twenty-first centuries. Some scholars and commentators look to the theoretical to explain liberalism's apparent weakness.[1] Others look to history.

James Davison Hunter, for instance, argues that the emergence of a secular understanding of political life lies at the heart of the instability of liberalism. Core to the cultural logic of liberal democracy is what Davison Hunter calls the 'fragile . . . synthesis of Reformed and Enlightenment traditions'.[2] Perhaps, then, we are living with the effects of the coming apart of this synthesis.[3] Davison Hunter's claim is problematic and difficult to prove. But there is a certain logic to the idea that something with a religious foundation would become unstable if that foundation were removed. If the roots of liberalism were religious, and specifically Christian, then the problem is that 'the cultural logic' of liberal democracy has 'lost credibility'.[4] This volume aims to provide some of the pivotal historical background to the philosophical and theological foundations of liberalism through an examination of the 'Reformed' part of Davison Hunter's synthesis. The following chapters outline how certain thinkers in the Reformed tradition conceptualised the nature of political life between the 1530s and the 1680s. More precisely, this work addresses the period between 1532, when John Calvin published his commentary on Seneca's *De clementia*, and 1689, when John Locke anonymously published *Two Treatises of Government*. My proposal is that looking at these early Reformed thinkers might help us understand how this particular tradition manifested an instability at the root of liberalism.

In sum, this volume focuses on Reformed Protestant political and legal thought. It places important thinkers in their theological and political contexts whilst arguing for a new understanding of key aspects of Reformed natural law jurisprudence through an interdisciplinary approach which draws on jurisprudence, theology and philosophy.[5] This results in important forerunners to the modern Protestant jurists being re-examined in light of the Reformed tradition. The significance of scholastic natural law in the formation of Reformed jurisprudence is also a pivotal theme in what follows. This historical examination of the emergence of Reformed natural law jurisprudence provides the grounds for reassessing the origins of secular natural law theories in light of their sacralised predecessors, whilst also raising fresh questions about the origins, and continuing viability, of western liberalism.

## Secularisation and Early Modern Political Thought

A key claim in this book is that Reformed Protestants maintained continuity with the medieval tradition which saw God as the founder of, and ultimate legislator for, political life. Political life was understood as natural in the sense that there was a natural causation for political existence. However, God had a concurring role through His creation of nature and the natural order.[6] Undergirding this 'theistic political naturalism' was a theistic natural law theory. However, a shift occurred in Reformed political thought when natural law was reimagined and, because of that reimagining, God was no longer understood as the primary agent in the origins of political life. This book argues that these desacralised theories of natural law and the origins of politics laid the foundation for the secularisation of political life more generally.[7] But what do I mean by 'secularisation' and 'desacralisation'? In the case of secularisation, the term is multivalent and highly contested. Further, both secularisation and desacralisation can be used alongside one another for similar purposes. By 'secularisation' and 'desacralisation' I have in mind the first of Charles Taylor's types of 'secularity': the removal of God from public spaces and, more specifically, the political sphere and political discourse.[8] These changes in ideas of natural law and, consequently, the desacralisation of the origins of politics contributed to the broader secularisation of political thought across the early modern period.

The chapters below focus on the political thought of five thinkers within the broad Reformed tradition, and their understanding of natural law and the origins of political life. This analysis of these exemplary thinkers will shed light on the question of how the desacralisation of ideas of political life came about in the early modern period. The ideas of 'the origins of society' and the related 'origins of political life' are central to this discussion. While a full account of this notion will emerge in the ensuing discussion, it is worth offering a cursory definition here. When we approach the question of the origins of society, we are really approaching the question of political anthropology. Thinkers who address the questions 'Why are we in society?' and 'Why are we political?'

are answering a set of questions which undergird it. They are questions about political anthropology; questions about human nature, humanity's relationship to the rest of nature, one human's relationship to another. The thinkers examined here approached the question of societal and political origins with detailed historical, mythological or speculative accounts of how humans joined together in society. Alternatively, they addressed the questions lying behind the question; they discussed human nature, the role of the natural law in providing social and political impulses in humanity, or even the role of an emotion, like fear, in their explanation for the existence of society and political life.

These commonplace, yet divergent, discussions of the origins of political life provide us with a powerful historical and theoretical lens through which we can analyse the relationship between natural law ideas, political thought, and secularisation.[9] At the beginning of the sixteenth century, natural law was generally linked to God's eternal law, with God himself as the legislator and enforcer of the natural law. Early Reformed thinkers held to this understanding of natural law whilst also believing that humans were, according to God's design, naturally political; they were 'theistic political naturalists'. In essence, political life was founded by God and in accordance with the natural law. However, this consensus in the Reformed tradition shifts during the seventeenth century and political life becomes understood as conventional. Political life becomes a human artefact; a human creation. I argue that this occurs because of an altered conception of natural law. The *lex naturalis* came to be understood as a summation of, and even a prop for, pre-political 'natural rights'. Natural law was understood to be directed towards human self-preservation and human sociability, whereas the older conception of natural law was directed towards conformity to God's eternal law. These pre-political natural rights were natural and divinely ordained, but they also demanded protection. Their defence required people to be political and humans were consequently presented as the chief instigator of political life. This understanding purported that political life, while not against God's law, was not divinely mandated as such. God was no longer understood as the primary agent in the creation of human society and, as a result, the idea of political life was desacralised. The transcendent foundation of political life was, therefore, undermined.

There have been numerous attempts by scholars to account for the emergence of a secular conception of political life in the west.

Ethicist and political theologian Oliver O'Donovan has traced the desacralisation of political life through the changing understandings of the role of civil government over time. His historical narrative is centred on the Judeo-Christian understanding of government, the earliest phase of which was characterised by a reliance on divine law for governmental juridical activity. Government was understood to be focused on the act of judgement rather than legislation.[10] O'Donovan argues, though, that this changes over the medieval period until we reach the seventeenth century. '[T]he act of human foundation ceased to depend on divine foundation' and political thinkers found themselves 'presupposing no prior law, no pre-existing social rationality'.[11] Humanity was now the creator and legislator of society, and political life was no longer sacred.[12] But what of the natural law's role in all of this? A similar argument, with a brief acknowledgement of the role of natural law theories, is mounted by Charles Taylor. He suggests that older conceptions of reality framed nature and society as having the duty to conform themselves to pre-existing transcendent norms. The early moderns, on the other hand, developed a view where society was understood as something that humans could construct (or reconstruct) according to reason.[13] Political life was, for Taylor, desacralised because it was no longer understood as a creation of God within His cosmological order, but a 'precipitate of common action'.[14]

A different position is maintained by medievalist and historian Francis Oakley, who addresses the emergence of secular western political thought through the lens of sacral kingship. The idea of sacral kingship was, according to Oakley, inherited from pagan peoples and baptised by Eusebian political theology.[15] The rediscovery of Roman law and Aristotelian naturalism broke the continuity of a political theology of sacral kingship which resulted in a much clearer demarcation between (political) things sacred and things secular.[16] In other words, the western conception of a desacralised political realm was founded upon a theological debate about divine right ecclesiastical authority, with Aristotelian political naturalism providing fertile ground for a secular conception of political life. Similarly, Quentin Skinner sees the rise of Aristotelian political naturalism as instrumental in the 'modern, naturalistic and secular view of political life'.[17] The Aristotelian insistence on the independence of civic philosophy, the idea of the kingdom (or commonwealth) as independent from an 'external superior', the acceptance of sole allegiance within the kingdom, and an emphasis on a temporal *telos*, or purpose, for politics, all played a role in the emergence of the idea of the modern state.[18] Skinner conceives of the secular nature of the early modern state as being caused by both a naturalising of how political life was understood and a desacralising of the purpose of political life. After removing the transcendent *telos*, God was also removed from politics. However, was Aristotelian naturalism quite so instrumental in the rise of secular conceptions of political life? The examples I expand upon in this volume demonstrate this was not necessarily the case.

There is a flowering of scholarship on early modern natural law which places it front and centre in the process of the secularisation of politics, with Ian Hunter being exemplary.[19] Hunter argues that the desacralisation of political thought was, in large part, driven by a recalibration of natural law theories around the need to defend the state 'against religious and moral deligitimation'.[20] Moves to 'detheologise politics' and separate civil and philosophical sciences from theological ones 'emerged as a response to the devastation of religious civil war'.[21] Natural law was reformulated around the concept of human sociability, becoming disconnected from the received conception of the *lex aeterna* as articulated by thinkers like Thomas Aquinas. Once natural law was decoupled from eternal law, theology was no longer connected to natural and civil jurisprudence.[22] In short, the desacralisation of political thought occurred via the pragmatic needs of the emerging modern state, a pattern exemplified by thinkers like Samuel Pufendorf (1632–1694) and Christian Thomasius (1655–1728).[23]

In what follows, I interact with these various accounts of the secularisation of early modern political ideas whilst challenging them at various points. My account recasts the role of natural law theories and political naturalism in the secularisation of political thought during the early modern period. Rather than being a harbinger of secularity, as is typically argued, political naturalism, be it of an Aristotelian or other variety, is shown to have been an outworking of a broadly scholastic approach to natural law which was a bulwark against secular conceptions of political life. Scholastic natural law theories were connected to an understanding that political life was natural and, therefore, connected to God through the natural law. This understanding of the nature of political life worked itself out in a sacral conception of political life. It also provides a counternarrative to the common claim that the Reformed Protestant tradition was a significant break from medieval scholasticism with regard to these questions. This might be true of some forms of later Reformed Protestantism, but the earliest thinkers examined here display substantial continuity with the earlier scholastic thinkers on questions of natural law and origins of politics.

Before continuing to the body of the argument, I will briefly enunciate the central concepts of the origins of political life and natural law, and offer a justification of my choice of historical subjects and historical method.

## Key Concepts

What do we mean by the origins of politics? Many early modern political thinkers addressed questions of human nature, the effects of the Fall of Adam, sociability, along with various other related issues. These fundamental questions then formed part of an answer to the question about human society's very existence, and the consequent existence of political life in that society. Theories of the origins of politics were attempts to answer the question about why humans are, to use Aristotle's famous dictum, political animals (*zoon politikon*). With the question of political origins, we are really asking: where did politics come from? This, in turn, informs how thinkers address normative questions about politics and society. These theories also point to an important distinction between society (that is, social life) and political life. The question has been addressed in numerous ways across history.[24] Cary Nederman has shown that the figures of Aristotle, Cicero and Augustine defined the approach to the question of societal and political origins throughout the medieval period.[25] These three figures, or some synthesis of their ideas, lie behind most of the reflections on political anthropology during the earliest decades of the early modern period. We shall observe a shift towards a different approach in the later chapters of this book, which I argue undergirds the secularisation of politics more generally.

A further key concept for the following chapters is 'natural law' or the law of nature. This venerable idea is evidenced in texts from classical Greece through to the early modern period, and is still a central *locus* of discussion in philosophy and jurisprudence today.[26] For example, Plato's god fashioned the previously disordered universe, taking 'it from disorder into order', with the goal of the universe 'by nature' reflecting the god's own orderly reason.[27] The idea of a teleological, ethical *kosmos* persisted, and eventually took on a juridical tone, with Greek, Roman and then Christian thinkers joining this concept of natural order to the divine mind.[28] This line of natural jurisprudence is exemplified by the thirteenth-century scholastic philosopher Thomas Aquinas

(1225–74). According to Thomas, natural law is the 'participation of the eternal in the rational creature'; that is, natural law is the rational creature grasping what is good and evil, and understanding the purpose of his own being implanted in his own nature.[29] In Thomas's concept of eternal law and natural law we can see two key elements of the Christian natural law tradition: God's governance of the entire universe through an overarching law, and the creature's participation in that eternal law through the natural law. For Thomas, practical reason is, to quote Christopher Tollefsen, 'reason directed toward action', a reason emanating from man's knowledge of the natural law and applied to particular circumstances.[30] Natural law and human law are connected, for Thomas, because human law is, like natural law, shaped according to the 'rule of reason'.[31] Here, we see a connection between natural law and political life. In Thomas's thought, the *polis* is a natural institution founded upon natural law, but that natural law is connected to the eternal law and, therefore, has a transcendent purpose.

It would be accurate to say, as J. P. Canning does, that the Aristotelian–Christian synthesis produced a natural law theory which provided 'an apparently complete and systematic naturalistic view of the world, the heavens and man's life purpose'. But Canning also notes that this naturalism was never consistently worked out. 'God remained in the background as the creator of the natural world.'[32] Therefore, God remained the creator and legislator of the natural law. Other scholastics, namely voluntarists, diverged in some important ways from this intellectualist rendering of the divine and natural order, and yet retained the basic connection between God's eternal law and the ordering and ends of nature. While the voluntarist privileged God's will above his reason, they also understood that natural law as a dictate of right reason.[33] In sum, we can say with a level of generality that in the long history leading up to the early 1500s, God was understood to be intimately involved in both the structuring and working of the world through the legislation of natural law, and a part of this natural law was, often, the establishment of political life. As will be demonstrated in the chapters below, things were understood very differently by the turn of the eighteenth century. Human political life became an artificial creation, and natural law became focused around a conception of basic human sociability and natural rights, rather than a transcendent moral order and eternal law. The predominant theory of politics then became desacralised.

## People, Texts and Contexts

The following chapters address themselves to these questions by tracing ideas through different texts across a period of just over 150 years. I have chosen five figures to examine who fit within the Reformed tradition, a tradition which numerous scholars take to be important to the shaping of western liberalism. The first chapter will focus on the thought of John Calvin (1509–64). Including Calvin in this list ought to be uncontroversial. While recent scholarship has certainly tempered the near obsession with Calvin in studies of the Reformed tradition, there is little question that he exerted a substantial influence on those that followed him in Reformed Protestantism.[34] Likewise, Calvin's writings contain distinctive contributions to the questions of natural law and political origins. English divine Richard Hooker (1554–1600) is the next subject, and he is the first who might raise some eyebrows due to the tendency in some circles to claim him for *via media* Anglicanism.[35] However, large swathes of scholarly work on Hooker endorse his affinity with magisterial Reformed Protestantism.[36] Johannes Althusius (1557–1638) occupies the next chapter and, like Calvin, his place within the Reformed tradition is hardly contestable.

Thomas Hobbes (1588–1679) and John Locke, whilst heterodox in important ways, can plausibly be placed in the broad English Reformed confessional culture. Hobbes, for example, self-identified his allegiance to the Church of England through his church attendance and his desire to receive the Lord's Supper.[37] He recognised only two sacraments, a key marker of Reformed Protestantism which was also in line with the Thirty-Nine Articles of the Church of England.[38] In certain key respects, Hobbes's understanding of how someone comes to faith in Christ cohered closely with Reformed theology.[39] He explicitly affirmed the 'doctors of the Reformed Churches', on their understanding of free will, necessity and constraint. Indeed, the general shape of his political thought is deeply imbued with Reformed theology.[40] Locke's inclusion, while less controversial, is similarly fraught. And yet he was raised in a Puritan household, attended Christ Church, Oxford under the leadership the Reformed scholastic John Owen, and maintained an association with the Reformed wing of Protestantism through his connections with the Remonstrants and Socinians in Holland.[41] Indeed, while Locke's theological views would not pass the Reformed orthodoxy test, his political thought can be readily characterised as 'Calvinist'.[42]

The most influential of the various arguments linking Protestant-ism with the modern social order is, of course, Max Weber's, who casts the followers of Calvin in a starring role.[43] Weber's remark-able statement is focused on the interaction of religious belief, theologies of vocation, and commercial activity. The idea that there could be a close connection between particular Protestant religious convictions and modern life has proven extremely provocative and, to many, compelling. However, this volume aims to avoid a Weberian methodological weakness, which places too much onus on one particular religious tradition's putative responsibility for a particular historical outcome. There are others who cast Reformed Protestants in different, but no less significant, roles more closely related to jurisprudence and political thought.[44] Davison Hunter's recent discussion of the instability of liberal democracy is a case in point.[45] The figure of John Locke (1632–1704) features at the centre of his discussion. Locke, so often cast as a precursor and progenitor of much western liberal political thought today, is the final figure considered in this book. His true influence on liberal ideals is rightly contested.[46] However, seen through the lens of hindsight, there seems little doubt that his thought is exemplary of Davison Hunter's synthesis between Enlightenment ideals (which are famously elusive and infamously wielded today) and Reformed Protestantism. It is the Reformed Protestant aspect of the historical story of western political thought that we are interested in here, with a key problem being the role this line of thought played in the secularisation of political thought.

What do I mean by 'Reformed'? A confessional label can mean any number of things, but here Reformed refers to the non-Lutheran branch of the magisterial reformations. Finding figures who fit the label 'Reformed' could become a fraught exercise and, to some, my selection will look like a rather motley crew. But to exclude some from this conversation on the basis of theology alone would require some kind of test of the truth claims of Reformed Protes-tant orthodoxy.[47] There is no doubt that a category like 'Reformed' requires some boundary markers and, with Richard A. Muller's methodological concerns in mind, we will certainly make use of confessional documents in this study as a way of placing think-ers' particular philosophical and theological *loci* within or without the orthodoxy of the Reformed tradition.[48] However, dealing with questions which are broader than academic divinity or ecclesiology necessitates the discussion of figures who are part of the Reformed tradition in a loose sense. As Philip Benedict has noted, to apply a test of orthodoxy would 'silence half of the ongoing dialogue' within what was ultimately a broad tradition of thought, practice and confessional culture.[49]

In terms of method, I implement (imperfectly, no doubt) a contextualist approach to intellectual history. What follows describes a set of ideas which change over time. The contention here is that there is, to use Oakeshott's phrase, an observable 'passage of historical change' in ideas on the origins of politics.[50] The thoughts of the people which stretch between Calvin and Locke are antecedent historical events which sometimes have contingent relationships. The relationship between these ideas, insofar as they show some coherence to one another, is circumstantial. They are not treated as inevitable or necessary. The ideas are certainly linked, in that past ideas help make antecedent ideas what they are. However, things did not have to eventuate as they did.[51] Historical context will (naturally) be used to reconstruct these ideas with sufficient accuracy so that they can be better understood.[52]

Good history should tell us something about ourselves. My claim, as iterated above, is that these past events do just that. Only when we reconstruct political ideas from the past accurately can they help us understand ourselves. Cary Nederman's profound answer to the question of the relevance and utility is that 'the very "otherness", the foreignness' of ideas from the past 'may have salutary decentring effects upon our complaisant contemporary assumptions about political life and its relation to a whole host of other philosophical questions'.[53] Contemporary political problems and questions are extant because of what happened in the past. If we are able to better understand history we shall, to quote Nederman again, 'be better qualified to assess some of the presuppositions that haunt our political world'.[54] In defending the procedure of intellectual history, Skinner writes that 'our own society places unrecognized constraints upon our imaginations'.[55] We can place 'limits on those constraints' by looking into the ideas of the past.[56] The removal of a creative God from ideas concerning where political life comes from is an unrecognised constraint which bears careful consideration, and will occupy us for the remainder of this volume.

## Notes

1. For some examples of this kind of commentary, see the following: Edward Luce, *The Retreat of Western Liberalism* (London: Little, Brown, 2017); cf. Patrick Lee Miller's excellent review, 'The Implosion

of Western Liberalism', *Quillette*, http://quillette.com/2017/11/05/implosion-western-liberalism/ (accessed 8 November 2017); Ryszard Legutko, *The Demon in Democracy: Totalitarian Temptations in Free Societies* (New York: Encounter Books, 2016); John Milbank and Adrian Pabst, *The Politics of Virtue: Post-Liberalism and the Human Future* (Lanham, MD: Rowman & Littlefield, 2016), 35 and Chapter 1 more generally; Patrick J. Deneen, *Why Liberalism Failed* (New Haven, CT: Yale University Press, 2018), 29–30.

2. James Davison Hunter, 'Liberal Democracy and the Unraveling of the Enlightenment Project', *The Hedgehog Review* 19.3 (2017): 22–37, here 28. The word 'Calvinist' is problematic and will be avoided in this book. See Willem J. van Asselt, 'Calvinism as a Problematic Concept in Historiography', *International Journal of Philosophy and Theology* 72.2 (2013): 144–50; Richard A. Muller, *Calvin and the Reformed Tradition* (Grand Rapids, MI: Baker Academic, 2012), 51–69.

3. Davison Hunter, 'Liberal Democracy', 28; cf. Adam B. Seligman, *The Idea of Civil Society* (New York: Free Press, 1992), 29.

4. Davison Hunter, 'Liberal Democracy', 35.

5. See, for a recent justification of this approach, David P. Henreckson, *The Immortal Commonwealth: Covenant, Community, and Political Resistance in Early Reformed Thought* (Cambridge: Cambridge University Press, 2019), 2–3.

6. On the question of God's concurrence, see Alfred J. Freddoso, 'God's General Concurrence with Secondary Causes: Why Conservation is Not Enough', *Philosophical Perspectives* 5, Philosophy of Religion (1991): 553–85.

7. Cf. Hans Blumenberg's rejection of the idea of 'secularization' (*Verweltlichung*), in Hans Blumenberg, *The Legitimacy of the Modern Age*, trans. Robert M. Wallace (Cambridge, MA: MIT Press, 1983). Cf. Karl Löwith, *Meaning in History* (Chicago: University of Chicago Press, 1949), 191–203; Peter E. Gordon, 'The Idea of Secularisation in Intellectual History', in *Companion to Intellectual History*, ed. Richard Whatmore and Brian Young (Chichester: Wiley Blackwell, 2016), 230–46.

8. Charles Taylor, *A Secular Age* (Cambridge, MA: Belknap Press, 2007), 2.

9. The seminal article which pointed me in this direction was Cary J. Nederman, 'Nature, Sin and the Origins of Society: The Ciceronian Tradition in Medieval Political Thought', *Journal of the History of Ideas* 49.1 (1988): 3–26.

10. Oliver O'Donovan, 'Government as Judgement', *First Things*, April 1999, 37.

11. Ibid., 38.

12. Cf. Oliver O'Donovan, *The Desire of the Nations: Rediscovering the Roots of Political Theology* (Cambridge: Cambridge University Press, 1996), 236–42.

13. Taylor, *A Secular Age*, 125–6.

14. Ibid., 193–4; cf. ibid., 188–95. Cf. Blumenberg, *The Legitimacy of the Modern Age*, 137–43. A different, and equally interesting narrative, is found in Rémi Brague, *The Kingdom of Man: Genesis and Failure of the Modern Project* (Notre Dame, IN: Notre Dame University Press, 2018).

15. Francis Oakley, *Empty Bottles of Gentilism: Kingship and the Divine in Late Antiquity and the Early Middle Ages (to 1050)* (New Haven, CT: Yale University Press, 2010), 1–110.

16. See more generally Francis Oakley, *The Mortgage of the Past: Reshaping the Ancient Political Inheritance (1050–1300)* (New Haven, CT: Yale University Press, 2012); Francis Oakley, *The Watershed of Modern Politics: Law, Virtue, Kingship and Consent (1300–1650)* (New Haven, CT: Yale University Press, 2015). Particularly ibid., 172–285.

17. Quentin Skinner, *The Foundations of Modern Political Thought*, vol. 1: *The Renaissance* (Cambridge: Cambridge University Press, 1978), 50.

18. Quentin Skinner, *The Foundations of Modern Political Thought*, vol. 2: *The Age of Reformation* (Cambridge: Cambridge University Press, 1978), 349–52. Cf. Oakley, *The Watershed of Modern Politics*, 51–90.

19. Knud Haakonssen, *Natural Law and Moral Philosophy* (Cambridge: Cambridge University Press, 1996); Ian Hunter, *The Secularisation of the Confessional State: The Political Thought of Christian Thomasius* (Cambridge: Cambridge University Press, 2007); Ian Hunter and David Saunders, eds, *Natural Law and Civil Sovereignty: Moral Right and State Authority in Early Modern Political Thought* (Basingstoke: Palgrave Macmillan, 2002); Thomas Ahnert, 'Introduction', in Christian Thomasius, *Institutes of Divine Jurisprudence: With Selections from Foundations of the Law of Nature and Nations*, ed. and trans. Thomas Ahnert (Indianapolis: Liberty Fund, 2011), xi–xxiv; T. J. Hochstrasser, *Natural Law Theories in the Early Enlightenment* (Cambridge: Cambridge University Press, 2000); T. J. Hochstrasser and P. Schröeder, eds, *Early Modern Natural Law Theories: Context and Strategies in the Early Enlightenment* (Dordrecht: Springer, 2003); Ian Hunter and Richard Whatmore, eds, *Philosophy, Rights and Natural Law: Essays in Honour of Knud Haakonssen* (Edinburgh: Edinburgh University Press, 2019).

20. Ian Hunter and David Saunders, 'Introduction', in Samuel Pufendorf, *The Whole Duty of Man According to the Law of Nature* (Indianapolis: Liberty Fund, 2003), xii.

21. Ian Hunter, *Rival Enlightenments: Civil and Metaphysical Philosophy in Early Modern Germany* (Cambridge: Cambridge University Press, 2001), 14.

22. Ian Hunter, 'Natural Law as Political Philosophy', in *The Oxford Handbook of Philosophy in Early Modern Europe*, ed. Desmond M. Clarke and Catherine Wilson (Oxford: Oxford University Press, 2011), 475–6.

23. Key works include Samuel Pufendorf, *De officio hominis et civis juxta legem naturalem libri duo* (1673), and Christian Thomasius, *Institutiones iurisprudentiae divinae* (1688).

24. For example, see Plato, *The Republic*, 369b–370a; Aristotle, *Politics*, 1253a1–1253a40; Cicero, *De republica*, I.39a–40; Cicero, *De inventione*, I.1–3; Philo, *Questions on Genesis*, 1.26, 1.27, 1.29; Augustine, DCD, 12:28, 14:11, 19:14–15; Wyclif, *De civili dominio*, 1.1–1.18; Thomas Aquinas, *De regimine principum*, 1.1; ST Ia-IIae, Q. 96; Marsilius of Padua, *Defensor pacis*, 1.3.1–1.3.5; John of Salisbury, *Policraticus*, 4.21; John of Salisbury, *Metalogicon*, 1.1.

25. Nederman, 'Nature, Sin and the Origins of Society', 3–26.

26. Merio Scattola, 'Before and After Natural Law: Models of Natural Law in Ancient and Modern Times', in *Early Modern Natural Law Theories*, ed. Hochstrasser and Schröeder, 1–30; Perez Zagorin, *Hobbes and the Law of Nature* (Princeton, NJ: Princeton University Press, 2009), chapter 1.

27. Plato, *Timaeus*, 29d–30c; translation from *Plato's Cosmology: The Timaeus of Plato*, trans. Francis McDonald Cornford (Indianapolis: Hackett, 1997), 33–4.

28. On this, see the detailed accounts in Rémi Brague, *The Wisdom of the World: The Human Experience of the Universe in Western Thought* (Chicago: University of Chicago Press, 2003); Rémi Brague, *The Law of God: The Philosophical History of an Idea* (Chicago: University of Chicago Press, 2007). Cf. Aristotle, *Physics*, II.1; Cicero, *De republica*, II.23; ibid., III.23; Seneca, *Naturales quaestiones*, 3.16.4, 3.29.4, 6.1.12; Genesis 1 & Romans 2:14; Augustine, *De Trinitate contra Arianos libri quindecim*, 14.15; Augustine, *De Sermone in Monte secundum Matthaeum*, II.19.32; Isidore, *Etymologies*, 5.2 & 5:4; Gratian, *Decretum*, 1; ibid., Dist. 1, C.7; ibid., Dist. 6, C.3; ST Ia-IIae, Q. 90–95.

29. ST Ia-IIae, Q. 91, a. 2; Hunter, 'Natural Law as Political Philosophy', 477.

30. ST Ia-IIae, Q. 91, a. 3; ibid., IIa-IIae, Q. 94, a. 2; Christopher Tollefsen, 'Natural Law, Basic Goods and Practical Reason', in *The Cambridge Companion to Natural Law Jurisprudence*, ed. George Duke and Robert P. George (Cambridge: Cambridge University Press, 2017), 134.

31. ST Ia-IIae, Q. 95, a. 2.

32. J. P. Canning, 'Introduction: Politics, Institutions, Ideas', in *Cambridge History of Medieval Political Thought*, ed. J. H. Burns (Cambridge: Cambridge University Press, 1988), 360–1.

33. Francis Oakley, *Natural Law, Laws of Nature, Natural Rights: Continuity and Discontinuity in the History of Ideas* (New York: Continuum, 2005), 69–80. Cf. Otto Gierke, *Political Theories of the Middle Age* (Boston, MA: Beacon Press, 1958), 172–3; Francis Oakley, 'Medieval Theories of Natural Law: William of Ockham and the Significance of the Voluntarist Tradition', *Natural Law Forum* 6 (1961): 66–70. A sprawling, largely unconvincing account of the

impact of nominalism and voluntarism is Michael Allen Gillespie, *The Theological Origins of Modernity* (Chicago: University of Chicago Press, 2008). Cf. Brad S. Gregory, *Unintended Reformation* (Cambridge, MA: Harvard University Press, 2012), 25–73.

34. Richard A. Muller, *Post-Reformation Reformed Dogmatics: The Rise and Development of Reformed Orthodoxy, ca. 1520 to 1725*, vol. 1: *Prolegomena to Theology* (Grand Rapids, MI: Baker Academic, 2003), 44–6.

35. Perhaps the foremost treatment of this comes from Lee W. Gibbs. See Lee W. Gibbs, 'Richard Hooker: Prophet of Anglicanism or English Magisterial Reformer?', *Anglican Theological Review* 84.4 (2002): 943–60; Lee W. Gibbs, 'Richard Hooker's *Via Media* Doctrine of Scripture and Tradition', *Harvard Theological Review* 95.2 (2002): 227–35.

36. For a good overview of this debate, see W. Bradford Littlejohn, 'The Search for Reformed Hooker: some modest proposals', *Reformation & Renaissance Review* 16.1 (2014): 68–82. Pre-eminent in asserting the magisterial Reformed Hooker is W. J. Torrance Kirby, *Richard Hooker's Doctrine of the Royal Supremacy* (Leiden: Brill, 1990); Nigel Atkinson, *Richard Hooker and the Authority of Scripture, Tradition and Reason: Reformed Theologian of the Church of England?* (Carlisle: Paternoster, 1997). More recently, see Paul Anthony Dominiak, *Richard Hooker: The Architecture of Participation* (London: T&T Clark, 2019). Cf. the various discussions of Hooker in Paul D. Avis, *The Church in the Theology of the Reformers* (London: Marshall Morgan & Scott, 1981).

37. Cf. A. P. Martinich, *Hobbes: A Biography* (Cambridge: Cambridge University Press, 1999), 207–8, 355; John Aubrey, *Brief Lives*, ed. Richard Barber (London: The Folio Society, 1975), 166.

38. *Lev* XXXV, 221:286.

39. Compare *Lev* XLIII, 323–43:405–6 with Calvin's *Commentary on Romans* 10:17, in CO 49:206–7. Also cf. Comm. John 6:45; CO 25:149–50.

40. For example, see Eldon J. Eisenach, 'Hobbes on Church, State and Religion', *History of Political Thought* 3.2 (1982): 215–43; Leopold Damrosch, Jr., 'Hobbes as Reformation Theologian: Implications of the Free-Will Controversy', *Journal of the History of Ideas* 40.3 (1979): 339–52. There is, I think, much more work to be done on the connections between Hobbes and Reformed Protestant theology, especially in relation to the architectonics of his political theory: state of nature, covenant, covenant head ('Sovereign'), and temporal salvation from the state of war.

41. Diego Lucci, *John Locke's Christianity* (Cambridge: Cambridge University Press, 2020), 50–8; Nathan Guy, *Finding Locke's God: The Theological basis of John Locke's Political Thought* (London: Bloomsbury, 2019), 54–9; Roger Woolhouse, *Locke: A Biography* (Cambridge:

Cambridge University Press, 2007), 198–9, 223–4, 350–4, 383–4; John Marshall, *John Locke: Resistance, Religion and Responsibility* (Cambridge: Cambridge University Press, 1994), 329–34.

42. Skinner characterises Locke's *Two Treatises* as 'the classic text of radical Calvinist politics', in *Foundations*, vol. 2, 239. Cf. John Dunn, *The Political Thought of John Locke: An Historical Account of the Argument of the 'Two Treatises of Government'* (Cambridge: Cambridge University Press, 1969), where he presents Locke's worldview, especially his social anthropology, as 'Calvinist'. Cf. the interesting analysis on Locke's critique of 'priestcraft' in Mark Goldie, 'John Locke, the Early Lockeans, and Priestcraft', *Intellectual History Review* 28.1 (2018): 125–44.

43. Max Weber, *Die protestantische Ethik und der Geist des Kapitalismus*, which was first published in *Archiv für Sozialwissenschaften* 20.1 (1904): 1–54; *Archiv für Sozialwissenschaften* 21.1 (1905): 1–110.

44. For example, see Gregory, *Unintended Reformation*; James Simpson, *Permanent Revolution: The Reformation and the Illiberal Roots of Liberalism* (Cambridge, MA: Belknap Press, 2019); Alec Ryrie, *Protestants: The Faith That Made the Modern World* (London: Penguin Random House, 2018); John Witte, Jr, *The Reformation of Rights: Law, Religion and Human Rights in Early Modern Calvinism* (Cambridge: Cambridge University Press, 2007).

45. Davison Hunter, 'Liberal Democracy'.

46. On Locke's reputation and the development of liberalism, see Duncan Bell, 'What is Liberalism?' *Political Theory* 42.6 (2014): 682–715, here 692–8; Samuel C. Rickless, *Locke* (Chichester: Wiley Blackwell, 2014), 169; John Baltes places Locke at the forefront of the development of liberalism, even if in a counter-intuitive way. See John Baltes, *The Empire of Habit: John Locke, Discipline, and the Origins of Liberalism* (Rochester, NY: University of Rochester Press, 2016). Cf. the role Alan Ryan gives Locke in his assessment of liberalism in Alan Ryan, *The Making of Modern Liberalism* (Princeton, NJ: Princeton University Press, 2012), 27–42. Further examples include Kim Ian Parker, *The Biblical Politics of John Locke* (Waterloo: Wilfrid Laurier University Press, 2004), 1–3; John Perry, *The Pretenses of Loyalty: Locke, Liberal Theory, and American Political Theology* (Oxford: Oxford University Press, 2011). An important contribution has recently been made by Tim Stanton. See his 'John Locke and the Fable of Liberalism', *The Historical Journal* 61.3 (2018): 597–622.

47. Cf. Jonathan Sheehan, 'Thomas Hobbes, D.D.: Theology, Orthodoxy, and History', *The Journal of Modern History* 88.2 (2016): 249–74.

48. Muller, *Post-Reformation Reformed Dogmatics*, vol. 1, 27–30.

49. Philip Benedict, *Christ's Churches Purely Reformed: A Social History of Calvinism* (New Haven, CT: Yale University Press, 2002), xxiv. For a more detailed discussion of the principles at play here, and the ideas

of a broader 'confessional culture', see Thomas Kauffmann, *Konfession und Kultur: Lutherischer Protestantismus in der zweiten Halfte des Reformationsjahrhunderts* (Tübigen: Mohr Siebeck, 2006), 3–26.

50. Michael Oakeshott, *On History and Other Essays* (Indianapolis: Liberty Fund, 1999), 121; cf. Quentin Skinner, *Visions of Politics,* vol. 1: *Regarding Method* (Cambridge: Cambridge University Press, 2002), 175–87.

51. Cf. Gregory, *Unintended Reformation*, 12, where he hints at this idea.

52. On the broader issue of historical method and importance of context for understanding ideas, see R. G. Collingwood, *The Idea of History* (Oxford: Oxford University Press, 1970), 215; Michael Oakeshott, *Lectures in the History of Political Thought*, ed. Terry Nardin and Luke O'Sullivan (Exeter: Imprint Academic, 2006), 32; cf. Quentin Skinner, 'Meaning and Understanding in the History of Ideas', *History and Theory* 8.1 (1969): 43. For a provocative argument in favour of the Cambridge School method, see Gordon J. Schochet, 'Why Should History Matter? Political Theory and the History of Discourse', in *The Varieties of British Political Thought, 1500–1800,* ed. J. G. A. Pocock, Gordon J. Schochet and Lois Schwoerer (Cambridge: Cambridge University Press, 1996), 321–57. More generally on the debate over the importance of context, influence and tradition in interpreting texts, see Francis Oakley, *Politics and Eternity: Studies in the History of Medieval and Early-Modern Political Thought* (Leiden: Brill, 1999), 1–24; Francis Oakley, 'In Praise of Prolepsis: Meaning, Significance and the Medieval Contribution to Political Thought', *History of Political Thought* 17.3 (2006): 416–18. My own approach, influenced by the Cambridge School, is summarised in Benjamin B. Saunders and Simon P. Kennedy, 'History and Constitutional Interpretation: Applying the "Cambridge School" Approach to Interpreting Constitutions', *Oxford Journal of Legal Studies* 40.3 (2020): 595–600.

53. Cary J. Nederman, *Lineages of European Political Thought: Explorations Along the Medieval/Modern Divide from John of Salisbury to Hegel* (Washington, DC: Catholic University of America Press, 2009), xv.

54. Ibid., 27.

55. Skinner, 'Meaning and Understanding', 53.

56. Ibid., 53.

# Chapter 1

# John Calvin's Political Naturalism

In 1532, a young humanist attempted to force his way into the illustrious upper echelons of classics scholarship by publishing a commentary on Seneca's *De clementia* (*On Clemency*). However, the commentary was received with no fanfare. The ambitious Frenchman's pride was wounded. This impressive work of classical scholarship would, in the end, recede into the background of the later theological works of that young Frenchman, John Calvin. As it turned out, more fame was to be had in his vocation as a Protestant Divine. Another thing related to the commentary that receded into the background, although remains present in Calvin's later works, is the Senecan emphasis on the social nature of humanity. In *De clementia*, Seneca states that '*hominem sociale animal communi bono genitum*'; that 'man' is a 'social animal begotten for the common good'.[1] Calvin, as we shall see, agreed with this sentiment in 1532, and he consistently reaffirmed it throughout his later theological and biblical writings. This embracing of the late Stoic understanding of humanity's social nature was consistent with a typical medieval Christian understanding of human nature, human society and natural law.

This chapter places Calvin within the broader sweep of Reformed Protestant ideas concerning natural law and politics. We will see that he articulated a natural law theory which maintained a close connection between God's governance of the universe and the natural law. In other words, the natural law is not secularised in Calvin's thought. And, because of this, his conception of political life is not secularised either, as he understands that humans are naturally political creatures as designed by God. For Calvin, humans are political because of the natural law. Calvin adhered to a form of theistic political naturalism, a naturalism which retained God's role in the establishment of human political life. This connection was ultimately broken later in the Reformed tradition, a fact which becomes evident in the latter part of the seventeenth century. However, for now, we can see quite clearly that the early Reformed thinkers like Calvin were political naturalists and retained a sacral view of political life.

Despite there being a wide range of scholarship on Calvin's natural jurisprudence, none of it draws the connection between his natural law thought and his understanding of the basis of political life.[2] This chapter aims to rectify this. To do this, and properly assess the key claim that Calvin was a political naturalist, there are two key questions we need to answer in this chapter. First, what is Calvin's view of natural law? We will find here that Calvin fits into the classical stream of natural law theory, rather than the more modern one which emerges in the antecedent Reformed thinkers we will consider in later chapters. Partly because of this view of natural law, Calvin retains a sacralised conception of political life. This leads to the second question: What was Calvin's understanding of the origins of politics? Here, we shall see that Calvin holds to the view, similar to that of the later Stoics, that humanity is naturally social. He also holds that humans are naturally political according to the prelapsarian order of creation. The grounds upon which this political nature manifests itself are altered post-Fall. However, what is most intriguing about Calvin's view of the origins of political life is the role of natural law. The role accorded to natural law in Calvin's thought undergirds a robust account of the continuity between prelapsarian and postlapsarian human relations. According to Calvin, God is the founder of human political life through his order of creation. This natural institution is given ongoing legitimacy and purpose in the postlapsarian world through the operations of the natural law, a law which is distinct from the divine and human positive law in Calvin's thought.

## The European Reformations, Calvin and Geneva

In his masterful social history of Reformed churches, Philip Benedict relates that, as a child, John Calvin would accompany his mother to a local abbey to venerate a fragment of the body of Saint Anne.[3] This is emblematic of Calvin's upbringing in a devout Christian household in northern France. Indeed, the young John, born in July 1509, was groomed for clerical life by his father through a thorough liberal education, supported by church benefices.[4] Calvin probably moved to Paris when he was fourteen, and began his university studies.[5] His place of learning, the Collège de Montaigu, provided a rigorous training, steeped in scholastic and Aristotelian logic and dialectic, and required its students to be skilled in Latin.[6] He pursued his studies in Paris until receiving a master's degree, and was then sent to study law at Orléans in 1528, moved to the University of Bourges in 1530, and then back to Paris in 1531.[7] Not only did he study law, but studying the trivium and quadrivium meant that Calvin almost certainly spent some time reading scholastic philosophers and theologians.[8] Being a law student meant that he would have had to deal with the question of natural law.[9]

The wildfire of Protestantism had well and truly spread across much of central and northern Europe by the time John Calvin published his commentary upon Seneca's *De clementia*. Here, we see Calvin's philosophical and scholarly interest in Stoic thought, an interest which continued his whole life. T. H. L. Parker writes that '[it] is said, perhaps without truth, that throughout his life he read all Cicero yearly'.[10] Even if the likelihood of Calvin reading all of Cicero on an annual basis pushes the limits of possibility, there is probably a seed of truth to this anecdote. Cicero was influential for Calvin, and his political anthropology reflects this Stoic influence, especially his understanding of humanity as naturally social.[11] However, the Stoics were not the only influence on the younger Calvin. Evangelical theology was to take a hold of his heart and mind as well. This came to affect his theology more generally, and his political anthropology in particular. It is unclear precisely when Calvin might have come to more 'Lutheran' convictions – some date it as early as 1528[12] – but his affinity with a speech by his university rector in 1533 which contained reforming themes gives us some indication of the trajectory of his thought and beliefs.[13] A wave of persecutions erupted in France in response to the spread of evangelical theology, and Calvin found it necessary to escape to the relative safe haven of Basle. The city was a bastion of reforming theology and could claim residents like Martin Bucer, Desiderius Erasmus and Johannes Oecolampadius. It was here that Calvin wrote and published the first edition of his *Institutio Christianae Religionis* (now known as the *Institutes of the Christian Religion*) in 1536.[14]

Elsewhere on the continent, the so-called Radical Reformation was taking a hold. Anabaptists were taking power in the Westphalian city of Münster in 1533, as well as spreading their ideas throughout the Low Countries. An Anabaptist monarchy was set up in Münster in 1534 under Jan van Leiden, who proclaimed a radical legal and social programme, including allowing polygamy and enforcing a sharing of all money and material goods. Leiden also announced his aim of world domination. Outside of Münster, the city's bishop, Franz of Waldeck, laid siege to the city for over a year, with it finally falling to the Roman Catholic forces in June 1535.[15] These tumultuous events would have a marked impact on Calvin's political ideas, as evident in his distaste for the anarchism implicit in much Anabaptist political theology. While much less violent and extreme in nature, confessional tensions also ebbed and flowed throughout the Swiss Confederation for the remainder of the decade.[16] Here we can see some of the experiential foundations for Calvin's insistence that politics is necessary for social life, and that politics mitigates human sin. Further, it certainly goes some way to explaining Calvin's concern for the stability of the political order in his political ideas. This concern is one which we see returning in a later chapter with Thomas Hobbes.

Calvin returned to France briefly to arrange some personal matters and, finding his path back to Basle blocked by military conflict, took an alternative route through Geneva. It was 1536, and his reputation as a theological mind, especially since the publication of the *Institutes*, went before him. When he passed through Geneva he was accosted by Guillaume Farel and virtually forced to remain in the city.[17] He accepted the office of 'reader' of scripture and helped cement the reforms that Farel had worked towards.[18] His time in Geneva was punctuated by controversy and a time of exile, but he earnestly began his project of religious and social reform in 1541.[19] His legal training, along with his theological fluency, allowed him to reshape both civil and ecclesiastical laws and regulations, and with the assistance of the city Council and his fellow pastors, Calvin enacted a practical and spiritual revolution in the city.[20] As a foreigner, he could not vote and was prevented from holding political office during the remainder of his time in Geneva. He was no dictator and had no right to coerce. And yet he managed to wield an unofficial influence through his moral and civic authority.[21] He had close involvement with the redrafting of Geneva's republican constitution, and he also constructed a new church law code, which included a consistory – a body designed to regulate and monitor the moral and spiritual conduct of congregants.[22] Most significantly for our purposes, Calvin continued to revise his *Institutes* until the final edition of 1559 which, amongst the dense theological reflections, contained various passages addressing the natural law, as well as a lengthy discussion of civil government. He also composed dozens of biblical commentaries, some of which shed light on his understanding of political anthropology, political life and the natural law.

## Natural Law and Divine Law

Even though the importance of Calvin's legacy is beyond doubt, various interpretations of his writings abound. Perhaps no area of Calvin's thought has been more contested than his understanding of natural law. His view of natural law is definitive, in certain respects, for my argument. I hope to demonstrate below that the natural law plays a positive role in Calvin's understanding of the nature and origins of politics. If, for Calvin, humans are naturally social and naturally political before the Fall, then the natural law will play an important role in providing continuity between the prelapsarian and postlapsarian social and political conditions for humanity.[23]

Calvin offers an outline of his jurisprudence in his commentary on Psalm 119:52 (1557). Here, we see his basic understanding of the divine law as a republication of God's law in creation; that is, the natural law. And he further joins the civil law to these. In Calvin's commentary, Psalm 119:52 reads 'I called to mind thy judgements of old, O Jehovah! and I comforted myself.'[24] Calvin inquires into why the psalmist stipulates that the law of God has been in place 'from everlasting'. And he suggests that these words 'may to some extent be accounted for from the righteousness here mentioned not being of recent growth, but truly everlasting, because the written law is just an attestation of the law of nature, through means of which God recalls to our memory that which he has previously engraven on our hearts'.[25] The 'written law' that Calvin refers to here is the divine law of God, and that law is simply an 'attestation' of the natural law. '[Civil] law penalties are called confirmations' in the sense that they are one way that God 'takes vengeance on the ungodly' and, in doing so, he 'confirms what he had spoken' in his divine law.[26] In short, the law of nature is God's law, which is republished in the divine law, which is further reinforced by human civil law. In this way, Calvin joins these three primary types of law together in a way that is consistent with medieval jurists and theologians, such as Thomas. These three types of law – natural, divine and civil – are expanded upon below.

But first, it is notable that there is no mention of a *lex aeterna* in this passage, nor is there a mention of such an idea in any other part of Calvin's corpus. For Thomas, the natural law was itself a 'rational creature's participation of the eternal law' and is manifested in the creature through its 'share of the Eternal Reason'.[27] Does the absence of an explicit *lex aeterna* in Calvin's thought disqualify him from adhering to a medieval understanding of natural law, which saw God as the governor of the universe through that law? This would be difficult to maintain for two reasons. First, Calvin uses terminology like 'the frame of the universe' to describe the natural order of creation, which presents a similar conception to Thomas's of God's governance of His creation. In the *Institutes* 2.6.1, he writes that '[the] natural order was that the frame of the universe [*mundi fabrica*] should be the school in which we were to learn piety'.[28] Elsewhere, he writes that 'the knowledge of God' is 'quite clearly set forth in the system of the universe [*mundi machina*]'.[29] The sense of the creation, indeed the entire universe, as an orderly whole governed by God is prevalent in Calvin's thought and there is present in his thought an understanding, consistent with the Stoic and Christian traditions, that there is one overarching divine law functioning as the foundation for all other laws.[30] Second, it is abundantly clear that Calvin was not afraid of polemics. However, as both Susan E. Schreiner and David VanDrunen point out, Calvin never engages in any polemics about natural law. Unlike several other points of scholastic theology and philosophy, natural law jurisprudence is not a contested point for him.[31] Why does Calvin pass over the idea of an eternal law? Matthew Tuininga suggests that Calvin rejected the scholastic emphasis on the efficacy of human reason in comprehending the natural law, which may go some way to explaining his omission of the eternal law category in his writings.[32] More plausible is the explanation that Calvin never systematically outlined his understanding of law, and therefore never had the need nor the opportunity to explicitly include, or exclude, the eternal law from his schema. As we will see below, Calvin is not entirely dismissive of human reason, especially when it comes to earthly matters. Furthermore, instead of emphasising reason in the apprehension of the natural law, Calvin sees an important role for the conscience.

In Book II of his *Institutes*, Calvin writes that '[there] is nothing more common than for a man to be sufficiently instructed in a right standard of conduct by natural law'.[33] Why is this so? It is not primarily human reason that allows people to know how to conduct themselves, but their conscience, which 'stands in place of [divine positive] law'.[34] Here, Calvin refers to the Apostle Paul's Epistle to the Romans, where he says that the 'Gentiles, who do not have the law, do the works of the law ... and show that the work of the law is written on their hearts'.[35] Calvin holds that this law that is 'written on the heart' is the natural law, apprehendable by human conscience. 'This', he writes, 'would not be a bad definition: natural law is that apprehension of the conscience which distinguishes sufficiently between just and unjust, and which deprives men of the excuse of ignorance.'[36] In his commentary on Romans 2:14 (1540), Calvin writes that 'all nations ... have some notions of justice and rectitude ... which are implanted by nature in the hearts of men'.[37] He uses similar language in other places to describe how humans know this natural law, instances which are reflective of his primacy of conscience over reason. The natural law is 'engraved upon their minds'.[38] The 'voice of nature, or the testimony of that equity' is 'engraven on the hearts of men'.[39] Humans have been 'endowed with this knowledge'.[40] They 'carry the distinction between right and wrong engraven on their conscience'.[41] Edward A. Dowey brings these various descriptors of Calvin's together by noting that what he holds to is 'an ability to know and actual knowledge, as well as an ability to judge and a criterion for judgement'.[42]

It is worth flagging at this point a difference between Calvin's natural law theory and the 'modern' natural law thinkers who follow (in both chronological and theoretical senses) those thinkers we shall encounter later in this study. Jennifer Herdt has pointed out that 'modern natural lawyers eroded Calvin's careful distinction between conscience as revealing our duty as duty, and instinct as guiding toward natural advantage'.[43] They collapsed them together, claiming that instinct revealed duty and doing away with the anthropological commitments we discuss later in this chapter, including the factor of the Fall into sin. To sum up this point about conscience and the natural law, Calvin holds that humans have an innate knowledge of, and sense of, the law of nature. This law provides people with a 'right standard of conduct' in the world which God has created, including matters related to human society.

The issue for us, then, is how Calvin related the natural law to God's divine law. In the passage from his commentary on Psalm 119:52, we saw that, for Calvin, 'the written law' was an 'attestation of the law of nature'.[44] In other words, the divine law is a republication of the law God had already written in His creation and, specifically, on the hearts of humans. There are numerous places in the *Institutes* which support this proposition. I will focus on just one, which reads: 'Now that inward law, which we have above described as written, even engraved, upon the hearts of all, in a sense asserts the very same things that are to be learned from the two Tables.'[45] Calvin goes on here to say that because of human sin, and the noetic effects of the same, humanity cannot properly discern the divine legislation stipulated in the natural law. Therefore, 'the Lord has provided us with a written law to give us a clearer witness of what was too obscure in the natural law'.[46] Elsewhere he writes that 'the law of God which we call the moral law is nothing else than a testimony of natural law and of that conscience which God has engraved upon the minds of men'.[47] Does this mean that the Decalogue (which is equivalent to the 'moral law' for Calvin) and the natural law are synonymous with each other?[48] Grabill argues that this is not the case. According to Grabill, the natural and divine laws are 'equally legitimate means *for accessing* the same basic content of morality' in Calvin's thought.[49] Grabill further observes that Calvin does not insist in the passage in *Institutes* 2.8.1 that 'all natural-law precepts ... must be reducible to a logical correlate in the decalogue'.[50] So, while Calvin identifies the natural law with the divine positive law, the connection is not one of absolute correspondence. Still, Calvin holds that the very same natural law, which he says is 'engraved upon the minds of men' and written in the Decalogue, is the prescriptive model for the 'equity' which is 'the goal and rule and limit of all laws'.[51] That is, the natural law is the model for the underlying principles of all laws, in particular the civil law.

The universal model of equity which the natural law provides is, in Calvin's political thought, vital to the maintenance and governance of temporal life in God's creation.[52] Irena Backus has observed that, while he closely (though not entirely) identifies the natural law with the Decalogue, the natural law was, for Calvin, an 'innate knowledge of right and wrong' which functionally 'enabled nations who do not know the Bible to have legal systems'.[53] However, just because nations do not have the Bible does not excuse them from implementing and enforcing civil laws reflective of the natural law and, therefore, the Decalogue. The Decalogue is divided into two tables by Calvin. The first table of commandments are God's instructions 'in piety and proper duties of religion'; the second 'prescribes how we ought to conduct ourselves in human society'.[54] Calvin holds that both tables are a part of the natural law and believes that the civil magistrate is obliged to uphold both in the form of positive law.[55] Therefore, the Decalogue serves to illustrate Calvin's understanding of the scope of the natural law as applied to human society. The overarching governance of creation by God is understood by Calvin to manifest itself in human society by way of the natural law.

Indeed, the governance of society is presumed to be done with reference to the natural law in pagan nations, according to Calvin.[56] He writes, in commenting on the sexual purity laws in the Mosaic law, that the 'prohibition of incests' in Leviticus 18 'flows from the fountain of nature itself, and is founded upon the general principle of all laws, which is perpetual and inviolable'.[57] He continues expounding on the same theme, focusing on the impossibility of civil legislators making just laws which are contrary to the natural law: '[No] legislator can effect that a thing, which nature pronounces to be vicious, should not be vicious', because 'the light of nature will presently shine forth and prevail'.[58] Here we can see how firmly Calvin believed that the order of nature, as set forth in God's natural law, was reliant upon and, further, must adhere to that natural law. And, as Susan Schreiner has pointed out, Calvin consistently utilised the categories of 'nature', the 'wisdom of the pagans', and the natural principles of justice and 'equity' in his discussion on civil government.[59]

We can see that the concept of nature and the natural law is present in Calvin's thought and that it plays an important role in how he understands the governance of creation, but also the governance of human society. It is also a theistic natural law, where God is ruling over his creation through His natural legislation. However, if the natural law is fundamental to the functioning of human society, is human society according to the natural law? Is human society 'natural', according to Calvin? Because if it is, it will have a bearing on whether Calvin understands the nature of human society as secularised or sacralised. In order to properly address these questions, we must investigate his anthropology and his view of the origins of society. More specifically, we must find out how Calvin conceives of prelapsarian and postlapsarian humanity and, connected to this, what the connection is between society and the natural law.

## Theological Anthropology and Calvin's View of Civil Government

Calvin's anthropology is very pessimistic. And yet, it is important not to forget his more positive framing of prelapsarian human nature, as this informs his understanding of society and the state. As related in Genesis 1 and 2, the prelapsarian condition of Adam was perfect. In his Commentary on Genesis (1554), Calvin affirms that Adam, the first human, was made in the likeness and image of God.[60] He enjoyed perfect fellowship with God and had no stain of sin in him. Eve, the first woman, was also made in the image and likeness of God, as Adam was. According to Calvin, '[man] proceeds spotless from God's hand'; he describes humans as having an 'originally upright nature'.[61] Based on the Apostle Paul's explication of the restored image of God in Jesus he says that Adam must have had 'righteousness and holiness'.[62] Calvin further adds that Adam was also endowed with 'right judgement, had affections in harmony with reason, had all his senses sound and well regulated, and truly excelled in everything'.[63]

However, the Fall into sin alters this perfection dramatically, and it is here that Calvin's anthropology slides into the pessimism he is so notorious for. Calvin relates the event of the Fall as a rebellion against God's command to Adam in Genesis 2:16. He states that 'Adam was denied the tree of the knowledge of good and evil to test his obedience and prove that he was willingly under God's command'.[64] Adam and Eve disobeyed God's command when they ate the fruit of the tree, and, according to Calvin, they correspondingly broke God's law.[65] This law required perfect obedience, and humanity's perfection was lost by Adam and Eve's rebellion against God's command. Calvin states in his commentary on Genesis that sin enters the world by the breaking of God's law.[66] This is commonly called 'the Fall', and Calvin relates that the Fall has a number of consequences. First, Calvin holds that in the Fall the image of God seen in humankind is 'obliterated'.[67] This consequence is foundational to his adoption of the Augustinian doctrine of original sin. Through the Fall of Adam, sin entered the world and all his progeny.[68] Calvin is not dissimilar to Martin Luther (1483–1546) on this point, who also holds that humans 'are sinners by nature – conceived and born in sin' and that 'sin has poisoned us through and through'.[69] Huldrych Zwingli (1484–1531) also writes that when Adam sinned 'he infected and corrupted his offspring'.[70] The likeness of God is lost in the first man, and therefore all men and women after him are tarred with the same brush. 'All of us', Calvin states, 'are born infected with the contagion of sin'.[71] It is 'a hereditary depravity' and a 'corruption of our nature, diffused into all parts of the soul', according to Calvin.[72] The fallen state of man is not a minor stain, able to be easily removed. It is a perpetual and ingrained feature of human existence and affects all aspects of life. This aspect of Calvin's anthropology, as we shall see, is central to his understanding of societal origins and the role of civil government.

A second consequence of the Fall is that Adam and Eve are cast out from the Garden of Eden. According to Calvin, this consequence has relational import for Adam and Eve, in particular their relationship to God. The relationship is now fundamentally broken and is described by Calvin in the following juxtaposition: 'Previously, direct communication with God was the source of life to Adam but, from the moment in which he became alienated from God it was necessary that he should recover life by the death of Christ, by whose life he then lived.'[73] Whereas Adam had perfect communion with God before the Fall, he was 'alienated from God' post-Fall. Calvin lists four spiritual qualities that humans lost in their fall from fellowship with God: faith, love of God, a desire for righteousness, and, most interestingly, 'charity toward neighbour'.[74] It is the latter of these qualities that bears most directly on Calvin's view of the origins of political life.

Calvin sees a breaking of fellowship not just between God and humanity, but also between humans themselves. This is a third consequence of the Fall. As André Biéler notes, Calvin holds that 'sin and its consequences destroys each [element] of the natural social order'.[75] Whereas before the Fall Adam and Eve enjoyed a perfect relationship between themselves, they now live in opposition to one another. Genesis 3 is a key text for Calvin on this. In his comments on Genesis 3:16, he describes the relational and social results of the Fall in stark terms.[76] Calvin writes that, in her prelapsarian state, Eve was in gentle and loving subjection to her husband. Conversely, Adam was in loving authority over his wife. After their rebellion, however, Calvin emphasises that Eve is now 'cast into servitude'.[77] Her position in relation to her husband is greatly diminished by the Fall. Calvin further says that Eve 'should not be free and at her own command'.[78] Calvin sees the severing of right relationship between her and her husband in God's curse upon Eve in Genesis 3. Authority and subjection are at the centre of the results of the Fall. But it is notable that there was still authority and subjection before the Fall. Indeed, Eve was happily under Adam's authority before the Fall. In the postlapsarian condition, she is subject to a sinful and broken version of this authority.

But how does this marring of Adam and Eve's relationship play out for the rest of humanity? Calvin universalises the problems which sin brought into the world as evidenced in Eve's postlapsarian subjection to Adam in his comments on the fifth commandment in

Exodus 20. This verse reads 'Honour your father and your mother, that your days may be long in the land that the Lord your God is giving you.' He says: 'Now this precept of subjection strongly conflicts with the depravity of human nature which . . . bears subjection grudgingly.'[79] Like Eve's subjection to Adam, which is marred by sin, Calvin here sees that all humankind now pushes against instituted authority. Calvin notes in his commentary on Romans that 'there are indeed always some tumultuous spirits who believe that . . . they cannot enjoy the liberty given by [God], except they shake off every yoke of human subjection'.[80] This is, of course, a sin and a grave error in Calvin's mind, and he suggests that the Apostle Paul emphasises the necessity of subjection to civil authority in Romans 13 because humans are wont to avoid it.[81] Here we see a fundamental social consequence of the Fall into sin: that people will resent and try to 'shake off' human authority.

A further social outworking of the Fall that Calvin identifies is that humans display antisocial behaviours in the postlapsarian condition. Humans, for Calvin, are entirely sinful and inclined towards wickedness.[82] One illustration of Calvin's emphasis on humanity's antisocial tendencies is in his exposition of Cain's violence towards his brother Abel in Genesis 4. Calvin here claims that Cain's sinfulness was a root cause of his violence towards Abel. He notes that, in order to trap Abel, Cain made an appearance of friendship. Indeed, Cain 'presented the appearance of fraternal concord, until the opportunity of perpetrating the horrid murder should be afforded'.[83] Then, in a revealing statement about the state of humanity's social nature, Calvin says: '[It] is by no means to be expected that they who are as savage beasts towards God, should sincerely cultivate the confidence of friendship with men.'[84] Cain's rebellious stance towards God is, according to Calvin, a precursor to his violent, antisocial stance towards his brother Abel.

But it is not only Cain who displayed this tendency. Calvin generalises it across the entirety of humankind. His commentary on Genesis 6:11 is telling in this regard. The narrative describes how 'the earth was corrupt in God's sight, and the earth was filled with violence'. Calvin writes of this that 'the light of equity' was 'extinct'.[85] That is, human sinfulness had brought about the loss of an understanding of justice. This led, says Calvin, to the prevalence of 'the love of oppression . . . frauds, injuries, rapines, and all kinds of injustice'.[86] According to Calvin, this is a result 'of impiety' and of man's revolt against God.[87] In another telling passage in his *Sermons on the Book of Job* (published in 1574), Calvin exposits Job 36:6–14 and explains 'that the nature of men is such that every man would be lord and master over his neighbours and that no man is willing to be subject'.[88] Indeed, 'all men are given to evil and their lusts are so boiling that every man wishes to have complete license and that no man should be under correction'.[89] Yet, this is exactly where civil government comes in, according to Calvin. God, he says, 'has created men in order that they should govern themselves honestly and modestly'.[90] Good civil government is, for Calvin, the epitome of order, which is itself the practical opposite of the chaos caused by sin. Order is at the forefront of Calvin's political thought, and this shows through in his emphasis on the necessity of civil government, as well as his distaste for Anabaptists and anarchy.[91]

These passages could, admittedly, be used to illustrate the post-lapsarian origins of civil government in Calvin's thought. However, further investigation demonstrates this is not the case. According to Calvin, the civil magistrate is a minister of God and is used by God to punish wickedness and prevent sinful people from destroying each other. He is most clear about this when arguing against those of his contemporaries who would do away with civil government. It is almost certain that he has Anabaptist radicals in mind when he writes: 'For since the insolence of men is so great, their wickedness so stubborn, that it can scarcely be restrained by extremely severe laws, what do we expect them to do if they see that their depravity can go scot-free – when no power can force them to cease from doing evil?'[92] In his commentary on 1 Timothy (1548) Calvin writes that those who oppose the existence of the civil magistrate are 'destitute of all humanity, and breathe nothing but cruel barbarism'.[93] As Susan Schreiner notes, Calvin understood that God had ordained the institution of civil government because 'if unbridled, the wickedness of men and women would destroy the human race'.[94] Without it, Calvin sees that evil would go virtually unrestrained and humanity would be wiped out, and he says that those who reject the necessity of civil government are effectively 'ushering in anarchy'.[95] This is a view not dissimilar to Martin Luther's, who writes that civil government ensures that people 'are unable to practice their wickedness, and if they do practice it they cannot do so without fear or with success and impunity'.[96] 'If it were not so,' writes Luther, 'men would devour one another.'[97] Finally, in a comment that is reminiscent of Aristotle's assessment of man's political nature, Calvin says that if one was to deny humankind the good of civil government, 'and if our pilgrimage [on earth] requires such helps, those who take these from man deprive him of his very humanity'.[98] The Anabaptists were arguing at this time that civil government was fundamentally evil and not to be meddled in. Calvin takes quite the opposite view. As Biéler says about this sentiment from Calvin, 'a man who is apolitical is a creature at odds with his very own nature'.[99] The Anabaptists, and any others who advocate anarchy, are promoting dehumanising doctrines. This is a sentiment we will return to again shortly, but the emphasis, in this case, ought to be placed on the need for humans to have civil government, which Calvin roots in their sinful nature.

Calvin further held that civil government was ordained by God for humanity's good, appointed 'for the preservation of mankind'.[100] In his comments on Romans 13:4, where the Apostle Paul says that the civil magistrate is 'God's minister for your good', Calvin notes that people should be thankful to God that civil government can protect them against evil people.[101] Regarding King David's words in Psalm 101:5, Calvin affirms the psalmist's sentiment that people who are invested with public authority are to punish evil deeds.[102] Elsewhere, Calvin writes that if the magistrate 'did not restrain the hardihood of wicked men, every place would be full of robberies and murders'.[103] Finally, Calvin holds the view, similar to that of Luther, that civil government is tasked by God with the 'establishment of religion'.[104] Civil government has a distinct role in preserving Christian religion amongst its subjects through the prevention of moral corruption.[105] It is clear, then, that Calvin holds the civil magistrate to be most necessary in a postlapsarian situation. In light of sin, God's ordination of the civil magistrate is necessary for the existence of society, for otherwise there would be moral and civic anarchy. Those who would do away with civil government entirely, particularly the Anabaptists, are enemies of civil order.

This brief exploration of Calvin's understanding of the role of the civil magistrate serves to demonstrate his insistence on the necessity for the existence of political life. Humans are fallen and would otherwise live in squalor and anarchy. God has ordained civil magistrates to prevent sin, punish evil and promote true religion for the good of their subjects. Calvin's pessimistic view of the natural sinfulness of humans seems to lead to the conclusion that he does not hold out any possibility for a prelapsarian origin for political life, nor a natural one. The emphasis in Calvin's writings on civil government is most certainly on its role in the postlapsarian world as a bridle on human sin.[106] He never grounds or explains civil government in prelapsarian terms. Does that mean that Calvin believed that civil government was purely a postlapsarian institution? It is this question that we will address next, and the answer I am inclined towards is 'No'. Calvin's thought contains strands and traces enough to suggest that he held to a form of political naturalism which, combined with his understanding of natural law, solidifies his sacralised view of society.

### 'Man is a social animal': Calvin's Political Naturalism

There is disagreement among scholars as to whether Calvin held that civil government would have existed in the prelapsarian condition. Susan Schreiner and Edward Dowey are good representatives of the two positions on the matter. For Schreiner, Calvin, while not addressing the question directly, sees the state as primarily a means by which God restrains the effects of sin in human society. Sin, she writes, 'was more than a secondary element in the role of the state; precisely in its function as a remedy . . . for sin Calvin saw the state as a divinely willed order'.[107] On the other hand, Dowey makes an interesting connection between Calvin's understanding of the human conscience and the intention for a prelapsarian political life. He rightly interprets Calvin as saying that God governs his creation, not 'by mere willing, but by revealing his will' which was originally done through 'the conscience'.[108] Additionally, Dowey contends that, for Calvin, God requires obedience to His will through, in some sense, an obedience to the divinely mandated authority of civil government, an obedience which was rendered necessary by the conscience.[109]

This link between this 'original endowment in man' (the conscience) and civil authority demonstrates, for Dowey, that Calvin saw 'the state as [belonging] to human society as God created it, apart from the Fall of man and his redemption'.[110] Dowey's linking of conscience with a prelapsarian political condition is convincing as far as it goes. However, there are several other points of evidence which suggest that Calvin held to a kind of political naturalism which entails the view that civil government is a part of the original creation order as ordained by God, and that humans are naturally political. First, we will see that Calvin held that humans were naturally social both before and after the Fall. Second, Calvin saw the postlapsarian role of the natural law in social relations as largely consistent with the prelapsarian natural law. Third, we will examine texts in Calvin's corpus which explicitly and implicitly provide evidence for the idea of a prelapsarian existence of politics in his thought.

Calvin's thought on the organic nature of human society is initially hinted at in his earliest printed work, his commentary on Seneca's *De clementia*. While Calvin remains a relatively detached commentator, his protégé and biographer Theodore Beza (1519–1605) made clear that Calvin admired Seneca, and Calvin's own comments occasionally betray an affinity with the Stoic.[111] In *De clementia*, Seneca (4 BC–65 AD) himself writes that 'man is a social animal'.[112] Calvin comments that with this statement by Seneca it is as if 'this one reason will be enough if someone were to dispute with the Stoics; that clemency is a sort of bond of human society and kinship'.[113] Calvin then quotes Cicero, Plato and Aristotle in support of Seneca's position that man is naturally social.[114] While the passage is far from conclusive regarding Calvin's own views, Backus rightly points out that he was 'obviously sufficiently interested in the Graeco-Roman concept of humans as social animals to make a comparative study of it'.[115]

In his commentary on Genesis 2, Calvin makes some telling remarks when discussing the narration of the creation of Adam and Eve. When discussing verse 18, which is prelapsarian, Calvin treats the principles he finds therein with universality. Verse 18 of Genesis 2 reads as follows: 'Then the Lord God said, "It is not good that the man should be alone; I will make him a helper fit for him."' In his comments on this verse, Calvin says that Moses (whom he takes to be the author of Genesis) 'now explains . . . that there should be human beings on the earth who might cultivate mutual society between themselves'.[116] At no point is there room for an idyllic individual in Calvin's view. In his *Institutes*, he affirms that Genesis 2:18 speaks of a 'universal condition', that 'it is not good for man to be alone'.[117] Luther makes a comparable observation when he says that in Genesis 2:18 God 'is speaking of the common good of the species, not of personal good'.[118] Luther is saying that the good that God speaks of applies not just to Adam, but to all humankind. It is also acknowledged by Calvin that, though the text in Genesis speaks specifically to Adam's isolation, it applies more generally to humankind. It is, as Calvin says, a 'common law of man's vocation'.[119] Therefore, we can conclude that Calvin holds to a universal application of this verse as relating to the necessity of human relationships. He does this by applying the prelapsarian state of humanity to the postlapsarian condition, still drawing the same universal conclusions.

At the creation of Eve in Genesis 2:19, Calvin understands that God is commencing the human social life. 'God begins', he writes of this creative act, 'at the first step of human society.'[120] Furthermore, and perhaps most revealingly, Calvin concludes the following: 'The commencement [of human society], therefore involves a general principle, that man was formed to be a social animal'.[121] Here we see Calvin's adoption of Seneca's social anthropology. Humans in their very nature are social, according to Calvin. Therefore, they are naturally, or organically, going to form into societies. He goes on to link not only the origins of human society but also the perpetuation of human society to the creation of Eve. Calvin holds that 'the human race could not exist without the woman'.[122] According to Calvin the ongoing existence and organic growth of human society are grounded in the origins of human society. Therefore, both the origins of society and the perpetuation of society are instituted pre-Fall.

The design of God is not only that humans should not be alone but, according to Calvin, humans are designed to be neighbourly and serve one another. In a 1559 sermon on Genesis 2:18–21, he asserts that 'if we had all we wanted' and if everything was always done for us, yet we were alone and without companionship, life would 'be very sad and seem half dead'.[123] So, says Calvin, God gave the first human a companion, therefore establishing the principle of what Nico Vorster calls 'the neighbourly nature of society'.[124] Human community is something that 'God has ordained for our well-being', according to Calvin; so much so, that if we are 'not united in true harmony to serve one another' we are guilty of 'shameful ingratitude'.[125] Marriage is a 'beautiful covenant', which Calvin maintains is, in part, intended to show humans that they are 'obligated to associate with [their] neighbours' and that they 'exist mutually through one another'.[126] In other words, human society from its very beginning in the first marriage was, according to Calvin, intended to cultivate neighbourly activity and interconnectedness between individuals.[127] A fundamental feature of Calvin's understanding of humans, and indeed human society, is the naturalness of human relationships and interconnectedness. And this natural interconnectedness is universal, both before and after the Fall.

Still, it remains to be seen whether this social nature of humanity carries over into the postlapsarian world. A key to this is establishing Calvin's view of the operations of the natural before and after the Fall. Thankfully, there are passages in Calvin's writings which address both the social nature of humanity and the natural law. They demonstrate that, according to Calvin, the laws of nature are not altered by the Fall.

The law of nature in Calvin's thought, as found in prelapsarian creation, is well described by Edward Dowey when he says that it is 'God's orderly will in creation' and 'the orderly, harmonious Creator–creature relationship'.[128] The law of nature might be less recognisable to the broken human mind, but it remains a consistent expression of God's creation ordinances. While there is a radical break in the conditions of creation between the pre- and post-Fall Edenic paradise, it is not the case that nature is fundamentally different, per se.[129] There are fundamental consistencies which carry over into postlapsarian nature, including a consistent natural law. God's activity as the one who sustains his creation does not cease after the Fall. According to Calvin, this is an ongoing work of God, who retains and restrains his creation order.[130] In what follows, I shall further demonstrate that Calvin saw much continuity between the prelapsarian and postlapsarian operations of natural law. The discussion focuses on the institution of marriage. This is in part because there are several examples where Calvin examines marriage in his writings. It is also because marriage is a key aspect of the social order, for Calvin, and so serves as a specific example of a pre-Fall institution that informs his views of the origins and nature of human society.

In his commentary on the Apostle Paul's theological exposition of marriage in the book of Ephesians (1548), Calvin clearly defines marital relations as being couched in nature. Commenting on the Apostle's detailed discussion in Ephesians 5, Calvin describes the use of the mystical union between Jesus and the Church as an illustration 'of the common law of marriage'.[131] This acknowledgement of the law of marriage as 'common' places postlapsarian marriage under the natural law. However, Calvin is more specific about the continuities between this pre-Fall and post-Fall 'common law' institution soon after this. He discusses the Apostle's quote from Genesis 2:24, and points to Paul's use of this quote as a statement of a law still built into nature. The quote is taken from a portion of the prelapsarian narrative and reads as follows: 'For this cause shall a man leave his father and mother, and shall be joined unto his wife, and they shall be one flesh.' Calvin begins his commentary on this by pointing to a different set of natural duties, that of a son's to a father. 'A son', Calvin states, 'is bound by an inviolable law of nature to perform his duties toward his father.'[132] Note that he considers this set of duties as part of the natural law, and the assumption is that those duties are extant in the prelapsarian condition, such as the quote from Genesis. He goes on to observe that, in utilising this text from Genesis, the Apostle is declaring that 'the obligations of a husband towards his wife are . . . stronger' than even those that a son has to a father.[133] Calvin holds that both sets of duties fall under the prelapsarian and 'inviolable law of nature', and that both remain in force despite the Fall.[134]

A further example of Calvin's view of the continuity between pre- and postlapsarian natural law is found in Calvin's commentary on 1 Timothy (1548). In chapter two of the letter, the Apostle Paul discusses the role of men and women in the corporate worship of the church, showing that the different roles he designates are derived from the ordered creation of God. In verse 12, the Apostle forbids women from having authority over men. Calvin writes regarding this that 'woman . . . by nature (that is, the ordinary law of God) is formed to obey'.[135] Here, again, Calvin affirms that it is according to the natural law that women are subject to men. This is not only a postlapsarian law, either. Note that Calvin says that woman was 'formed' to be in subjection to man, thereby grounding the law in the prelapsarian creation order. Paul goes on in verse 13 to write that 'Adam was first formed, then Eve.' Calvin's discussion of this verse serves as further evidence that he held that the order within marriage was consistent both pre-Fall and post-Fall. He writes that 'God enacted this law at the beginning', thereby acknowledging a natural, prelapsarian hierarchy within marriage.[136] He then notes that God 'also inflicted [subjection to Adam] as punishment on the woman'.[137] Here, Calvin acknowledges that the postlapsarian pattern was similar to the prelapsarian one but was also meted out as a punishment for Eve's disobedience. His position on whether this postlapsarian pattern is properly according to the natural law is clear in what follows in his commentary. He writes that 'although mankind had stood in their first and original uprightness', that is, that even though the order of creation was good before the Fall, 'the true order of nature, which proceeded from the command of God, bears that women shall be subject'.[138] Calvin is clarifying how Eve's subjection can be both according to the natural law and a punishment. He shows that it is both: that the hierarchical ordering of marriage pre-Fall was good, and that the punishment given to Eve was also consistent with this insofar as it was according to what was in nature already. Calvin is again affirming that prelapsarian and postlapsarian marriage hierarchies are consistent and according to the natural law.

A final example of this continuity in the operations of the natural law before and after the Fall will be drawn from Calvin's commentary on Paul's letters to the Corinthians (1548). In a discourse in 1 Corinthians 11 on the use of head coverings in worship, the Apostle Paul writes about the nature of men and women at some length. In verses 7–10, the Apostle writes the following:

> For a man ought not to cover his head, since he is the image and glory of God, but woman is the glory of man. For man was not made from woman, but woman from man. Neither was man created for woman, but woman for man. That is why a wife ought to have a symbol of authority on her head, because of the angels.[139]

This injunction draws out further thoughts from Calvin on natural law and marriage. There are two key points in his comments on these verses that I will focus on. First, Calvin notes the Apostle's utilisation of the prelapsarian creation order as an authoritative pattern for gender relations in the postlapsarian world. He says that as 'woman derives her origin from man, she is therefore inferior in rank'.[140] Note his specification of the origin of woman, which is, according to the Genesis narrative, both prelapsarian and from Adam. He goes on to comment that the 'woman was created for the sake of the man', hence she is 'subject to him'. So, according to Calvin, the prelapsarian order of creation still informs social relations in a post-Fall world. Second, Calvin goes on to write a response to commentators who claim that the passage does not refer to unmarried women but only married women, and he attempts a refutation of their view. The principle Calvin argues is one of the universality of the authority of men and subjugation of women, and he reasons on the basis of natural law. Calvin says 'it is a mistake' to restrict the Apostle's teaching to married women only, 'for Paul looks beyond this'.[141] He looks to 'God's eternal law which has made the female sex subject to the authority of men'.[142] Note the description of the law in this passage: 'eternal'. Calvin grounds his view of the differences between men and women in the prelapsarian natural order and the 'eternal law' of God and applies the principle to the postlapsarian context. This is further evidence of Calvin's conviction of the natural law's presence before the Fall, and its continuing, consistent application after the Fall.

Finally, we come to address passages in Calvin's writings to directly address the civic order and the nature of prelapsarian civil government. The first passage, from his *Institutes*, deals with humankind's ongoing capacity to excel in earthly matters, despite the effects of sin. In his discussion of man's ability to know God in

His works of creation, Calvin concedes that despite God's clarity of revelation in creation, these works 'flow away without profiting us'.[143] With regard to man's knowledge of nature and creation, Calvin holds that man has lost the knowledge that we should have had if we had not rebelled.[144] He writes that sinful humanity, 'having forsaken the truth of God, they turned to the vanity of their own reason'.[145] As a result, they 'understand nothing aright' and 'are carried away headlong, in various ways, into errors and delusions'.[146] He states that human reason 'by which man distinguishes between good and evil, and by which he understands and judges . . . was weakened and partly corrupted, so its misshapen ruins appear'.[147] According to Calvin, human understanding and knowledge are, broadly speaking, broken and significantly weakened in the wake of the Fall.[148] However, it is not the case for Calvin that humans are entirely without noetic ability. He ultimately enunciates a view of human knowledge that allows for humankind's postlapsarian natural faculties to form true ideas about human society and politics.

In his discussion about 'man's natural endowments', Calvin observes that it would be mistaken to 'so condemn human understanding for its perpetual blindness as to leave it no perception of any object whatever'.[149] Indeed, man naturally longs for truth and does look for it, but still 'wanders through various errors and stumbles repeatedly, as if it were groping in the darkness'.[150] However, there is a distinction within Calvin's thought between earthly matters, on the one hand, and spiritual matters related to knowing God, on the other. This distinction is crucial in properly characterising Calvin's view of human noetic ability. His highly negative view of humanity's abilities takes a different turn when he states that 'its efforts do not always become so worthless as to have no effect, especially when it turns its attention to things below'.[151] With regard to knowledge of 'earthly matters', Calvin holds out some possibility for human success. This success is partly based upon an implanted knowledge. In his careful distinction between earthly and heavenly things, Calvin lists 'government, household management, all mechanical skills, and the liberal arts' as earthly matters.[152] These are matters where humans can know truth in accord with their natural capacity for reason. Crucially for this discussion, Calvin holds that all men have 'universal impressions of a certain civic fair dealing and order'.[153] Indeed, there is not a single individual or nation which does not know that human organisation must be governed by laws.[154] Calvin does acknowledge that there are people who dissent from widely understood principles of law and equity, but this is to be accounted for by human sinfulness and not by a lack of understanding.[155] We can garner from this that, according to Calvin, sinfulness does not immediately impinge upon human understanding of civil affairs, only on human behaviour in civil affairs. Despite some disagreement and sinful behaviour, Calvin holds that 'men . . . agree on the general conception of equity' and that 'some seed of political order has been implanted in all men'.[156] Was this seed implanted before the Fall? And if so, does this mean that the political order was intended for prelapsarian conditions? This text is not clear on this question. There are two other texts which can be read as implying that this 'seed of political order' was a prelapsarian part of human nature.

The first passage which implies that civil government is not merely an institution created to stifle human sin, but had a prelapsarian purpose, is from Book VI of the *Institutes* in the chapter on civil government. Calvin's concern is to establish the credibility and necessity of the civil magistrate in the eyes of those (particularly the Anabaptists) who would reject the goodness and godliness of the civil magistrate. He uses various scriptural texts to demonstrate that God has given the civil magistrate 'most honorable titles' and 'commends it to us'.[157] God, Calvin says, affirms in his word that kings and authorities rule according to his own ordination. 'This', he writes, 'amounts to the same thing as to say: it has not come about by human perversity that the authority over all things on earth is in the hands of kings and other rulers, but by divine providence and holy ordinance.'[158] This intriguing statement is set in the midst of a series of polemical assertions about the God-approved and God-created institutions of civil authority, and its purpose, as Schreiner correctly points out, is not to outline a theoretical stance about the prelapsarian nature of civil government.[159] Nonetheless, it does indicate with some clarity that 'human perversity' is not responsible for the creation of civil authority. This could merely be a statement about the agency of God in the creation of the civil magistrate, but it does also hint at a prelapsarian political order for humanity.

A similarly intriguing statement can be found in Calvin's commentary on Romans 13:1. The polemical context for this text is similar to the one above, and Calvin takes aim at those who '[attempt] to invert the order of God, and thus resist God himself'.[160] His concern is, once again, to establish that civil authority always comes from God, an idea denigrated by the Anabaptists.[161]

It is not a sinful act of humanity to institute civil government, according to Calvin, and nor is civil government a punishment from God. 'Understand further', he writes, 'that powers are from God, not as pestilence, and famine, and wars, and other visitations for sin, are said to be from him.'[162] Civil government is not, argues Calvin, in the same category as natural disasters and other manifestations of God's judgement for sin. On the contrary, '[God] has appointed them for the legitimate and just government of the world.'[163] It would be reasonable to interpret Calvin as, at this point, simply indicating that civil authority is from God, but not as a judgement or punishment for sin. However, if read in light of the above passages, the first indicating that humankind enjoys an implanted knowledge of political order, and the second, like this one, indicating that human sin is not the cause of civil government, this passage might be understood as indicating a prelapsarian political life for humanity.

Indeed, having assembled the above evidence and considered the picture of Calvin's thought on this matter, it appears that Calvin was a political naturalist. In the first place, he held to the Stoic doctrine that humans are naturally social creatures. Second, he understood that the law of nature governing social relations is consistently applied both before and after the Fall. Third, he seems to have understood that the 'seed of political order' implanted in postlapsarian humankind was a hangover from the prelapsarian condition. According to Calvin, the law of nature governing social relations also governs political life, a law which is consistently applied both before and after the Fall.

## Conclusion

At the beginning of this chapter, I posited that Calvin's view of human nature might have been influenced by his study of Seneca. 'Man', write both Seneca and Calvin, 'is a social animal.' The question that was not clear at that point in the chapter was whether Calvin holds to the view that 'man' was also 'a political animal'. The case has been put forward in this chapter that Calvin did, indeed, hold that view, in part because of his understanding of natural law. In his theory of natural law, he maintained a close connection between God's governance of the universe and the natural law. The natural law is not secularised in Calvin's thought. Further, because of his theistic understanding of natural law, his conception of political life was not secularised either, as he understood that humans are naturally political creatures as designed by God. For Calvin, humans are in political life because of the natural law, and would have been in political life whether Adam and Eve had sinned in the Garden, or whether they had remained holy. Calvin exemplifies, then, early Reformed political naturalism. For Calvin, God is the founder of human society and political life through his creation order, and this natural institution is given ongoing legitimacy and purpose in the postlapsarian world through the operations of the natural law.

Calvin is, then, found to be the earliest proponent of Reformed political naturalism in the bigger story of this volume. If, by the time of Locke, the tradition had shifted from naturalism to conventionalism, the obvious problem to solve is how this shift occurred. Calvin was not the culprit, as it were.[164] Principally, Calvin's theory of natural law is Christian and theistic, and was generally consistent with the received medieval theories of natural law which identify God's reason or His will with the legislation written in nature. At some point, this understanding of natural law starts to be usurped and, with this change, the understanding of who founded political life changes. As C. Scott Pryor states, Calvin 'disagrees with later natural law writers . . . who ground the natural law solely in "order in nature"'.[165] Calvin's understanding of both the law of nature and of civic order was, ultimately, sacred. It is the later writers, who are exemplified by Hobbes and Locke, who changed the ground of natural law, and who shifted the foundation of political order towards humanity and away from God. It is this, I argue, which led to a secular understanding of political life. Richard Hooker, our next subject, is sometimes considered a forerunner to Hobbes and Locke, particularly with his emphasis on consent in his theory of political legitimacy. We will consider the latter two later. But we next turn to the thought of the judicious Hooker, to consider whether his thought separated God from the foundations of political life.

## Notes

1. Seneca, *De clementia*, 3.2.
2. Irenca Backus, 'Calvin's Concept of Natural and Roman Law', *Calvin Theological Journal* 38.1(2003): 7–26; André Biéler, *Calvin's Economic and Social Thought*, trans. James Greig (Geneva: World Council of Reformed Churches, 2005), 247, but cf. 185; Edward A. Dowey, *The Knowledge of God in Calvin's Theology* (Grand Rapids,

MI: Eerdmans, 1994), 61–3; Jennifer A. Herdt, 'Calvin's Legacy for Contemporary Reformed Natural Law', *Scottish Journal of Theology* 67.4 (2014): 414–35, here 414–28; Harro Höpfl, *The Christian Polity of John Calvin* (Cambridge: Cambridge University Press, 1982), 179–84; John T. McNeill, 'Natural Law in the Teaching of the Reformers', *The Journal of Religion* 26.3 (1946): 182; Susan E. Schreiner, *The Theatre of His Glory: Nature and the Natural Order in the Thought of John Calvin* (Grand Rapids, MI: Baker Academic, 2001), 82–3; cf. Josef Bohatec, *Calvin und das Recht* (Feudingen in Westfalen: Buchdruckereri u. verlagsanstalt, 1934), 57ff.

3. Benedict, *Christ's Churches Purely Reformed*, 9. The best scholarly biography of Calvin is Bruce Gordon, *Calvin* (New Haven, CT: Yale University Press, 2009).

4. Alexandre Ganoczy, 'Calvin's Life', in *The Cambridge Companion to John Calvin*, ed. Donald K. McKim (Cambridge: Cambridge University Press, 2004), 3.

5. François Wendel, *Calvin: The Origins and Development of His Thought* (London: Collins, 1963), 18. This is challenged by Alister E. McGrath, 'John Calvin and Late Mediaeval Thought: A Study in Late Mediaeval Influences on Calvin's Theological Development', *Archiv für Reformationsgeschichte* 77 (1986): 62.

6. Alister E. McGrath, *A Life of John Calvin: A Study in the Shaping of Western Culture* (Oxford: Blackwell, 1990), 31–47.

7. Wilhelm H. Neuser, 'Stations – France and Basel', in *The Calvin Handbook*, ed. Herman Selderhuis (Grand Rapids, MI: Eerdmans, 2009), 24. An account of life at these universities can be found in Gordon, *Calvin*, 6–8. Gordon seems uncertain about Calvin's move to Bourges. See ibid., 19.

8. Alister McGrath speculates about the influence of the *via moderna* in Calvin's university education in McGrath, 'John Calvin and Late Mediaeval Thought', 58–78.

9. A reasonable assumption, given that Calvin studied law, and in particular the *Corpus Iuris Civilis*. See Gordon, *Calvin*, 18–22. Ganoczy rejects this, although cf. Alexandre Ganoczy, *The Young Calvin*, trans. David Foxgrover and Wade Provo (Philadelphia: Westminster Press, 1987), 174–8.

10. T. H. L. Parker, *Portrait of Calvin* (Minneapolis: Desiring God, 2012), 55.

11. Peter J. Leithart has a series of articles on the subject of Cicero's influence on Calvin in particular, and the Stoic influence on Calvin more generally. See Peter J. Leithart, 'That Eminent Pagan: Calvin's Use of Cicero in *Institutes* 1.1–5', *Westminster Theological Journal* 52.1 (1990): 1–12; Peter J. Leithart, 'Stoic Elements in Calvin's Doctrine of the Christian Life, Part I: Original Corruption, Natural Law, and the Order of the Soul', *Westminster Theological Journal* 55.1

(1993): 31–54; Peter J. Leithart, 'Stoic Elements in Calvin's Doctrine of the Christian Life, Part II: Mortification', *Westminster Theological Journal* 55.2 (1993): 191–208; Peter J. Leithart, 'Stoic Elements in Calvin's Doctrine of the Christian Life, Part III: Christian Moderation', *Westminster Theological Journal* 56.1 (1994): 59–85. Also cf. Egil Grislis, 'Calvin's Use of Cicero in the *Institutes* I:1-5 – A Case Study in Theological Method', *Archiv für Reformationsgeschichte* 62 (1971): 5–37.

12. Neuser, 'Stations', 25.

13. Ganoczy, 'Calvin's Life', 7.

14. Ibid., 8–9.

15. Sigrun Haude, 'Anabaptism', in *The Reformation World*, ed. Andrew Pettegree (London: Routledge, 2002), 244–5; R. E. McLaughlin, 'The Radical Reformation', in *Cambridge History of Christianity*, vol. 6: *Reform and Expansion 1500–1660*, ed. R. P. Hsia (Cambridge: Cambridge University Press, 2007), 51–2.

16. Bruce Gordon, *The Swiss Reformation* (Manchester: University of Manchester Press, 2002), 146–56.

17. CO 31:23; cf. John Calvin, 'Author's Preface', in John Calvin, *Commentary on the Book of Psalms,* vol. 1, trans. James Anderson (Grand Rapids, MI: Eerdmans, 1963), xlii.

18. Ganoczy, 'Calvin's Life', 10.

19. Frans P. Stam, 'Stations – Calvin's First Stay in Geneva', in *The Calvin Handbook*, ed. Herman Selderhuis (Grand Rapids, MI: Eerdmans, 2009), 34–5; Benedict, *Christ's Churches Purely Reformed*, 95–6.

20. Carter Lindberg, *The European Reformations* (Malden: Wiley-Blackwell, 2010), 247–9.

21. McGrath, *A Life*, 109.

22. Benedict, *Christ's Churches Purely Reformed*, 96–105; William Naphy, 'Calvin's Church in Geneva', in *Calvin and His Influence, 1509–2009*, ed. Irena Backus and Herman Selderhuis (Oxford: Oxford University Press, 2011), 109–11.

23. The debate over Calvin's view of natural law is complex. Some representative scholarship includes Emil Brunner and Karl Barth, *Natural Theology: Comprising 'Nature and Grace' by Professor Dr. Emil Brunner and the Reply 'No!' By Dr. Karl Barth*, trans. Peter Fraenkel (Eugene, OR: Wipf and Stock, 2002); August Lang, 'The Reformation and Natural Law', in *Calvin and The Reformation*, ed. William Park Armstrong (New York: Fleming H. Revell, 1909), 56–98. Also see Michael Walzer, *The Revolution of the Saints: A Study in the Origins of Radical Politics* (London: Weidenfeld & Nicolson, 1966), 31–2; T. F. Torrance, 'Interpreting the Word by the Light of Christ or the Light of Nature? Calvin, Calvinism and Barth', in *Calviniana: Ideas and Influence of Jean Calvin*, ed. Robert V. Schnucker (Kirksville, MO: Sixteenth Century Journal

Publishers, 1988), 256–7; Wilhelm Neisel, *The Theology of Calvin* (Grand Rapids, MI: Baker Book House, 1980), 102–3; Gene Haas, 'Calvin, Natural Law, and the Two Kingdoms', in *Kingdoms Apart: Engaging the Two Kingdoms Perspective*, ed. Ryan G. McIlhenny (Phillipsburg, NJ: Presbyterian and Reformed Publishing, 2012), 33–47; Wendel, *Calvin*, 206–8; also see Charles Partee, *Calvin and Classical Philosophy* (Leiden: Brill, 1977), 20–1; McNeill, 'Natural Law in the Teaching of the Reformers', 168–82; more generally Schreiner, *The Theatre of His Glory*; William Kempa, 'Calvin on Natural Law', *John Calvin and the Church: A Prism of Reform*, ed. Timothy George (Louisville, KY: Westminster/John Knox Press, 2001), 72–95; Stephen J. Grabill, *Rediscovering the Natural Law in Reformed Theological Ethics* (Grand Rapids, MI: Eerdmans, 2006), 70–97; Paul Helm, *John Calvin's Ideas* (Oxford: Oxford University Press, 2004), 367–88; C. Scott Pryor, 'God's Bridle: John Calvin's Application of Natural Law', *Journal of Law and Religion* 22.1 (2006–2007): 225–54; David VanDrunen, *Natural Law and the Two Kingdoms: A Study in the Development of Reformed Social Thought* (Grand Rapids, MI: Eerdmans, 2010), 99–118; Matthew J. Tuininga, *Calvin's Political Theology and the Public Engagement of the Church: Christ's Two Kingdoms* (Cambridge: Cambridge University Press, 2017), 101–12; Dowey, *The Knowledge of God in Calvin's Theology*, 135–47; Herdt, 'Calvin's Legacy', 414–35. For recent assessment of the relationship between Reformed theology and natural law, see Johnathan Stonebraker and Sarah Irving, 'Natural Law and Protestantism: A Historical Reassessment and Its Contemporary Significance', *Oxford Journal of Law and Religion* 4.3 (2015): 421–41.

24. Comm. Psalm 119:52; CO 32:235; translation from *Calvin's Commentaries: Commentary on the Book of Psalms*, vol. 4, trans. James Anderson (Grand Rapids, MI: Eerdmans, 1949), 436.

25. Comm. Psalm 119:52; CO 32:236; *Commentaries on Psalms*, vol. 4, 438.

26. Comm. Psalm 119:52; CO 32:236–7; *Commentaries on Psalms*, vol. 4, 438–9.

27. *ST* Ia-IIae, Q. 91, art. 2.

28. *Institutes*, 2.6.1.

29. Ibid., 1.10.1.

30. Cf. Schreiner, *The Theatre of His Glory*, 73–9.

31. David VanDrunen, 'Medieval Natural Law and the Reformation: A Comparison of Aquinas and Calvin', *American Catholic Philosophical Quarterly* 80.1 (2006): 81–3; Susan Schreiner, *The Theatre of His Glory*, 2–3; Pryor, 'God's Bridle', 240. Pryor points out that Calvin rejects both intellectualism and voluntarism. Cf. David C. Steinmetz, 'Calvin and the Absolute Power of God', *Journal of Medieval and Reniassance Studies* 18.1 (1988): 6.

32. Tuininga, *Calvin's Political Theology*, 104; Backus, 'Calvin's Concept', 11–12.

33. *Institutes*, 2.2.22.

34. Ibid.

35. Comm. Romans 2:14–15; CO 49:37; translation from *Calvin's Commentaries: Commentaries on the Epistle of Paul the Apostle to the Romans*, trans. John Owen (Grand Rapids, MI: Eerdmans, 1959), 96.

36. *Institutes*, 2.2.22.

37. Comm. Romans 2:14; CO 49:37; *Commentaries on Romans*, 96–7.

38. *Institutes*, 2.2.22.

39. Comm. Habakkuk 2:6; CO 44:540; translation from *Calvin's Commentaries: Commentaries on the Twelve Minor Prophets*, trans. John Owen (Grand Rapids, MI: Eerdmans, 1950), vol. 4, 92–3.

40. *Institutes*, 2.2.22.

41. Comm. John 1:9; CO 47:9; translation from *Calvin's Commentaries: Commentary on the Gospel According to John*, trans. William Pringle (Grand Rapids, MI: Eerdmans, 1949), vol. 1, 38.

42. Dowey, *The Knowledge of God in Calvin's Theology*, 58; Peter Leithart makes the observation that Calvin's emphasis on the 'universal consensus of morality' is influenced by the Stoics, and especially Cicero. See Leithart, 'Stoic Elements, Part I', 44.

43. Herdt, 'Calvin's Legacy', 417.

44. Comm. Psalm 119:52; CO 32:236–7; *Commentaries on Psalms*, vol. 4, 438–9.

45. *Institutes*, 2.8.1. 'Two tables' is a reference to the Decalogue.

46. Ibid., 2.8.1; cf. Comm. Deuteronomy 27:1–4, 8; CO 24:230; translation from *Calvin's Commentaries: Commentaries on the Four Last Books of Moses arranged in the Form of a Harmony*, trans. Charles William Bingham (Grand Rapids, MI: Eerdmans, 1950), vol. 1, 369–70.

47. *Institutes* 4.20.16; Wendel, *Calvin*, 206.

48. As argued by R. S. Clark, 'Calvin on the *Lex Naturalis*', *Stulos Theological Journal* 6.1–2 (1998): 13–18; cf. VanDrunen, *Natural Law and the Two Kingdoms*, 109.

49. Grabill, *Rediscovering the Natural Law*, 89, emphasis original.

50. Ibid.

51. *Institutes* 4.20.16.

52. Tuininga, *Calvin's Political Theology*, 103–4.

53. Backus, 'Calvin's Concept', 10–11. Although, cf. Höpfl, *The Christian Polity*, 184–5, who argues that, for Calvin, the 'natural law is thus neither a necessary nor a sufficient guide for magistrates in their performance of their duty', which means Calvin leant towards theocratic biblicism, but not consistently.

54. *Institutes* 2.8.11.

55. Ibid., 4.20.9.

56. Cf. Thomas, *ST* Ia-IIae, Q. 91, art. 3.

57. Comm. Leviticus 18:6; CO 24:662; translation from *Calvin's Commentaries: Commentaries on the Four Last Books of Moses arranged in the Form of a Harmony*, trans. Charles William Bingham (Grand Rapids, MI: Eerdmans, 1950), vol. 3, 100.

58. Comm. Leviticus 18:6; CO 24:662; *Harmony Books of Moses*, vol. 3, 101.

59. Susan Schreiner, *The Theatre of His Glory*, 89; Leithart, 'Stoic Elements, Part I', 43; cf. *Institutes* 4.20.

60. Comm. Genesis 1:26; CO 23:25–27.

61. *Institutes* 1.15.1.

62. Ibid., 1.15.4; cf. Comm. Genesis 1:26; CO 23:26–7. 'in mente lux rectae intelligentiae vigebat ac regnabat, huic comes aderat mentis rectitudo, sensus omnes ad moderatum rationis obsequium prompti et formati'.

63. Comm. Genesis 1:26; CO 23:26; *Commentaries on Genesis*, 95.

64. *Institutes* 2.1.4.

65. Comm. Genesis 2:16; CO 23:44; Comm. Romans 5:13; CO 49:96–7.

66. Comm. Genesis 2:16; CO 23:44–5.

67. *Institutes* 2.1.5; Ronald S. Wallace, *Calvin's Doctrine of the Christian Life* (Edinburgh: Oliver and Boyd, 1959), 106; Wendel, *Calvin*, 105.

68. *Institutes* 2.1.5; cf. Comm Romans 5:12; CO 49:95; Wendel, *Calvin*, 195–6.

69. Martin Luther, *Table-Talk* (London: George Bell and Sons, 1909), CCXLIV, 111; *LW*, 1:161.

70. Huldrych Zwingli, 'On the Education of Youth', in *Zwingli and Bullinger: Selected Translations*, ed. G. W. Bromiley (London: SCM Press, 1953), 105.

71. *Institutes* 2.1.5.

72. Ibid., 2.1.8.

73. Comm. Genesis 3:22; CO 23:79; *Commentaries on Genesis*, 184.

74. *Institutes* 2.2.12.

75. Biéler, *Calvin's Economic and Social Thought*, 213–14.

76. 'To the woman he said, "I will surely multiply your pain in childbearing; in pain you shall bring forth children. Your desire shall be for your husband, and he shall rule over you."'

77. Comm. Genesis 3:16; CO 23:72; *Commentaries on Genesis*, 172.

78. Comm. Genesis 3:16; CO 23:72; *Commentaries on Genesis*, 172.

79. *Institutes* 2.8.35.

80. Comm. Romans 13:1; CO 49:248; *Commentaries on Romans*, 477.

81. Comm. Romans 13:1; CO 49:249.

82. Wallace, *Calvin's Doctrine*, 106; Schreiner, *The Theatre of His Glory*, 85–86; John H. Leith, *John Calvin's Doctrine of the Christian Life* (Louisville, KY: Westminster/John Knox Press, 1989), 166.

83. Comm. Genesis 3:16; CO 23:91; *Commentaries on Genesis*, 204.

84. Comm. Genesis 3:16; CO 23:91; *Commentaries on Genesis*, 204.

85. Comm. Genesis 6:11; CO 23:120; *Commentaries on Genesis*, 253. 'sed extincta iustitiae luce . . .'

86. Comm. Genesis 6:11; CO 23:121; *Commentaries on Genesis*, 253.

87. Comm. Genesis 6:11; CO 23:121; *Commentaries on Genesis*, 253.

88. CO 35:267; translation from John Calvin, *Sermons on the Book of Job*, trans. Arthur Golding (Edinburgh: Banner of Truth Trust, 1993), 657; cf. Schreiner, *The Theatre of His Glory*, 85–6.

89. CO 35:267; *Sermons on Job*, 657.

90. CO 35:267; *Sermons on Job*, 657.

91. Cf. Taylor, *A Secular Age*, 104–7 for an interesting reflection on Calvin's influence on the idea of a 'disciplinary society'.

92. *Institutes* 4.20.2.

93. Comm. 1 Timothy 2:2; CO 52:267; translation from *Calvin's Commentaries on the Epistles to Timothy, Titus and Philemon*, trans. William Pringle (Grand Rapids, MI: Eerdmans, 1948), 481.

94. Schreiner, *The Theatre of His Glory*, 82.

95. *Institutes* 4.20.5; cf. Comm. Micah 4:3; CO 21:348.

96. *LW*, 45:90; Duncan B. Forrester, 'Martin Luther and John Calvin', in *History of Political Philosophy*, ed. Leo Strauss and Joseph Cropsey (Chicago: Rand McNally, 1969), 288.

97. *LW*, 45:91.

98. *Institutes* 4.20.2.

99. Biéler, *Calvin's Economic and Social Thought*, 251.

100. Comm. 1 Timothy 2:2; CO 52:266; *Commentaries on Timothy*, 51; cf. Comm. Romans 13:1; CO 49:248–9. On the wider purpose of Calvin's political thought, see Marta Garcia-Alonso, 'Calvin's Political Theology in Context', *Intellectual History Review* (2020), doi: 10.1080/17496977.2020.1790149.

101. Comm. Romans 13:4; CO 49:251; *Commentaries on Romans*, 481.

102. Comm. Psalm 101:5; CO 31:56.

103. Comm. 1 Timothy 2:2; CO 52:267; *Commentaries on Timothy*, 51.

104. *Institutes* 4.20.3; cf. T. H. L. Parker, *Calvin: An Introduction to His Thought* (Louisville, KY: Westminster/John Knox Press, 1995), 157–8.

105. *Institutes* 4.20.3; Comm. 1 Timothy 2:2; CO 52:267–8; Comm. Isaiah 49:23; CO 37:210–12.

106. Cf. *LW*, 1:115: 'There was no need of civil government, since nature was unimpaired and without sin.'

107. Schreiner, *The Theatre of His Glory*, 82–3; cf. Bohatec, *Calvin und das Recht*, 57ff.; Biéler, *Calvin's Economic and Social Thought*, 247, cf. 185.

108. Dowey, *The Knowledge of God in Calvin's Theology*, 61.

109. Ibid., 62–3.

110. Ibid., 63.

111. Theodore Beza, 'Life of Calvin', in *Tracts and Treatises on the Reformation of the Church*, trans. Henry Beveridge (Grand Rapids, MI: Eerdmans, 1958), lxii.

112. Seneca, *De clementia*, 3.2.

113. John Calvin, *Commentary on Seneca's De Clementia*, trans. Ford Lewis Battles and Andre Malan Hugo (Leiden: Brill, 1969), section 28, 83–5.

114. Calvin cites the following works in ibid.: Cicero, *De Officiis*, 2.2; Plato, Epistle 9 to Artchytam as quoted in Cicero, *De Finibus*, 2.14.45ff; Aristotle, *Politics*, 1278b19.

115. Backus, 'Calvin's Concept', 20.

116. Comm. Genesis 2:18; CO 23:46; *Commentaries on Genesis*, 128.

117. *Institutes* 4.13.3.

118. *LW*, 1:115–16.

119. Comm. Genesis 2:18; CO 23:46; *Commentaries on Genesis*, 128. 'sed potius existimo communem esse humanae vocationis regulam'.

120. Comm. Genesis 2:18; CO 23:46; *Commentaries on Genesis*, 128.

121. Comm. Genesis 2:18; CO 23:46; *Commentaries on Genesis*, 128.; cf. *Institutes* 2.2.13, where he uses the same phraseology. Andrew Fulford points out that Calvin is referring to postlapsarian society at this point, in Andrew Fulford, 'Participating in Political Providence: The Theological Foundations of Resistance in Calvin', in *For the Healing of the Nations: Essays on Creation, Redemption and Neo-Calvinisn*, ed. Peter Escalante and W. Bradford Littlejohn (Charleston: Davenant Press, 2014), 112. This only further illustrates the continuity being discussed.

122. Comm. Genesis 2:18; CO 23:46; *Commentaries on Genesis*, 128.

123. John Calvin, *Sermons on Genesis: Chapters 1:1–11:4*, trans. Rob Roy McGregor (Edinburgh: Banner of Truth Trust, 2009), 180–1.

124. Nico Vorster, 'Symbiotic Anthropology and Politics in a Postmodern Age: Rethinking the Political Philosophy of Johannes Althusius (1557–1638)', *Renaissance and Reformation* 38.2 (2015): 32, n21.

125. Calvin, *Sermons on Genesis*, 181.

126. Ibid., 191–3.

127. Comm. Genesis 2:18; CO 23:46–8; Comm. Ephesians 5:21; CO 51:221–2; Nico Vorster, '"United but not Confused": Calvin's Anthropology as Hermeneutical Key to Understanding his Societal Doctrine', *Journal of Church and State* 58.1 (2016): 134.

128. Dowey, *The Knowledge of God in Calvin's Theology*, 223.

129. Comm. Romans 8:20; CO 49:152–3.

130. Comm. Romans 8:20; CO 49:152; Schreiner, *The Theatre of His Glory*, 29.

131. Comm. Ephesians 5:31; CO 51:226; translation from *Calvin's Commentaries on The Epistles of Paul to the Galatians and Ephesians*, trans. William Pringle (Grand Rapids, MI: Baker Book House, 1984), 323.

132. Comm. Ephesians 5:31; CO 51:226; *Commentaries on Ephesians*, 324.
133. Comm. Ephesians 5:31; CO 51:226; *Commentaries on Ephesians*, 324.
134. Comm. Ephesians 5:31; CO 51:226.
135. Comm. 1 Timothy 2:12; CO 52:276; *Commentaries on Timothy*, 68.
136. Comm. 1 Timothy 2:12; CO 52:276; *Commentaries on Timothy*, 68.
137. Comm. 1 Timothy 2:12; CO 52:276; *Commentaries on Timothy*, 68.
138. Comm. 1 Timothy 2:12; CO 52:276; *Commentaries on Timothy*, 68.
139. 1 Cor. 11:7–10.
140. Comm. 1 Cor. 11:8; CO 49:476; translation from *Calvin's Commentaries: Commentary on the Epistles of Paul the Apostle to the Corinthians*, trans. John Pringle (Grand Rapids, MI: Eerdmans, 1948), 357.
141. Comm. 1 Cor. 11:10; CO 49:477; *Commentaries on Corinthians*, 358.
142. Comm. 1 Cor. 11:10; CO 49:477; *Commentaries on Corinthians*, 358.
143. *Institutes* 1.5.11.
144. For an excellent discussion of this see Peter Harrison, *The Fall of Man and the Foundations of Science* (Cambridge: Cambridge University Press, 2007), 59–64.
145. Comm. Romans 1:21; CO 49:25; *Commentaries on Romans*, 72–3.
146. Comm. Romans 1:21; CO 49:25; *Commentaries on Romans*, 73.
147. *Institutes* 2.2.12.
148. Cf. Schreiner, *The Theatre of His Glory*, 66–7.
149. *Institutes* 2.2.12.
150. Ibid.
151. *Institutes* 2.2.13.
152. Ibid., 2.2.13; cf. *LW*, 2:160; *LW*, 26:123–4; Althaus, *The Theology of Martin Luther*, trans. Robert C. Schultz (Philadelphia: Fortress Press, 1966), 143.
153. *Institutes* 2.2.13; cf. William R. Stevenson Jr., 'Calvin and Political Issues', in *The Cambridge Companion to John Calvin*, ed. Donald K. McKim (Cambridge: Cambridge University Press, 2004), 174.
154. *Institutes* 2.2.13.
155. Ibid.
156. Ibid.
157. *Institutes* 4.20.4.
158. Ibid.
159. Schreiner, *The Theatre of His Glory*, 83.
160. Comm. Romans 13:1; CO 49:249; *Commentaries on Romans*, 478.
161. Cf. Calvin's response to *The Schleitheim Articles* of 1527, *Brieve instruction pour armer tous bons fideles contre les erreurs de la secte commune des Anabaptistes* (Geneva: Iehan Girard, 1544); CO 7:49–142; A good English translation of Calvin's response to article 6 of the *Confession* is found in John Calvin, *Treatises Against the Anabaptists and Against the Libertines*, ed. and trans. Benjamin Wirt Farley (Grand Rapids, MI: Baker Book House, 1982), 76–91.

162. Comm. Romans 13:1; CO 49:249; *Commentaries on Romans*, 479.
163. Ibid.
164. Cf. Herdt, 'Calvin's Legacy', 435, who cautiously suggests that Calvin's natural law theory, 'given key alterations', might have provided a path to the development of modern natural law theory.
165. Pryor, 'God's Bridle', 249.

# Chapter 2

# Richard Hooker's Theistic Naturalism

In the opening chapters of his *Second Treatise of Government*, published in 1689, John Locke quotes the Elizabethan divine Richard Hooker at some length in support of his anthropology and his doctrine of the state of nature.[1] Humans, writes Locke, are equal 'by Nature', something which 'the Judicious Hooker looks upon as self-evident'.[2] Locke begins to paint Hooker as a proto-contractarian in this passage. Later, Locke goes on to bring this assertion home with a long quote about the truth of his own conception of the state of nature. Locke's method of rebuttal to those who object to his conception of the state of nature is to paint his opponents as also opposing 'the Authority of the Judicious Hooker'.[3] Was Locke citing him accurately? Or was he, as Robert Eccleshall put it, 'unacquainted with the substance of Hooker's thought', and was instead using him 'as a stick with which to beat Anglican royalists'?[4] In my estimation, Eccleshall is correct, at least insofar as Locke's motivation for using Hooker, even if he underestimates his familiarity with Hooker's ideas.

Locke's citation of Hooker with regard to the origins of political life gets to the core question of this book. How did the idea of political life become desacralised during the early modern period? And what role did Reformed natural law ideas play in this? In a later chapter, we will consider Locke in more detail, whose thought regarding natural law and the origins of political life effectively removes God from having a role in the foundation of political life. But Locke's use of Hooker raises the possibility that it was Hooker who laid the groundwork for the secular conceptions of political life that were to follow him. The contention of this chapter is that this interpretation is mistaken. As demonstrated below, Hooker's understanding of law and his theory of the origins of society were quite different from Locke's social contractarian ideas. We shall see that Hooker's thought was much closer to that of Calvin than Locke. Hooker had an Aristotelian understanding of humanity's political anthropology, mixed with an Augustinian theological anthropology. Like Calvin, Hooker maintained a sacred understanding of civic existence. Indeed, contrary to some Hooker commentators, I will argue that he eschewed a conventionalist account of the origins of politics, embracing instead a theistic political naturalist account of political life. In Hooker's thought, God creates political life through the means of the natural law. In this sense, then, Hooker was a political naturalist, though not an Aristotelian naturalist. Humans are granted a subordinate agency in Hooker's thought by the law of reason, which is itself a subset of the natural law. If he was an Aristotelian naturalist, he would have held to the Aristotelian view that political life is a final end or purpose for humans. Contra Aristotle, Hooker's naturalism was not based on the final cause of politics, but is a naturalism based on the efficient cause.[5]

Another similarity between Calvin and Hooker was their Augustinian anthropology. Hooker emphasised human sin in his account of the nature and purpose of civil government, and this will be expanded upon below. One important discontinuity between Calvin and Hooker was the role Hooker gives humankind in the establishment of society. Hooker emphasised the role of consent in the framing and functioning of political life. This sets the tone, in some ways, for the contract theories of Reformed Protestants a century later, including Locke. Indeed, as we will see, Hooker's emphasis on consent and Johannes Althusius's emphasis on covenant (*pactum*) indirectly provide the theoretical tools undergirding the conventionalist contract theories of Hobbes and Locke. But this chapter, and the one that follows on Althusius, will show that neither Hooker nor Althusius can be labelled as conventionalists or contractarians. In Hooker's case, his understanding of the natural law and the role it plays in the establishment of politics means that he retained the understanding that God is the founder of political life. Therefore, Hooker was not an early advocate for a desacralised foundation for political life within the Reformed Protestant tradition. Human society and politics remained sacral in his thought.

To paint the above picture, we shall do the following. First, we will examine the context for Hooker's thought, emphasising his role in the intramural polemics of the Elizabethan Church of England.

Second, there will be a demonstration of Hooker's Augustinian anthropology, an often-overlooked aspect of his thought. Third, we shall examine his theory of law, which will focus on his exposition of the natural law. This section will provide the basis for the fourth and final section, which will be an exposition of his theory of the origins of politics.

## Reformation, Renewal and Polemics

The brief and bloody reign of Queen Mary left the English church, and England herself, reeling from a certain religious and civic disorientation. Mary was loyal to the Church of Rome and suppressed and reversed the reforming activity that had begun during the Henrician Reformation. Her untimely death in 1558 meant that Elizabeth, her half-sister, became the sovereign. Being a Protestant, Elizabeth set about restoring the Henrician relationship between the church, the commonwealth and the crown. However, while her ascension was widely welcomed by Protestants, her half-sister's reign had set the scene for ecclesiastical conflict.

Richard Hooker was born during the early years of the Marian regime, in 1554. He was bred and educated in Exeter and, despite not being well-off, was able to find a place at Corpus Christi College, Oxford, through his well-connected uncle, John Hooker.[6] Hooker's patronage came from ecclesiastical circles, first John Jewel (Bishop of Salisbury) and then Edwin Sandys (Bishop of London). He earned his Bachelor of Arts in 1573 and his Master of Arts in 1577, finally becoming a Fellow of Corpus Christi in 1579.[7] His academic career was a flourishing one, but he soon made a move into ecclesiastical life.

Hooker's ministerial life began in a church which was fraught with discord, debate and division, which Hooker would attempt to assuage in his own work. As Macaulay puts it, '[the] spirit of Protestantism was . . . far fiercer and more intolerant after the cruelties of Mary than before them'.[8] Many Protestant divines fled to the continent during Mary's reign and sat under the tutelage of influential reformers, including those in the Swiss city-states such as Calvin. Notably, their number included John Hooker and John Jewel.[9] While they returned happily to Elizabeth's England after her ascension to the throne in 1558, they were armed with new theological convictions which would set the tone for intramural conflict within the Church of England. Purity of worship was important for many of these divines, including matters of clerical dress, liturgical aesthetics and church government. However, the order set down by Elizabeth in her religious settlement, particularly in the Act of Supremacy and the Act of Uniformity of 1559, failed to smooth out the latent differences between the gathering clerical factions.[10]

There had been a disagreement brewing about priestly vestments, whereby more reform-minded Protestants were pushing back against the requirement to wear certain garments as defined by the rules under the Elizabethan Settlement.[11] As Patrick Collinson writes, 'the chief bone of contention was acknowledged to be the surplice and the outdoor clerical dress' forced upon ministers.[12] Clerical dress was not the only point of disagreement, though. An especially defining controversy, one which Hooker himself would later respond to, was ignited by a young theologian by the name of Thomas Cartwright. During a series of lectures in 1570 at Cambridge, on the biblical book of Acts, he expounded the presbyterian doctrine of church government.[13] While we know very little of the substance of the lectures, it does appear it was the first public salvo in the question over the government of the English church.[14] However, even more important was the publication of John Field and Thomas Wilcox, the *Admonition to Parliament*, in 1572.

The *Admonition* called for the institution of biblical standards in church government and worship and brought together the various elements of the Puritan disagreement with the church establishment.[15] This pamphlet forced a response from John Whitgift (later to become Archbishop of Canterbury), who, contrary to the *Admonition*, defended the episcopal government of the church. This prompted Cartwright to weigh in, beginning a long and drawn-out debate.[16] The nub of the question bouncing between Whitgift and Cartwright was the role of scripture in the determination of 'things indifferent'. The Latin word commonly used for this concept is *adiaphora*.[17] If scripture is not ultimately determinative on an issue, then questions of reason, tradition and law arise when seeking guidance. Hooker's own contribution to this debate came much later, but it is the Cartwright and Whitgift controversy which brings context to Hooker's own writings.

Hooker's public profile built gradually during the 1580s, as he was ordained, preached at the famous Paul's Cross on predestination, and was made 'Master of the Temple' in 1585.[18] This latter post was an influential one, being as it was the parish for lawyers and law students in the Temple, London.[19] It was also the site of a significant public dispute between Hooker and the

Reader at the Temple church, Walter Travers. Travers was the author of the anti-episcopal *Book of Discipline*, composed during the winter of 1584–5.[20] The new ministry team at the Temple church proceeded to give the differences between the Puritans and establishment thinkers, as Collinson writes, 'some theological definition in the parallel courses of sermons . . . preached from the same pulpit'.[21] Travers was eventually banished from the pulpit, leaving Hooker with a divided congregation. Hooker took an opportunity to move to a quieter parish in Wiltshire in 1591, in part so that he could work on the conclusion to the debate which he himself had lived out at the Temple.[22] Indeed, Izaak Walton writes that 'the foundation of [*The Laws of Ecclesiastical Polity*] was laid in the Temple, but he found it no fit place to finish what he had there esigned'.[23]

It is in this context, as a country parson but dealing with issues affecting the national church, that Hooker wrote the *Laws of Ecclesiastical Polity*.[24] He addressed the foundation and kinds of law in Book I, the role of scripture in questions of church government in Book II and Book III, and defended the Church of England against charges of having 'Popish Orders, Rights and Ceremonies' in Book IV.[25] Most strikingly, throughout these early books, he defended the principles of *adiaphora*, different kinds of law and the role of human reason.[26] Each of these principles was applied readily to the questions before Cartwright and Whitgift about the role of the Bible and the question of church government. These first four books were published in 1593, although not without some last-minute political manoeuvring from Hooker's old friend Edwin Sandys, who asked Hooker to add sections which paralleled the puritan demands with those of the more radical continental Anabaptists.[27] Book V, published in 1597, was on a similar theme to Book IV but addressed more specific objections relating to liturgy, the sacraments, the church calendar and set prayers.

After what Walton describes as a 'long and sharp sickness', Hooker died at Bishopsbourne in 1600.[28] He was only 46 years old. At the time that he died, Hooker was part way through the writing of the final books of the *Laws*. Because of the unfinished condition of the manuscripts that form the basis for these books, there have been concerns about the validity of what we now know as Books VI, VII and VIII. Add to these the emerging seventeenth-century political and ecclesiastical theories of divine-right kingship and divine-right apostolic succession, both of which are more or less undermined by Hooker's accounts in these later books, the confusion over the actual contents and delayed publication of these books is understandable.[29] Locke, in his own writing, only drew on Book I of the *Laws*, even though he appears to have had access to the entirety of the extant work. But the general scholarly consensus holds that what we have in the last three books is Hooker's work and Hooker's own considered thoughts on the subjects at hand.[30] Hooker's stated intention for Book VI is to refute the importance of lay-eldership in the church, but the surviving text is taken up almost entirely with the question of the purported sacramental status of confession and penance. Book VII is a historical and exegetical defence of episcopacy as a form of church government. The final book, Book VIII, is the most fragmentary of the texts that survive. Nonetheless, it remains a fascinating and robust defence of the Elizabethan arrangement of the headship of the civil magistrate over the church. Books VI and VIII were first published in 1648, and Book VII reached the public eye in 1662.[31]

This excursus into Hooker's life, as well as the biography of his *Laws of Ecclesiastical Polity*, sets the scene for the discussion of his ideas on the nature and origins of political life. Hooker's concern for the role and function of law, nature and scripture, as well as the interweaving of these, all played an important part of his polemic against the nonconformist critics of the Elizabethan church. Hooker's brief was, in part, to refute the grounds upon which these critics attacked the liturgy and government of the church, and Hooker did so by first clearly outlining the role of law in the world, and then the role of law in the formation of 'politic societies'.

Indeed, as Arthur S. McGrade states, 'Hooker's distinctive contribution to the English Reformation debate consisted of . . . carrying disputed issues back to first principles.'[32] In this context, we can trace the threads of his Thomistic theory of natural law. We can also see that he, like Calvin, places great stock in natural sociability of humans and, despite his emphasis on consent and human reason in the formation of political community, is a theistic political naturalist. This is the foundation of his sacral understanding of politics. Political life is of a sacred origin, even though humans have a distinct role in its establishment. However, this account of the Thomistic, Aristotelian bent to Hooker's ideas must be balanced by his emphasis on the Fall and sin in his anthropology. As W. Bradford Littlejohn puts it, Hooker 'takes with the utmost seriousness . . . the intractable clay of fallen humanity with which we have to work'.[33] It is this concept of 'fallen humanity' in Hooker's thought that we turn to first.

## The Fall and Sin in Hooker's Thought

In order to properly understand Hooker's ideas on the origins of politics, they must be considered alongside his theological anthropology. The Fall is a significant element in Hooker's understanding of human nature, as is usually the case with most theologically minded Christian thinkers. His understanding of human nature, when addressing the question of the impact of the Fall, is basically Augustinian.[34] The role that this part of his thought plays in his political ideas has received scant scholarly attention.[35] In this chapter, I seek to rectify this lack of attention to the relationship between Hooker's anthropology, his jurisprudence and his theory of political origins. In doing this, I hope to show that his theological anthropology is nuanced and balanced by an Aristotelian political anthropology, which means he finds a middle way between Augustine and Aristotle on the question of the origins of political life. Political life is necessary after the Fall, but that does not mean it is not possible before the Fall. To understand this distinction in Hooker's thought, we must understand his doctrine of sin.

The first key point in Hooker's hamartiology is his affirmation of the Augustinian conception of original sin, wherein all humanity is sinful because of their familial connection to Adam. The clearest statement of this comes in a surviving fragment of an undated letter, first published in 1836, where Hooker responds to a previous letter from some clergymen who disputed his fidelity to the Thirty-Nine Articles of the Church of England.[36] In the midst of an argument about the universal efficacious atonement of Christ, and this in spite of the sovereign decree of God to elect some to salvation and not others, Hooker says that all of Adam's posterity are sinful. He writes, '[the] whole masse which conteyneth . . . Adam and Adams naturall posteritie without exception of any one, wee find from the first to the last none in whome there is not unrighteousness, eyther actuall, or att the least originall'.[37] In another passage, Hooker parallels the redemptive blessings of Christ with the lapsarian curse of Adam. The blessings of Jesus 'passe from him to his whole race as malediction came from Adam unto all mankinde'.[38] In other words, all humanity is affected by Adam's first sin and all are, therefore, unrighteous. Hooker further describes the deep sinfulness of humanity by asserting that all sin originates in humanity itself, not in God, who is innocent of evil. He writes that no terrible event or 'calamity' originates in God himself but, on the contrary, 'his owne most sacred will, directeth us unto sinne as the verie roote out of which it originallie groweth; and because wee are sinfull, therefore the [burden] under which wee groane, wee impute to none butt ourselves only'.[39] All evil in human life originates in human sin. This illustrates the import of Hooker's doctrine of human sin.

He writes elsewhere, in his response to the critics of his *Laws*, of the will in human nature, saying that it is 'soe indisposed through a native evill habit that if God's speciall grace did not aid our imbecilitie, whatsoever wee doe or imagine would only be continuallie evill'.[40] In his exploration of human law, he notes that humans cannot 'learne of our selves' nor learn from others how to enjoy a good life because 'wickedness and malice have taken deepe roote'.[41] This wickedness is so ingrained in human nature, according to Hooker, that even when there was only one family on the earth (referring to Adam, Eve and their sons, Cain and Abel), 'no instruction humane or divine could prevent effusion of bloud'.[42] When he preached on Habakkuk 2:4, focusing on pride, he emphasised that '[we] are not dust and ashes but wourse, our mindes from the highest to the lowest are not right'.[43] Indeed, '[all] being wrapped up in sinne and made therby the children of death'.[44] The picture painted by Hooker of the effects and extent of human sin is, as Egil Grislis notes, 'strikingly radical'.[45]

Despite the depth of human depravity, Hooker holds that people can know the natural law of God. This ability is important as we approach his conception of the natural law's role in establishing political life. This capacity to know the natural law is, according to Hooker, a special grace of God, even if it is one separate from the saving grace offered through Jesus Christ. In his *Answer* to the critics of his *Laws*, Hooker affirms that 'without God's preventing and helping grace we are nothing at all able' to do any good at all.[46] However, humankind is still capable of natural knowledge. That is, Hooker affirms the ability of people to discern God's law as set down in nature, but special intervention is needed to bring them to salvation. God graciously '[bestows] gifts, to take away those impediments which are growne into Nature through sin'.[47] Humankind's 'naturall powers and faculties' are 'through our native corruption soe weakened' that we need God's 'speciall grace' to produce 'blossoms [and] buds that tende to the fruit of eternall life'.[48] Indeed, '[there] is no kind of faculty or power in man . . . which can rightly performe the functions allotted to it, without the perpetuall aid and concurrence of [God]'.[49] In other words, sin has so marred humanity's ability to function and reason that our grasp of the natural and moral law of God is, in Littlejohn's words, 'no longer clear and reliable'.[50]

But humanity still retains 'a reasonable understanding, and a will thereby framable to good things', and with God's help, people can pursue goodness and virtue.[51] This makes political life possible after the Fall, which obviously means it was possible before the Fall. Indeed, I would argue that Hooker holds, like Calvin, that political life is a possibility in the prelapsarian world, even if it is not a necessity. However, to return to our point, things that are good are knowable for humans 'if Reason were diligent to search it out'.[52] 'He is the author of all that we thinke or doe by vertue of that light, which he himselfe hath given', writes Hooker.[53] Moreover, these gifts from God, which illumine humanity's natural capacities and abilities, Hooker identifies with the Apostle Paul's statements about people knowing God's law 'by the light of nature' in Romans 1 and 2.[54] This, too, is similar to Calvin's understanding of the noetic effects of sin; humans are depraved but not incapable of temporal good. Indeed, according to Hooker, '[that] little sparke of the light of nature which remayneth in us may serve us for [the affairs] of this life'.[55] This 'little sparke' can be logically linked to Hooker's understanding of human reason and the role it plays in his jurisprudence. Despite the depravity of humankind, Hooker saw that people still had use of reason and, as discussed below, reason is linked with an understanding of the law of nature. It is to Hooker's jurisprudence that we now turn, where we will observe the links between Hooker's doctrine of sin, his understanding of law, and his understanding of the origins of political life.

## Law: Eternal, Divine and Natural

The foundation for Hooker's ideas on the origins of politics is found in his exposition of the multiple forms of law in his *Laws of Ecclesiastical Polity*. This foundation supplies the basic structural content of his theory of the origins of political life, while also providing material for his polemic against presbyterian arguments about church government.[56] His jurisprudence is, fundamentally, Thomist, although there are some small differences.[57] Hooker also displays a variation in the typical Aristotelian and Thomist understanding of political origins. He places great emphasis on human reason in the formation of society and, thereby, retains the primary agency of God in his theory while allowing humanity a significant role. This emphasis on human reason as well as consent is latched onto by Locke in his framing of political origins. But that need not distract us from the central point that, unlike Locke, Hooker is found to be a theistic, political naturalist. As will be demonstrated below, Hooker's conception of law affirms the goodness of the natural order as well as the necessity of civic life. God's eternal law is understood to be prior to and underneath everything, including humanity itself. Political life flows naturally out of the orderly, law-filled universe which Hooker describes in the opening chapters of the *Laws*. Despite human sin and the occasional departure from the natural order, political life is a natural, good outworking of his God-ordered universe.[58]

A key problem for Hooker was the relationship between ecclesiastical law, civil law and natural law.[59] Hooker was concerned to show that his presbyterian opponents were right to say that people are obliged to obey God's law, but he was principally concerned to show they were wrong in thinking there was only one law to obey.[60] Divine law, as revealed in the scriptures, was not the only source of authoritative law which guided action. The polemical needs of the moment required a response which balanced the need to defend the Elizabethan Settlement with still appealing to the opponents of that settlement. Hooker did this by adopting a broadly Thomistic approach to law, as outlined below.[61] However, as noted by Littlejohn, Hooker's Thomistic approach to legal theory was not without some deliberate modifications. These modifications suited both his polemical context and his theological tradition.[62] There is not adequate space here to go into much detail about this. Still, it is worth noting that Hooker's systematisation of legal theory and theology was in the same line as continental Reformed Protestant jurists like Franciscus Junius and Girolamo Zanchi. The latter's legal theory treatise was composed in the mid-1570s at Heidelberg and published in 1597 as a part of his *Operum theologicorum*, while the former wrote *De Politiae Mosis Observatione* in 1592 for the city magistrates at Leiden.[63] Both Junius and Zanchi adopted a broadly Thomistic approach to the question of law, with aspects of their thought cohering closely with Hooker's. These two examples lend weight to what will be demonstrated below: that Hooker's jurisprudence fits within the emerging 'Reformed Scholastic' school.[64]

Hooker's definition of law is 'that which doth assign unto each thing the kind, that which doth moderate the force and power, that which doth appoint the form and measure, of working'.[65] In short,

Hooker's understanding of law is that it is a rule directing or limit-ing something in order to guide it to its *telos*.[66] The similarities to Thomas are obvious upon comparison. Thomas writes that law is 'a rule and measure of acts, by which man is induced to act or is restrained from acting' by which humans, guided by practical rea-son, are directed to a particular purpose.[67] Further, it is, for Thomas, 'an ordinance of reason for the common good, made by him who has care of the community'.[68] The role of reason in relation to Hooker's understanding of law will be expanded upon below, but the parallels are significant enough to suggest Hooker's reliance on Thomists, if not Thomas himself, for this basic formulation. As A. S. McGrade points out, Hooker's conception of law is, like Thomas's, a non-coercive one, which has the virtue (for Hooker, at least) of '[allowing] him to apply the idea to God'.[69] Therefore, when Hooker recapitulates his definition of law at another point in the *Laws*, he includes God. Thus: 'A law therefore generally taken, is a directive rule unto goodnes of operation.' God determines the rule of 'divine operations' in himself, and '[the] rule of naturall agents . . . is the determination of the wisedome of God, known to God himselfe the principle Director of them'.[70] So, Hooker's con-ception of law is that of the ancient, or classical, variety, and God is a foundational and providential agent in the operation and enforce-ment of law.

The primary assertion of Hooker's legal theory is that God him-self is law.[71] God has internal workings which operate according to a kind of law, and he is the unmoved mover, the 'first cause, where-upon originally the being of all things dependeth'.[72] This is the 'law eternall' founded in God himself which, according to Hooker, is the cause and working of all things.[73] However, even though God is himself law, in the sense that all law is founded upon him, Hooker also understands that God binds himself to observe this eternal law, but is not subject to it, properly speaking. That is, 'the author and observer [of the eternal law] is one'.[74] This statement places Hooker firmly within the 'intellectualist' school of jurisprudence, of which Thomas's statement about God's relationship to law is archetypal: '. . . God's will is His very Essence, it is subject neither to the Divine government nor to the eternal law, but is the same thing as the eter-nal law.'[75] Here, Thomas makes the same equivalence between God and the eternal law: God is the law. However, Thomas concedes that 'we may speak of God's will as to the things themselves that God wills about creatures', and therefore God observes His own eternal law with respect to his will for created things.[76] Despite this submission to the eternal law, which is also immutable, Hooker maintains that God is voluntarily placing himself within the limits of that law and remains perfectly free.[77] However, Hooker distinguishes himself from Thomas by making a distinction between two kinds of eternal laws: the first is one by which God is a law in relation to himself, the second, God is a law in relation to all created things.[78]

Hooker purports that there are multiple types of law which are all derived in some sense from the second eternal law. The first two of these are the celestial law and the natural law. The celestial law is the law which is observed by heavenly beings, namely angels.[79] The natural law is the law 'which ordereth natural agents'. This law of nature undergirds the formation of political life, as we shall soon see. Within this law of nature, there is a division between the law which governs creatures who are reasonable and voluntarily keep the law and those who 'keep the law . . . unwittingly'.[80] In both cases of natural law, which governs both types of agents, the agent working through the law is God. Hooker writes that 'ever since the beginning' nature has been used by God 'to work his own will and pleasure withal'. Indeed, 'Nature . . . is nothing else but God's instrument.'[81] This is vital for our understanding of Hooker's account of the origins of political life. In Hooker's view, the natural law is God's implement through which he governs and guides his creatures. He even calls God's use of the natural law 'Providence', which implies God's active government in the created order.[82] At this point, it is worth noting that Hooker's focus on the natural law also has a polemical purpose. As Cargill Thompson observes, Hooker's discussion of natural law 'has an important role' in his debate with Puritans about church government and 'was intended to provide a philosophical basis for the . . . concept of "things indifferent"'.[83] Hooker wants to show his readers and, surely, his opponents that good and just laws have true force behind them, and that they are derived from God himself.[84] All of these explorations contribute, he says, to the 'question [concerning] the quality of ecclesiastical laws'.[85] In other words, his discussion of natural law and then the formation of political life all contributes what is of first importance for Hooker in the *Laws*: the validity and wisdom of episcopal church polity and practice.

Along with the natural and celestial laws, Hooker also posits two kinds of positive laws under the rubric of the 'second eternal law'. There are human laws and divine laws. The former are laws laid down by humans themselves, and the latter are those revealed by God through special revelation.[86] Hooker is here concerned to accurately decipher the relationship between the natural law and these latter two laws. How does God's positive law as revealed in the scriptures relate to human law as laid out in the civil and ecclesiastical realm? And how does the natural law relate to the same? As already noted, the natural law is, according to Hooker, fundamentally drawn up and enacted by God. Just as natural, irrational agents are guided by the natural law 'to their owne perfection', so too the rational agent, humanity, has a similar law for its own perfection.[87] In other words, humanity has a *telos* which the natural law drives them towards.[88] The *telos* is ultimately spiritual, in that it is 'participation in God himselfe'.[89] However, there is a temporal, ethical element to humanity's *telos* as well. The natural law is observable by humanity, and Hooker sees that, with training and education, humans are better 'able to judge rightly betweene truth and error, good and evill'.[90] Therefore, it is by reason that people can understand things 'that are and are not sensible'.[91] Accordingly, humans follow their reason to ascertain truths of ethical and social conduct. Here we must note a further variant on the Thomist schema in Hooker's legal theory, although, as Littlejohn notes, his 'reasoning is thoroughly Aristotelian'.[92] Hooker divides the natural law into one law for irrational agents, and one for rational agents, which he terms the 'Law of Reason'. Natural law is accessible and provides humans with evidence and guidance as to right conduct, and sin is the deliberate disordering of conduct in light of this. 'There is not that good which concerneth us, but it hath evidence enough for it selfe, if reason were diligent to search it out.'[93] The good dictates of natural law are available by human reason. It is here, in the inclusion of human reason in the working out of the natural law, that Hooker offers humans a limited role in their establishment of politics, as we shall see below.

But there seems to be a tension. The natural law is, according to Hooker, '[the] rule of natural agents' that works towards their good, and God is the 'Director' of those operations. If this is so, how can humans have agency in the outworking of a natural law-driven formation of society? If God directs the natural operations of humanity towards the good of human political life, where does humanity fit in? This is where Hooker balances, whether successfully or otherwise, the question of God's ordination and founding of political life with human action. It is through the category of human reason that Hooker provides a release from the tension. Human reason also plays an important role in Hooker's overall

polemic against the presbyterian and puritan claims against episcopal church government. We shall not go into this in any detail,
as others have done so already.[94] It suffices to note that Hooker
intended human reason to fill the gap between humanity's finite
capacity and his opponent's emphasis on the sufficiency of scripture. Reason would lead to clarity and resolve the debate. Hooker
writes in the 'Preface' to the *Laws*; 'Nor is mine own intent any
other ... than to make it appeare unto you, that for the ecclesi-
asticall lawes of this land, we are led by great reason to observe
them.'[95] Further, Hooker believed that his argument in favour
of the Elizabethan Settlement would be vindicated if his readers
'follow the light of sound and sincere judgement'.[96]

But more specific to our purposes, reason plays a mediating role
between human sinfulness and the interpretation of the natural law,
while also giving humanity a role in the establishment of political
life. For Hooker, reason is the 'rule of voluntary agents', whereby
they discern 'the goodness of those things which they are to do'.
In other words, reason guides action towards the good ends which
are evident by understanding the natural law. Indeed, the law of
nature is itself the 'law of reason'. Hooker writes that the 'Law
rationall' is that law which people 'commonly use to call the law
of nature', and is the law which human nature knows by reason.[97]
It 'may be termed most fitly the lawe of reason' and encapsulates
everything which people know they ought to do through their own
natural understanding.[98] Further, obedience to the law of reason is
righteous, whereas the contravention of it is sinful.[99] So, the natural
law is also the law of reason, meaning that the natural law is both
accessible to human reason and useful to humans in understanding natural things. This is important as we explore Hooker's ideas
about the origins of politics because Hooker holds that it is natural and, by virtue of his natural law framework, God-ordained.
However, because political life (as we shall see) is formed by nature
and, accompanying and equivalent to this, by reason, humans are
also implicated in the act.

Following Hooker, we shall deal with the question of human
laws next. Hooker has, up until this point in the outline of the different types of laws, dealt with the eternal law of God, and the types
of laws deriving from that eternal law. The eternal law establishes
the overall order and structure of all law in the universe and even
within the Godhead itself. The celestial and natural laws flow out
from this, with the former governing angelic beings and the latter
governing temporal beings. The latter law, the natural law, is itself

divided into the law governing irrational and rational creatures, with the latter law being named the law of reason. All of these laws are implemented and enforced by God himself, according to Hooker. 'Rewards and punishments' for obedience and contravention of laws are, in Hooker's words, in 'the hands of such as being above us have power to examine and judge our deedes'.[100] The obvious question for Hooker's readers at this point is how humans come to have this kind of power over other humans.[101] How does human law come about? And what are the appropriate grounds for such a law to be made and enforced?

This question touches on the core of Hooker's answer to the presbyterian opponents of the Elizabethan Settlement. A large part of Hooker's case for episcopal government and, indeed, the royal supremacy over the Church of England, is the legitimacy of the human law which shapes and governs the church. He begins addressing this question by, first, addressing the origins of human government. It this question that we turn to next.

## Human Law and the Origins of Political Life

Hooker's discussion of the origins of human government precedes his discussion of human law because he understands that human government is not a product of human law; it is a product of natural law. The legislator of the natural law is, of course, God. This makes God the originator of politics in Hooker's thought. Humans are granted a subordinate agency by the law of reason, which is itself a subset of the natural law. Hooker's theory of government is discussed in a number of works and, as mentioned above, has raised questions with regard to his relationship to social contract theory, not least due to the explicit use of him by John Locke.[102] While this will be addressed in greater detail below, it suffices to say that Locke's use of Hooker has muddied the waters of interpretation on this question.[103] Alexander S. Rosenthal is adamant that 'Hooker's compact theory . . . preceded these latter theories [of Hobbes and Locke] and to a large degree influenced them.'[104] Indeed, Rosenthal goes on to conclude that Hooker was a Thomist, but a modified one who introduced a conventionalist account of human government.[105] Ernst Troeltsch draws a strong link between Hooker's theory of consent with regard to the royal supremacy and Locke's contractarian ideas.[106] Peter Munz is comfortable with linking Hooker to Locke in the same vein that Locke himself does. According to Munz, they agree on 'the basic principles of constitutional government', including the question of the origins of politics.[107] In short, these scholars and others like them maintain that Hooker is essentially a proto-contractarian. Upon this interpretation, Hooker is a conventionalist with regard to political origins, who 'anticipated' thinkers like Hobbes and Locke.[108]

It is my contention in this section that Hooker's framework for the origins of political life demonstrates that he is a theistic political naturalist.[109] His theory of natural law feeds his theory of political origins and is balanced with the anthropological necessity of human fallenness flowing from his Augustinianism.[110] Hooker does indeed hold that human government is, in the words of Rosenthal, a 'human arrangement'.[111] However, the contention here is that because human government is prior to human law in Hooker's thought, human government is not made according to human law. Instead, it is made according to God's law. Politics remains sacralised and natural in Hooker's political thought. Like Calvin's theory, it is sacralised and natural despite his Augustinian anthropology.

To demonstrate this point, we will now unpack in some detail the argument surrounding the origins of political life in Book I of the *Laws*, before addressing the relevant statements in the remaining Books. Book VIII will garner special attention, as these texts are where Hooker seems to offer a conventionalist account of human government. However, the following evidence will, hopefully, demonstrate why this conclusion ought to be unconvincing. In short, my case regarding the texts in Book VIII is that taken on their own and out of context, they seem to justify the claim that Hooker believes political life to be a human artefact. If that were true, those who believe him a forerunner to Hobbes and Locke would have a very strong case. However, these texts must be read in light of the carefully constructed jurisprudence of Book I, in which case they are understood rather differently. But first, we continue our trek through Book I.

As noted above, Hooker has up until this point been outlining his theory of natural law and the 'law of reason'. Instead of continuing on the typically Thomist route by theorising on divine law, Hooker's next stop is human law. For our purposes, it is most notable that, in Hooker's account, human law is not possible without the consent of a properly formed commonwealth.[112] If the commonwealth must precede the existence of human positive law, then human government must be formed apart from human law. Indeed, it is pertinent that Hooker begins his discourse on human law by reinforcing the existence of laws above those made by humanity, and that 'nature it selfe teacheth lawes and statutes to live by'.[113] Hooker is stating that the foundation for what follows is the natural law. The natural law is effective and binding, says Hooker. However, because humanity is not able to 'furnish' those things which are necessary for the life 'which our nature doth desire', we 'naturally' seek community with others.[114] This concept that a person on their own cannot sufficiently provide for themselves is a common trope in political thought, stemming from Aristotle and echoed by Althusius below. This natural desire to seek community sets up a key distinction in Hooker's thought on the question of the origins of society: the distinction between pre-political society and post-political society. Or, put another way, between society (as in, social life) and government (as in, political life).

The distinction is important, but I would contend it is so in a different way to some scholars. For example, Joan Lockwood O'Donovan says that, for Hooker, society springs from the above-mentioned insufficiency of humans in and of themselves, whereas human government 'originates in the sinful depravity of individuals'.[115] However, O'Donovan does not acknowledge that Hooker allows for the possibility of political life before the Fall. According to his own jurisprudence, and his stated theory of the origins of society and government, both society and government spring from the same natural root. The root has two aspects, and both are aspects of human nature. One is human sin, the other is human insufficiency. First, Hooker states that the prelapsarian condition did not require political life as such. Indeed, he writes that 'men might have lived without any publike regiment', even if political life was not contrary to the sinless human condition.[116] Even though there might have been no specific requirement for political life flowing out of prelapsarian human nature, it was still consonant with it. Still, the Fall altered things so much that 'the lawe of nature doth now require of necessitie some kinde of regiment'.[117] Instead of being simply a possible arrangement, political life is now absolutely necessary, according to Hooker, because of the Fall.

The second aspect of Hooker's explanation for the natural origins of human society is humanity's natural lack of self-sufficiency. Hooker holds that '[humans] are naturally induced to seeke communion and fellowship with others'.[118] This natural inclination was 'the cause of men's uniting themselves at the first into politique societies'.[119] The thing which compelled humans to pursue political fellowship was their perfectly natural desire to live with others. Indeed, 'Civill society doth more content the nature of man than any private kind of solitarie living.'[120] Here, the law of nature is the foundation upon which the origins of political life are built. However, there is one more foundation. Hooker writes of 'an order expressly or secretly agreed upon touching the manner of their union in living together'.[121] This latter foundation is human positive law, agreed upon by either explicit or tacit agreement.[122] It seems, from this, that Hooker holds that human law precedes the formation of human government or human political life. If both the natural inclination towards social life and this agreed-upon form of law governing that social life are the 'foundations' of 'public societies', surely Hooker intends for human law to be the means by which political life comes about. However, this is not the case.

Instead, as will now be demonstrated, human law comes after the formation of political life in Hooker's thought. This is, admittedly, a truism. It might be too obvious a point because it makes way for his political naturalism. So how can it be a foundation if it is consequential to the formation of political life? Human law is a foundation for political life in the sense that it undergirds all human societies in an ongoing way. But Hooker does not hold that it plays an important role in the origins of politics. Rather, it is nature that establishes the grounds for the origins of politics. Hooker's theological anthropology plays an important role in understanding this. According to Hooker, all human laws should be framed with human fallenness in mind.[123] It is evident, according to Hooker, that humanity is evil, so much so that without human government there is the inevitable spread of 'envy, strife, contention and violence'.[124] Such being the case, Hooker posits that humans saw it entirely necessary to '[ordain] some kind of government publike', and to do so by consent.[125] Consent is necessary because the nature of political power is, according to Hooker, different from the nature of familial, or patriarchal, power. Political authorities do not enjoy the same 'naturall superioritie' as fathers do in their families.[126] At first glance, this seems to undermine my central claim, but that would be mistaken. Political power is still founded upon the natural law. Hooker allows for the possibility of there being no 'public regiment' if 'nature' is 'considered by it selfe', but because of the Fall and the resulting human evil, 'the lawe of nature doth now require of necessitie some kind of regiment'.[127] So, despite the difference in the nature of patriarchal and political authority, and despite the necessary presence of consent in the right constituting of political authority, it is 'the lawe of nature' that 'doth require' political life because of human sin.[128]

It is only at this point in his argument that Hooker examines the nature, extent and purpose of human laws as utilised in a political life. This reinforces my earlier point that human government precedes human law in Hooker's thought, implying that the formation of human government is not itself subject to human law but is subject to natural law. Hooker also does not hold that human government originates in human sinfulness; he holds that human government is necessary because of human sinfulness. Yet they are two different things. Hooker holds most fundamentally that human government originates in humanity's impulse to seek community, and in the postlapsarian world human community must be political community. In other words, the efficient cause of politics is natural for Hooker. He never denies the naturalness of political authority as such. Certainly, his political naturalism is not an Aristotelian naturalism because Aristotle's naturalism is focused on teleology and the 'final cause'. For Hooker, politics is natural when considered in light of the 'efficient cause'. It is natural to the human condition but is not (as with Aristotle) the highest purpose or end of human life.

We will now briefly examine some key texts in Book VIII of Hooker's *Laws* and show that these do not preclude a conventional understanding of political life. In each case, Hooker places the consent of the people in the given society in the pre-political condition, a condition governed by the natural law. Therefore, even these cases of consent are evidence for his political naturalism and, therefore, evidence for him holding a sacral view of political life. Hooker notes, in Book I of the *Laws*, that there are some 'very great and judicious men' who hold that there is a kind of natural right to rule 'in the noble, wise and vertuous'.[129] He is, of course, referring to Aristotle, and those who follow him. It seems that Hooker does not disagree. Rather, he thinks that some kind of consensual agreement is necessary for this natural right to be better enacted. Indeed, 'strifes and troubles would be endlesse' if people were not able to give 'their common consent all to be ordered by some whom they should agree upon'.[130] This mechanism of consent looms large in Hooker's thought, especially in Book VIII of the *Laws*, when he turns to the question of the royal supremacy over the Church of England.

The royal supremacy was disputed by his opponents on the grounds that no one but Jesus Christ could be the head of the church. Therefore, making the monarch the titular head usurped the role properly given to Christ himself.[131] It was Hooker's aim to prove the legitimacy of the crown's claim to be the constitutional head of the church and state. He did this, in part, by emphasising the role of the people in the establishment of political authority, showing that government can only be legitimised by consent.[132] The church and the commonwealth in England are personally one and the same, in Hooker's understanding.[133] Indeed, because, as Littlejohn puts it, 'religion is central to the life of virtue, and thus the life of the commonwealth' in Hooker's thought, the monarch can legitimately see to the betterment of both under his or her reign.[134] It was by consent that the English monarch ruled both the church and the commonwealth.[135]

One of Hooker's primary claims regarding the necessity for consent is that 'every independent multitude before any certaine forme of regiment established, hath . . . full dominion over it self'.[136] This dominion, or what might be called sovereignty in today's language, entails an ability and right for a group to decide for itself how they will live in community. Indeed, 'God creating mankinde did indue it naturally with full power to guide it self in what kindes of societies soever it should choose to live.'[137] So the 'independent multitude' can choose the shape and form of their social life, and they do so because God has 'indued' them naturally with the capacity and 'dominion' to do so. So, while the agency and 'dominion' is placed upon the shoulders of the human 'multitude' in this passage, Hooker believes God has 'indued' them naturally with this agency. In accordance with the jurisprudence outlined above, this is all occurring under the governance of the natural law and not human law.

Hooker then goes on to outline two further ways that a group of humans can come under a particular regime: by conquest and by divine fiat. Notably, 'it is God who gives the victory on the day of war', so that even in the case of conquest, God is the principal founder of the political life.[138] So there is a very important, fundamental sense in which God is always the author of political life in Hooker's thought. This is the case whether he uses the means of nature or other nations and peoples. Furthermore, this is the case even when the temporal means he uses to do so are people. Even in the principal instance of societal formation, where the multitude chooses its own political formation and submits to a ruler, Hooker says that God acts as the arch-authority who ratifies the people's decision to submit to that ruler.[139]

In another passage, Hooker reaffirms the 'dominion' of the people when he writes that '[the] naturall subject of power civill all men confesse to be the bodie of the Commonwealth'.[140] The people are the natural possessors of civil power, which is again grounded by Hooker in nature itself. Furthermore, 'the naturall subject of power to make lawes civill is the Commonwealth', and similarly for ecclesiastical laws, where the power is founded upon the 'whole intire body of that church'.[141] Indeed, regarding ecclesiastical laws, even the 'positive laws of the apostles' can be laid aside with the 'general consent' of the church.[142] The theme of consent is prominent in these passages, to be sure. However, the necessity for consent to form civil laws is based not on human convention, first and foremost, but on nature. This human consensus is formed, according to Hooker's jurisprudence, in the context of the rule of the natural law, not human law. For Hooker, God is the giver of the natural power to make laws.

This marries quite comfortably with the jurisprudence in Book I of the *Laws*. Hooker understands that the formation of political life precedes the making of human law, therefore political life is formed naturally, being under the natural law. God is the author and enforcer of the natural law and is, therefore, the primary agent in the formation of political life in Hooker's thought. Consent dominates Hooker's discussion regarding human law and political arrangements, but this is all in the context of humans being secondary agents in these matters. For Hooker, political life remains natural and sacralised.

## Conclusion

Alessandro d'Entrèves is, then, correct to say that in Hooker's thought, 'political organization may only claim a secondary, not primary value', and is not 'natural in the Aristotelian sense, as being a condition of human perfection'.[143] But whether Hooker was Aristotelian is not the primary question as we consider his doctrine of the origins of politics. Rather, we are interested in the relationship that Hooker might have to the emergence of a desacralised theory of the origins of politics. I have argued that, whether he was strictly Aristotelian or not, Hooker understood politics to be natural to the human condition. It is natural insofar as humanity is naturally inclined towards social life and that the law of nature requires that they form political societies. Further, the formation of political life occurs under the auspices of the natural law in Hooker's jurisprudence, not under the auspices of human law. The natural law is administered and enforced by God himself, making God the primary agent in the formation of political life. Of course, Hooker did not ignore or diminish the role of humanity. But he held that any agency humans have in the formation of political life occurs under the auspices and power of the natural law, and is not an act of human law.

Consent loomed large in Hooker's thought, but it did so because of his polemical context. His emphasis on consent countered his opponents' arguments about the unlawfulness of episcopal church government and royal supremacy. However, I would argue that it did not play an important role in his jurisprudential account of the origins of politics. Interestingly, it is this secondary element of consent which was later picked up by Locke and used to undergird his conventionalist theory of political life. Hooker also did not diminish the role of the Fall in his theory of the origins of politics. It is clear, according to Hooker, that political life is a counterweight to the effects of the Fall and that humanity is deeply sinful. However, politics does not exist simply because of the Fall. Hooker's thought was similar to Calvin's on this question. The Fall has had a significant impact on human social relations, and human government mitigates the effects of this degradation. But, as we have now seen, this did not rule out the naturalness of politics in either Calvin's or Hooker's thought. For Hooker, the natural law is in operation both before and after the Fall. The Fall does not destroy the natural law; it simply alters its operations. Therefore, the role of human government is altered too. It is still natural and is still required by natural law, but it has an altered role in the face of postlapsarian human sin.[144] In conclusion, Hooker was neither a conventionalist nor an Aristotelian on the question of the origins of political life. Instead, he represented a different kind of *via media* to the one usually attributed to him. God was still the author and founder of human political life, in Hooker's thought, and his theory of the origins of political existence remained sacral. We now turn to consider whether the same can be said of Johannes Althusius. As we do this, we will see that, as with Hooker, a core concept of Althusius's, that of covenant, was co-opted by later thinkers to shape a conventionalist, desacralised understanding of political life.

## Notes

1. The substance of this chapter has been previously published as Simon P. Kennedy, 'Richard Hooker as Political Naturalist', *The Historical Journal* 62.2 (2019): 331–48. The material appears here with the gracious permission of the editors.

2. TT, 2:5, 270.
3. TT, 2:15, 277.
4. Robert Eccleshall, *Order and Reason in Politics: Theories of Absolute and Limited Monarchy in Early Modern England* (Oxford: Oxford University Press, 1978), 129. Cited in Kirby, *Richard Hooker's Doctrine*, 11. Also see Michael Brydon, *The Evolving Reputation of Richard Hooker: An Examination of Responses* (Oxford: Oxford University Press, 2006), 139–40; Leo Strauss, *Natural Right and History* (Chicago: University of Chicago Press, 1953), 207. Strauss is on target when he suggests that Locke 'took every advantage of his partial agreement with Hooker'. However, I do not agree that Locke was being subversive in the typically Straussian sense.
5. Oakley, *Mortgage of the Past*, 78–80; cf. more generally Nederman, 'Nature, Sin and the Origins of Society', 3–26.
6. Lee W. Gibbs, 'Life of Hooker', in *A Companion to Richard Hooker*, ed. W. J. Torrance Kirby (Leiden: Brill, 2008), 9.
7. W. Bradford Littlejohn, *Richard Hooker: A Companion to His Life and Work* (Eugene: Wipf and Stock, 2015), 24; Izaak Walton, 'The Life of Mr Richard Hooker', in *The Works of that learned and judicious divine, Mr. Richard Hooker: with an account of his life and death by Isaac Walton*, ed. John Keble (Oxford: Oxford University Press, 1845), vol. 1, 17. Walton places it as 1577. However, this is clarified by Gibbs, who notes that he was made a 'scholar' in 1577 and 'a full fellow in 1579', in Gibbs, 'A Life of Hooker', 9.
8. Lord Macauley, *The History of England from the accession of James the Second* (London: Longman, Green, and Co., 1899), 29.
9. Both Gary Jenkins and Charles Miller place John Hooker as an exile, although they provide no documentary evidence for this. See Charles Miller, *Richard Hooker and the Vision of God: Exploring the Origins of 'Anglicanism'* (Cambridge: James Clarke & Co, 2013), 18; Gary Jenkins, 'Peter Martyr and the Church of England after 1558', in *Peter Martyr Vermigli and the European Reformations: Semper Reformanda*, ed. Frank A. James III (Leiden: Brill, 2004), 63.
10. For an overview of these Acts, see Joan Lockwood O'Donovan, *Theology of Law and Authority in the English Reformation* (Grand Rapids, MI: Eerdmans, 1991), 111–14.
11. For some general background to Hooker's polemical and ecclesiastical context, see the following: Patrick Collinson, *The Elizabethan Puritan Movement* (Oxford: Oxford University Press, 1990); W. Bradford Littlejohn, *The Peril and Promise of Christian Liberty: Richard Hooker, the Puritans, and Protestant Political Theology* (Grand Rapids, MI: Eerdmans, 2017), 50–124; O'Donovan, *Theology of Law*, 109–36; John F. New, 'The Whitgift–Cartwright Controversy', *Archiv für Reformationsgeschichte* 59 (1968): 203–12; Felicity Heal, *The Reformation in Britain and Ireland* (Oxford: Oxford University

Press, 2005), 353–424; Torrance Kirby, '"Relics of the Amorites" or "Things Indifferent"? Peter Martyr Vermigli's authority and the Threat of Schism in the Elizabethan Vestiarian Controversy', *Reformation & Renaissance Review* 6.3 (2004): 313–26.

12. Collinson, *The Elizabethan Puritan Movement*, 68.
13. Heal, *The Reformation in Britain and Ireland*, 373; Littlejohn, *Richard Hooker*, 20–1.
14. Collinson, *The Elizabethan Puritan Movement*, 112–13.
15. O'Donovan, *Theology of Law*, 119.
16. Heal, *The Reformation in Britain and Ireland*, 373; Littlejohn, *Peril and Promise of Christian Liberty*, 87–124; New, 'The Whitgift–Cartwright Controversy', 203–12.
17. Cf. Calvin, *Institutes* 3.19.7.
18. Walton, 'The Life of Mr Richard Hooker', 22–7; Littlejohn, *Richard Hooker*, 25; Gibbs, 'A Life of Hooker', 9–11.
19. Littlejohn, *Richard Hooker*, 25.
20. Heal, *The Reformation in Britain and Ireland*, 399.
21. Collinson, *The Elizabethan Puritan Movement*, 295.
22. Gibbs, 'A Life of Hooker', 13–14.
23. Walton, 'The Life of Mr Richard Hooker', 66.
24. This work is not Hooker's only work but it is the most relevant to the questions at hand. See P. G. Stanwood, 'Works and Editions I', in *A Companion to Richard Hooker*, ed. Kirby, 27.
25. Richard Hooker, *Of the Laws of Ecclesiastical Polity*, Book IV, from *Works of Richard Hooker*, ed. Keble, 416. I will cite the *Laws* as *LEP* [Book].[Chapter].[Section] herein.
26. See Littlejohn, *Richard Hooker*, 39, for a simple summary of the purpose of the book.
27. Gibbs, 'A Life of Hooker', 15.
28. Walton, 'The Life of Mr Richard Hooker', 84.
29. Gibbs, 'A Life of Hooker', 23. For an excellent overview of the textual debates and concerns surrounding these books, see ibid., 18–23.
30. For more on the historical and textual problems for books VI through VIII, see W. Speed Hill, 'Works and Editions II', in *A Companion to Richard Hooker*, ed. Kirby, 41–6.
31. Gibbs, 'A Life of Hooker', 17.
32. A. S. McGrade, 'Introduction', in *Hooker: Of the Laws of Ecclesiastical Polity*, ed. A. S. McGrade (Cambridge: Cambridge University Press, 1989), 15.
33. Littlejohn, *Peril and Promise of Christian Liberty*, 271.
34. Egil Grislis, 'The Role of Sin in the Theology of Richard Hooker', *Anglican Theological Review* 84.4 (2002): 881–96; Ranall Ingalls, 'Sin and Grace', in *A Companion to Richard Hooker*, ed. Kirby, 152–83. W. J. Torrance Kirby addresses Hooker's use of an Augustinian framework in his theories of law and sovereignty but leaves

aside the question of anthropology. See W. J. Torrance Kirby, 'From "Generall Meditations" to "Particular Decisions": The Augustinian Coherence of Richard Hooker's Political Theology', in *Sovereignty and Law in the Middle Ages and Renaissance*, ed. Robert Sturges (Turnhout: Brepols, 2011), 43–65.

35. Cf. O'Donovan, *Theology of Law*, 129–52; more generally, Kirby, *Richard Hooker's Doctrine*; W. D. J. Cargill Thompson, 'The Philosopher of the 'Politic Society': Richard Hooker as a Political Thinker', in W. D. J. Cargill Thompson, *Studies in the Reformation: Luther to Hooker* (London: Athlone Press, 1980), 131–91; more generally, Littlejohn, *Peril and Promise of Christian Liberty*.

36. John E. Booty, 'Introduction', in Richard Hooker, *Of the Laws of Ecclesiastical Polity: Attack and Response*, ed. John E. Booty, in *Folger Library Edition of The Works of Richard Hooker*, ed. W. Speed Hill, (Cambridge, MA: Belknap Press, 1982), IV, xiii–xiv. Booty notes that the anonymous letter critiquing Hooker is dated 1599, that 'Hooker died in November 1600' and that 'he had been preparing an answer to it' before he died. So, the dating is likely to be 1600, though possibly earlier. See ibid., xiii.

37. The fragment is reproduced in ibid., 147, lines 12–15. Subsequent citations of the Folger edition shall be in the form of *FLE* [volume]:[page]. [line]. So *FLE* 4:147.12–15.

38. *LEP* 5.56.10; Richard Hooker, *Of the Laws of Ecclesiastical Polity: Book V*, ed. W. Speed Hill, in *Folger Library Edition of The Works of Richard Hooker*, ed. W. Speed Hill (Cambridge, MA: Belknap Press, 1977), II, 241.23.

39. *FLE* 4:146.18–23.

40. Ibid., 101.15–18.

41. *LEP* 1.10.3; Richard Hooker, *Of the Laws of Ecclesiastical Polity: Preface, Books I to IV*, ed. Georges Edelen, in *Folger Library Edition of The Works of Richard Hooker*, ed. W. Speed Hill (Cambridge, MA: Belknap Press, 1977), I, 98.6–7.

42. *LEP* 1.10.3; *FLE* 1:98.8–9.

43. Richard Hooker, *Of the Laws of Ecclesiastical Polity: Tractates and Sermons*, ed. Laetitia Yeandale and Egil Grislis, in *Folger Library Edition of The Works of Richard Hooker*, ed. W. Speed Hill (Cambridge, MA: Belknap Press, 1990), V, 312.24–6.

44. Ibid., 312.30–1.

45. Grislis, 'The Role of Sin', 882.

46. *FLE* 4:101.4–6.

47. Ibid., 103.8–9.

48. Ibid., 103.12–17.

49. *LEP* 1.8.11; *FLE* 1:92.25–8.

50. Littlejohn, *Peril and Promise of Christian Liberty*, 214.

51. *FLE* 4:103.19–29.

52. *LEP* 1.7.7; *FLE* 1:80.30–1.

53. *LEP* 3.9.3; *FLE* 1:238.30–1.

54. *LEP* 3.9.3; *FLE* 1:239.2.

55. *LEP* 3.11.18; *FLE* 1:266.1–3.

56. W. J. Torrance Kirby, 'Richard Hooker's Theory of Natural Law in the Context of Reformation Theology', *Sixteenth Century Journal* 30.3 (1999): 684.

57. The problem of using 'Thomist' as a distinctive is parsed out in Paul Dominiak, 'Hooker, Scholasticism, Thomism, and Reformed Orthodoxy', in *Richard Hooker and Reformed Orthodoxy*, ed. W. Bradford Littlejohn and Scott Kindred-Barnes (Göttingen: Vandenhoeck & Ruprecht, 2017), 111–13; Lee W. Gibbs, 'Book I', in *Of the Laws of Ecclesiastical Polity: Introductions; Commentary, Preface and Books I–IV*, ed. W. Speed Hill, in *Folger Library Edition of The Works of Richard Hooker*, ed. W. Speed Hill (Binghamton, NY: Medieval & Renaissance Texts & Studies, 1993), VI, 92.

58. Cf. McGrade, 'Introduction', 22–3.

59. E.g. *LEP* 1.1.3. Also see 1.16.5.

60. Atkinson, *Richard Hooker and the Authority of Scripture*, 27–8; Littlejohn, *Peril and Promise of Christian Liberty*, 157; *LEP* 1.16.5.

61. The best recent study on this is Dominiak, 'Hooker, Scholasticism', 101–26; Alessandro P. d'Entrèves, *The Medieval Contribution to Political Thought: Thomas Aquinas, Marsilius of Padua, Richard Hooker* (New York: Humanities Press, 1959), 118–21.

62. Littlejohn, *Richard Hooker*, 135; cf. McGrade, 'Introduction', 17–19, where he suggests that Hooker may have had Scotus in mind when he formulated his jurisprudence, not Thomas. Dominiak also notes some similarities to Scotus, but emphasises Hooker's obvious reliance on Thomas, in 'Hooker, Scholasticism', 112–17.

63. Girolamo Zanchi, *Operum theologicorum*, vol. 4: *De primi hominis lapsu, de peccato, & de lege Dei* (Geneva: Samuelis Crispini, 1617), Cap. X, 'De lege in genere', 185–221; Girolamo Zanchi, *On the Law in General*, trans. Jefferey J. Veenstra (Grand Rapids, MI: CLP Academic, 2012); Franciscus Junius, *De Politiae Mosis Observatione: Quid in populo Dei obseruari, quid non obseruari ex ea oporteat, postquàm gratia & veritas per Christum facta est, & Euangelio promulgata* (Lugduni Batavorum: Officina Plantiniana Raphelengius, 1593); Franciscus Junius, *The Mosaic Polity*, trans. Todd M. Rester (Grand Rapids, MI: CLP Academic, 2015).

64. More generally, see Dominiak, *Architecture of Participation*, chs. 2 and 3; Bradford Littlejohn, 'Cutting Through the Fog in the Channel: Hooker, Junius, and a Reformed Theology of Law', in *Richard Hooker and Reformed Orthodoxy*, ed. Littlejohn and Kindred-Barnes, 221–40.

65. *LEP* 1.2.1; *FLE* 1:58.26–9.

66. *LEP* 1.2.1.

67. *ST* Ia-IIae, Q. 90, art. 1.
68. *ST* Ia-IIae, Q. 90, art. 4.
69. McGrade, 'Introduction', 19.
70. *LEP* 1.8.4; *FLE* 1:84.16–22.
71. *LEP* 1.1.2; cf. W. J. Torrance Kirby, 'Reason and Law', in *A Companion to Richard Hooker*, ed. Kirby, 251.
72. *LEP* 1.2.3; *FLE* 1:60.1–2.
73. *LEP* 1.2.5; *FLE* 1:61.28–62.1.
74. *LEP* 1.2.5; *FLE* 1:62.8–9.
75. *ST* Ia-IIae, Q. 93, art. 4.
76. Ibid., Ia-IIae, Q. 93, art. 4.
77. *LEP* 1.2.6.
78. *LEP* 1.3.1; cf. Kirby, 'Reason and Law', 253; cf. Littlejohn, 'Cutting Through the Fog', 234–6. Kirby's insight that Hooker's use of the 'logic of hierarchical *disposition* in Aquinas's theological method' in Book I of the *Laws* is '*contained* . . . within a broad Augustinian theological frame' is vital in understanding this unusual division of the *lex aeterna*. See Kirby, 'From "Generall Meditations"', 49–56.
79. *LEP* 1.3.1.
80. *LEP* 1.3.2; *FLE* 1:64.6–7.
81. *LEP* 1.3.4; *FLE* 1:68.17–19; cf. *LEP* 1.8.3; Dominiak, *Architecture of Participation*, 79: '"nature" remains a thenomous term for Hooker'.
82. *LEP* 1.3.4.
83. Cargill Thompson, 'Philosopher of the "Politic Society"', 147.
84. *LEP* 1.16.1.
85. Ibid., 1.16.1; *FLE* 1:135.24–5; cf. McGrade, 'Introduction', 17, who questions whether this is the scope of the *Laws*, as at *LEP* 2.1.1.
86. Ibid., 1.3.1; compare Aquinas at *ST* Ia-IIae, Q. 90, art. 4, especially reply 1.
87. *LEP* 1.3.5; *FLE* 1:69.9; cf. *LEP* 1.5.1.
88. *LEP* 1.5.1ff.
89. Ibid., 1.5.2; *FLE* 1:73.10.
90. *LEP* 1.6.5; *FLE* 1:76.23–4.
91. *LEP* 1.7.1; *FLE* 1:77.1–2.
92. Littlejohn, 'Cutting Through the Fog', 248; O'Donovan, *Theology of Law*, 137. As Cargill Thompson notes, 'Hooker . . . was far from being a doctrinaire Thomist.' Cargill Thompson, 'Philosopher of the "Politic Society"', 149.
93. *LEP* 1.7.7; *FLE* 1:80.29–31.
94. On Hooker's use of reason in these ecclesiastical debates, see Daniel Eppley, *Defending Royal Supremacy and Discerning God's Will in Tudor England* (Aldershot: Ashgate, 2007), 168–76; M. E. Perrott, 'Richard Hooker and the Problem of Authority in the Elizabethan Church', *Journal of Ecclesiastical History* 49.1 (1998): 29–60, especially at 45–56; Littlejohn, *Peril and Promise of Christian Liberty*, 163–6 and 179–90.

95. *FLE* 1:34.15–18.
96. Ibid., 1:34.22.
97. *LEP* 1.8.9; *FLE* 1:90.19–20.
98. *LEP* 1.8.9; *FLE* 1:90.22.
99. *LEP* 1.9.2; O'Donovan, *Theology of Law*, 138.
100. *LEP* 1.9.2; *FLE* 1:95.6–7.
101. *LEP* 1.9.2.
102. TT, 2:5, 270.
103. See Chapter 5 below, but also see George Bull, 'What Did Locke Borrow from Hooker?', *Thought* 7.1 (1932): 122–35.
104. Alexander S. Rosenthal, *Crown under Law: Richard Hooker, John Locke, and the Ascent of Modern Constitutionalism* (Plymouth: Lexington Books, 2008), 98.
105. Rosenthal, *Crown under Law*, 98.
106. Ernst Troeltsch, *The Social Teaching of the Christian Churches* (Louisville, KY: Westminster/John Knox Press, 1992), 638.
107. Peter Munz, *The Place of Hooker in the History of Thought* (London: Routledge & Kegan Paul, 1952), 205–6.
108. For a recent and nuanced assessment of Locke's relation to Hooker, see Alan Cromartie, 'Theology and Politics in Richard Hooker's Thought', *History of Political Thought* 21.1 (2000): 41–66, but especially 55. Cromartie's interpretation is different to my own on the question of the origins of politics in Hooker.
109. Cargill Thompson notes Hooker's adherence to Aristotelianism in 'his general philosophical assumptions', but thinks he departs from Aristotle at this point. See Cargill Thompson, 'Philosopher of the "Politic Society"', 162.
110. The connection and tension between Hooker's Aristotelianism and his Augustinianism is made in Rosenthal, *Crown under Law*, 98; see also Cargill Thompson, 'Philosopher of the "Politic Society"', 161–2; Cromartie, 'Theology and Politics', 55.
111. Rosenthal, *Crown under Law*, 98 and 110.
112. Cf. O'Donovan, *Theology of Law*, 140.
113. *LEP* 1.10.1; *FLE* 1:96.4.
114. *LEP* 1.10.1; *FLE* 1:96.8–14.
115. O'Donovan, *Theology of Law*, 138.
116. *LEP* 1.10.4; *FLE* 1:100.10.
117. *LEP* 1.10.4; *FLE* 1:100.12–13.
118. *LEP* 1.10.1; *FLE* 1:96.12–13.
119. *LEP* 1.10.1; *FLE* 1:96.13–14.
120. *LEP* 1.10.12; *FLE* 1:107.15–16.
121. *LEP* 1.10.1; *FLE* 1:96.19–20.
122. Cf. Aristotle, *Politics*, 1278b19–23.
123. *LEP* 1.10.1.
124. *LEP* 1.10.3; *FLE* 1:98.11–12.

125. *LEP* 1.10.4; *FLE* 1:98.26.
126. *LEP* 1.10.4; *FLE* 1:99.23; Littlejohn, *Peril and Promise of Christian Liberty*, 182–4.
127. *LEP* 1.10.4; *FLE* 1:100.9–13.
128. *LEP* 1.10.5.
129. *LEP* 1.10.4; *FLE* 1:99.11–13.
130. *LEP* 1.10.4; *FLE* 1:99.6–8.
131. *LEP* 8.1.2; Kirby, *Richard Hooker's Doctrine*, 98–105.
132. Cromartie, 'Theology and Politics', 58.
133. *LEP* 8.1.2. Put another way, 'church and common can be united as "accidents" within a single "subject"'. See Kirby, 'From "Generall Meditations"', 61.
134. W. Bradford Littlejohn, '"More than a swineherd": Hooker, Vermigli, and an Aristotelian Defence of the Royal Supremacy', *Reformation & Renaissance Review* 15.1 (2013): 68–83, especially at 71; *LEP* 5.1.2 and 8.1.4.
135. *LEP* 8.2.5–8.2.6; Eppley, *Defending Royal Supremacy*, 176–9. On Hooker's two kingdoms theology, see Kirby, *Richard Hooker's Doctrine*, 122–4; Littlejohn, *Peril and Promise of Christian Liberty*, 144–8. On the royal supremacy, see Littlejohn, '"More than a swineherd"', 69–72. Cf. Perrott, 'Richard Hooker and the Problem of Authority', 56–7.
136. *LEP* 8.2.5; Richard Hooker, *Of the Laws of Ecclesiastical Polity: Books VI, VII, VIII*, ed. P. G. Stanwood, in *Folger Library Edition of The Works of Richard Hooker*, ed. W. Speed Hill (Cambridge, MA: Belknap Press, 1981), III, 334.3–6.
137. *LEP* 8.2.5; *FLE* 3:334.8–10.
138. *LEP* 8.2.5; *FLE* 3:334.18–22.
139. *LEP* 8.2.6.
140. *LEP* 8.6.1; *FLE* 3:385.19–20.
141. *LEP* 8.6.1; *FLE* 3:386.1–6. Also see *LEP* 8.6.11.
142. Ibid., 7.5.8; *FLE* 3:167.7–17; Avis, *The Church in the Theology of the Reformers*, 117.
143. d'Entrèves, *The Medieval Contribution*, 128; cf. Dominiak, *Architecture of Participation*, 51 on the efficient cause in Hooker.
144. Cf. O'Donovan, *Theology of Law*, 47, where she discusses this idea in relation to John Fortescue.

# Chapter 3

# Johannes Althusius and Political Society as *Pactum*

In 1880, the German intellectual historian Otto von Gierke published a book entitled *Johannes Althusius und die Entwicklung der naturrechtlichen Staatstheorien.*[1] Those few who were familiar with the main protagonist of Gierke's volume would have wondered at his choice of subject, for Althusius's thought was outdated almost as soon as it was published.[2] The societal and political theories of the German jurist were based largely on soon-to-be-outdated modes of analysis and understanding. Only a decade after his death, the Treaty of Westphalia ended the so-called Thirty Years War, and a series of new national and international orders were gradually ushered in. Althusius's death in 1638 was a kind of harbinger of the death of the pre-modern European political order. Both his ideas and the medieval structures of European society which he was reflecting on seemingly became obsolete. Given all of these facts, Gierke's attempt to resurrect Althusius seems all the more puzzling.

Rather than attempting a rehabilitation of Althusius by arguing for his significance as a political thinker (as per Gierke) or dismissing him as largely irrelevant (as per most others), this chapter aims to demonstrate Althusius's role in the desacralisation of the confessional state in Europe and the broader secularisation of political thought. The role of Althusius in this story is mixed. He displays continuity with earlier Reformed thinkers in his theory of natural law and his understanding of the origins of political life. This is, in part, because Althusius's ideas were deeply imbued with Aristotelianism. These aspects of his thought, his Aristotelianism and his natural law theory, will occupy the initial sections of this chapter. First, we will examine his conception of natural law. As we will see, this aspect of Althusius's thought is reminiscent of Thomas, as well as Calvin and Hooker. He retained a strong connection between God and the purpose and operations of the natural law. Second, we shall address Althusius's theory of the origins of political society, a theory which was clearly Aristotelian and naturalist. I will argue that these two key elements mean that Althusius retained a sacred foundation for political life.

However, in the third instance, we will see that Althusius played a part in introducing an idea into the Reformed Protestant political theory vocabulary which would influence the tradition in a secular direction. This idea is that of *pactum*. This concept of *pactum* gets developed in the later Reformed tradition and comes to resemble a 'social contract', which we shall see undergirds a non-sacred theory of political life. However, Althusius should not be blamed for this appropriation of *pactum*. Rather, Althusius's idea of *pactum* (or 'covenant') was quite different from the social contractarian renderings of Thomas Hobbes and John Locke, even though the early Reformed rendering of *pactum* was ultimately turned towards imagining a desacralised concept of political society.

Althusius's death in 1638 marks, in a way, the death of theistic political naturalism which permeated the Reformed tradition up until the middle of the seventeenth century. After this, pre-political natural rights came to the fore of Reformed thought, and the foundation of political society came to be understood as laid by man and not by God. The roots of this change are not found in Althusius, but his political thought shows how the Reformed concept of *pactum* paved the way for this to occur. However, in order to understand the figure in question, we cannot dwell on his death. His life will provide some illumination as to where and why he wrote what he wrote.

## Wittgenstein-Berleburg to Emden

Althusius was born in Wittgenstein-Berleburg, in the Holy Roman Empire, in 1557, two years after the Treaty of Augsburg. The Treaty, among other things, conferred upon territorial rulers the legal capacity to determine the confessional allegiance of their territory.[3] Althusius's home county was known to be Reformed Protestant, even though the Reformed faith did not have legal standing in the Empire at that time. This did not prevent Althusius from receiving an excellent education which, considering his humble origins, could indicate he had links to the nobility. He is known to have studied at Cologne, Basle and then Geneva.[4] He had personal connections to key Reformed thinkers, such as the theologian Johann Grynaeus (1540–1617) and French jurists Denis Godefroy (1549–1622) and Francis Hotman (1524–90).[5] The latter figures no doubt had some influence on the shape and content of his first published work, *De jurisprudentiae Romanae* (1586), which appeared in the same year he received his doctorate in law from Basle.[6] His studies and connections afforded him exposure to the ideas which would shape his thought, including the ideas of Aristotle, Calvin, and various expressions of Reformed jurisprudence. His book would serve, in many ways, as the basis upon which he built his reputation and his natural law thought.

Aristotle was to continue as an important influence on Althusius, and the Thomist framework for natural law would also have a deep impact on him. This Thomist and Aristotelian influence was, in part, due to those Reformed thinkers who were Althusius's colleagues in the academy. In 1586, Althusius was appointed to the faculty of the Herborn Academy. The Academy was one of the fruits of what has become known as the 'Second Reformation'.[7] It was founded by the Count of Nassau-Dillenburg in 1584. The establishment of educational institutions such as Herborn was an important measure for rulers intent on instilling their particular confessional identity in their territory, as well as for training the expanding civil service and consolidating territorial claims.[8] The proliferation of gymnasiums, academies and universities during this period was remarkable and without historical precedent.[9] Althusius's time at Herborn Academy corresponded with a period of remarkable confessional consolidation by Count Johann VI of Nassau-Dillenburg. Around the time the Academy was founded, the count restructured the administrative, legal and ecclesiastical institutions in Nassau-Dillenburg in order to reform government, the church, and the lives of the entire population of subjects.[10] The Academy was to provide the pedagogical means to achieve this reform in a comprehensive fashion.[11] Herborn was both a result of, and a tool for, Reformed Protestant reformation.

It was in this confessional academic context that Althusius's ideas about natural law were further formed and consolidated. This Reformed context is crucial for properly understanding Althusius's philosophical and theological development. He was writing and operating within an existing Reformed natural law tradition, imbibing the ideas of leading Reformed thinkers, and producing a theory that responded to the confessional tensions of his day.[12] Importantly for this chapter, it is this confessional context which frames Althusius's most significant contribution, his *Politica methodice digesta* (*Politics Methodically Set Forth*, herein *Politica*), the first edition of which was published in Herborn in 1603.[13] *Politica* can easily be read as an abstract expression of political theory, with its carefully reasoned construction of a multi-layered political society.[14] However, its composition was linked closely with the administrative and political aims of the Reformed confessional state in Nassau-Dillenburg.[15] It must be understood, at least in its early form, as a student textbook rather than a revolutionary handbook.[16] The *Politica* is not, fundamentally, a tract of 'Calvinist Resistance Theory'.[17]

However, the implications of the theories explored by Althusius in the *Politica* changed somewhat over the various editions of the work. He was appointed as syndic of Emden in 1604 by the City Council and the Assembly of the Forty.[18] Althusius performed this role, which involved leadership of the northern city's legal and political administration, until his death in 1638. Over the same period, he produced two more revised editions of *Politica* (a significantly expanded one in 1610 and another in 1614) and composed his enormous *Dicaeologicae libri tres, Totum & universum Jus* (*Complete Theory of Law*, 1617).[19] Both of these works contain a well-developed theory of natural law, and his theistic-naturalist account of the origins of political life is clear once both are analysed together. This what we will proceed to do now, focusing first on Althusius's theory of natural law.

### Althusius on the Natural Law

If one reads Althusius, the question of public law appears to stand front and centre. His *Politica* is dominated by the questions of the constitution of a polity.[20] But it should be evident upon the following analysis that Althusius was far from fixated on public law. His jurisprudence is founded upon the natural law and, like Calvin and Hooker, he has a naturalist understanding of human society. But does his natural law theory and the consequent political naturalism remove God from the picture? Is his jurisprudence a secularising force in the movement of Reformed ideas? Some certainly see him that way.[21] However, I would argue that quite the opposite is true. Althusius's theory of natural law and his understanding of the nature and origins of political society demonstrate that Althusius continued the pattern witnessed to by Calvin and Hooker of a divine origin and purpose for political society. Political life was sacralised, not secularised, in Althusius's thought.

To understand Althusius's theory of natural law, we should first establish what he means by the word 'law'. Althusius's definition of law is that it is 'something that is established after coming into being because of an action'.[22] This admittedly obtuse statement boils down to an affirmation that laws come about as things are done, and is a concept reminiscent of Thomas's idea of law being a precept of practical reason.[23] Further, what makes something law is its connection to humanity, because the thing is 'established in a human affair, or by some individual' for the purposes of living properly.[24] Furthermore, law is a 'precept for doing those things that pertain to living a pious, holy, just and suitable life'.[25] What is this precept founded upon, according to Althusius? It is sacred; it is founded upon, or by, God. The precept is 'solely God's will for men manifested in his law'.[26] He writes, further, that law is a 'rule of living, obeying and administering' which is 'the will of God alone' and is 'the law of things to be done and to be omitted'.[27] Law is, for Althusius, a precept founded upon God, which reflects God's will for humankind to live well, and is established by human actions.

This formulation of law finds significant parallels within the Reformed tradition. Fellow Reformed jurist Jerome Zanchi, who taught theology at Heidelberg between 1568 and 1577, has a similar definition of law, and Althusius's debt to him is evident in a number of ways.[28] The passage just quoted is one demonstration of this. Zanchi, in his 1605 *Opera theologicorum* (*Theological Works*), writes that 'Natural law is the will of God [*Lex naturæ est voluntas Dei*], and, consequently, the divine rule and principle for knowing what to do and what not to do. It is, namely, the knowledge of what is good or bad.'[29] The lengthy quote is important, as it demonstrates parallels to Althusius's definition of law. Where Zanchi says that natural law 'is the will of God', Althusius writes that it is 'the will of God alone [*Regula vivendi . . . est sola Dei voluntas*]'.[30] And where Zanchi states that natural law is the 'rule . . . for knowing what to do and what not to do', Althusius writes that it is 'the law of things to be done and to be omitted [*lex faciendorum & omittendorum*]'.[31] The likely influence of Zanchi demonstrates the prevalence of theistic natural law in the early Reformed Protestant tradition, in these cases expressed as *Dei voluntas* – the will of God.

Not only is natural law the 'will of God', but, according to Althusius, God is also the source of that law.[32] This divine source for law in general sets up the basis of his theistic theory of law which then undergirds his understanding of societal origins. Beneath this over-arching banner of law, Althusius recognises two types of law. He differs from his fellow jurists in his own day on this point.[33] Typi-cally, jurists would divide law into three types: natural law (*ius natural* and *lex naturae*), the law of nations (*ius gentium, ius com-mune, lex communis*) and civil law (also called positive law: *ius civile, ius positivum*). Althusius collapses the law of nations into the natural law, and typically uses the terminology of natural law and common law interchangeably when discussing what we are terming natural law.[34] As a result of this structuring of his legal the-ory, Althusius divides law into only two kinds, rather than three: natural law and civil law.[35] What is the difference between natural and civil law? The natural law is, according to Althusius, produced by right reason 'for the common necessity and welfare of human social life in general' and has been 'inscribed on human hearts' or 'naturally implanted . . . in men' by God.[36] Civil law is differenti-ated from natural law by the fact that it provides for the common good of a particular place rather than humanity in general, and is 'enacted by a magistrate'.[37] We will leave civil law at this point, and continue expanding upon Althusius's theory of natural law.

As with Calvin and Hooker, Althusius sees the natural law as connected to civil law in that it influences the shape and content of it. It does this by metaphorically working its way through the human heart, and into human law. This is evident when we look at Althusius's most pithy definition of natural law, which is found in his *Dicaeologicae*:

> [Natural] law [*ius commune*] is that which has been inscribed on human hearts by nature or by God from birth and that by which human beings are moved either to act or avoid actions, which is sufficient for preserving the common good of human society, con-victs wrongdoers of evil, or excuses the innocent.[38]

In other words, the natural law is written on the human heart, guides human action, and guides humans to act for the good of society. The parallels between Althusius and Calvin, as well as Hooker, are notable. Calvin emphasised the implanting of the nat-ural law in human hearts, whilst Hooker echoed the Thomist fram-ing of natural law as connected to human reason. Althusius affirms both the natural law written on the heart, and also the knowability of natural law through human reason.

In order to adequately see these connections and affirm that Althusius had a theistic understanding of the law of nature, I will examine the above definition in more detail. It has three elements which we will consider in turn. First, we will see how Althusius understands the inscription of the natural law on the human heart by nature and by God. This will raise the question of the relationship between natural law and divine law. Second, we will briefly examine the idea that humans are 'moved' by the natural law to act. Third, we will note Althusius's framing of the role that natural law plays in human society, thereby connecting the natural law and civil law.

Althusius holds that the natural law is implanted in all people and that it informs people as to what is just and unjust.[39] It is God who has given humans this innate knowledge of the natural law. 'Natural law [lex communis]', writes Althusius, 'has been naturally implanted by God in all men.'[40] There is a 'knowledge and natural inclination' embedded in humans, also described as a 'secret impulse'.[41] Who is it who has implanted this knowledge, or given this impulse to humans? God himself. Referring to Romans 1:19 where Paul says that God 'made it manifest to them', Althusius asserts that God gives humans 'knowledge' and 'inclination'.[42] Note that it is implanted by God, and it is done naturally. Althusius believed that God works through nature to give humans knowledge of natural law. Further, 'God teaches and inscribes on human hearts general principles of fairness and justice and unfairness and injustice'.[43] God is the enforcer and legislator of the natural law and has, according to Althusius, an active role in imparting the knowledge of it to humanity.

How does Althusius envisage the natural law impelling people to follow it? According to Althusius, God 'urges' people to live according to the natural law.[44] We will cover this further when we look at the second element of Althusius's definition. Most relevant to this element, God also convicts people of their transgressions of the natural law by way of their conscience.[45] This raises the spectre of the 'moral law'. In a fashion similar to Calvin, Althusius uses the term 'conscience' to explain the way that people know the moral law – it is imprinted or implanted in humankind.[46] Furthermore, like Hooker, Zanchi, Calvin and another Reformed jurist, Franciscus Junius (1545–1602), Althusius makes the moral law of God (the Decalogue) equivalent in some respects to the natural law.[47] Althusius argues that the natural law is 'the general theory and practice of love, both for God and for one's neighbour'.[48] This natural law, Althusius says, was propagated by Christ under 'two headings': first, 'our duty immediately to God', and second, 'our duty . . . to what is owed to our neighbour'.[49] Althusius's explicit reference to Christ's summary of the Decalogue in two parts demonstrates that he holds to a tight equivalence between natural law and divine moral law, which he says expresses 'duties' that we have towards God and neighbour.[50]

Because Althusius makes a tight equivalence between the natural law and the moral law, he suggests that all people understand the moral law and, therefore, the natural law. 'The Decalogue', Althusius asserts, 'has been prescribed for all people to the extent that it agrees with and explains the common law of nature for all peoples [*lege naturae omnibus gentibus communi*].'[51] However, here is where Althusius's Reformed theological anthropology begins to make its mark. In a 1603 *oratio panegyrica* (panegyric speech), given as an inaugural lecture at Herborn, Althusius sounds very Calvinist notes with regard to the state of humanity.[52] He says that 'man is hopeless, ignorant, oblivious and dull'.[53] The heart and mind of humanity are bent towards evil and all people are repulsive, abusive, impure, an immoral dubious rabble (*sentina vitiorum*), lacking self-control.[54] Elsewhere he writes that people are fickle, untrustworthy, easily influenced, constantly changing their mind, easily distracted, slothful, fearful, lacking judgement, lacking discernment, lacking wisdom, impulsive and rash.[55] It is, to say the least, hardly a catalogue of compliments. This pessimistic anthropology, which is reflective of his theological tradition, leads Althusius to moderate the extent to which the natural law is known by all people. Although all people know and have access to the same natural law, 'they differ in the level and means of their inscribing [on the heart] and urging [to do what is just]'.[56] 'The knowledge of [natural law] is communicated more abundantly to some and more sparingly to others' by God himself.[57] Indeed, some people, according to Althusius, 'exert themselves more strongly, others less so, in their desire for [obedience to the natural law]'.[58] It is this exertion to act according to the natural law which we will address next.

The second element of Althusius's definition of natural law is that he says that natural law somehow impels people to act or avoid actions. Althusius uses active language when describing this part of God's activity in relation to natural law. He says that God, through the work of the natural law upon their hearts and minds, 'urges' (*impellit*), and he 'incites' (*incitat*) people to do good and just things.[59] Elsewhere, he writes that God 'excites' (*exitandi*) people to follow the natural law.[60] There is a link, here, to Thomas's concept of natural law as human practical reason participating in divine reason.[61] Perhaps Althusius is readier to ascribe to God some active agency in the human participation in his own reason than Thomas. Nonetheless, Althusius's description of God's active encouragement of human adherence to the natural law fits within the Thomist conception of natural law and practical reason, and his conception demonstrates an adherence to not only a Thomistic tradition, but also the precedents in the Reformed tradition.

Calvin, for example, understood that God had given all people 'the natural light of righteousness', or 'preconceptions' of justice, which play a role in compelling them towards obedience to the natural law.[62] Another example comes from Franciscus Junius, who writes in Thomistic fashion that the purpose of natural law is to encourage the creature to seek 'the good' and avoid 'evil'. There is no question that a level of compulsion is at work here in Junius's understanding.[63] Zanchi, likewise, holds that God's writing of the natural and moral law on the hearts of humanity is not simply a passive action designed to induce conviction of sin; it is also intended to alter human behaviour such that social and political life is possible after the Fall.[64] Indeed, Zanchi's conception is remarkably similar to Althusius's, in that he says that natural law 'pushes' people to do good.[65] However, the thinker who is most illustrative of this idea remains Althusius, who writes in his definition of natural law that 'human beings are moved to act or to avoid actions', with the end of preserving and fostering human society.[66]

This leads us to the third element in Althusius's definition of natural law: that it is directed towards the existence and maintenance of a political and social group. The first element of the definition saw God implanting the natural law into people. The second saw God using the natural law to actively compel and 'urge' people to live in accordance with it. This final element demonstrates that Althusius sees God acting through his natural law to establish and cultivate political life. That God establishes political life in Althusius's thought will occupy us in the final section when we address Althusius's conception of societal origins. In the next, we will focus on the cultivation of human community, or what Althusius calls the 'preserving [of] the common good of human society'.[67] This preserving of the common good demonstrates that Althusius's theory of natural law is directed towards the goods of political life. Indeed, according to Althusius, God has created human beings to be in political society. It is an entirely natural thing for people to live in community. In showing this, we shall see that Althusius understood society to be natural, and because it is natural it is also sacral.

## Political Life and Human Nature

But how can society be natural? And what kind of role does the natural law play in Althusius's thought to make this apparent? Althusius is emphatic that laws in general, and the natural law in particular, exist to make human society a good place to be.[68] With God as its author, Althusius understands the cultivation of human society to be a divine activity done through the natural law. Part of how Althusius understands how this cultivation of human society works out in political life is through human nature. We will examine two key elements of Althusius's view of human nature which bear most directly on the question of this chapter. First, we will examine his key theoretical concepts of *consociatio* and *symbiosis*. Second, we will look at Althusius's preference for the *vita activa* (the 'active life') of the political citizen.

The purpose of politics for humankind, according to Althusius, is happy, just, commodious and holy 'symbiosis'.[69] The Latin term *symbiosis* translates straightforwardly as 'living together'. Therefore, the purpose of politics is that people live together to make a social life and to conserve that social life (*vitam socialem ... conservandam*).[70] Politics also exists to establish and cultivate that society.[71] The similarity between this and Althusius's statement of purpose regarding the natural law is striking. Both the natural law and politics exist for the cultivation of society, and human social life, for Althusius, is necessarily linked with politics. In a clear allusion to Aristotle's use of αὐτάρκης (*autarkês*, or self-sufficient) in the *Politics*, Althusius writes that no human can be naturally gifted to live alone. Indeed, he writes that 'in living this life, no man is αὐτάρκης (self-sufficient)'.[72] A human cannot provide for all of his or her own needs if they live alone; 'He is unable', writes Althusius, 'to help himself without the intervention and assistance of another.'[73] Even if an adult was to find himself in such a situation, Althusius holds that he could not supply everything needed for a 'comfortable and holy life'.[74] Political life, that of symbiotes in *consociatio* (which we will come to soon), is the only way to gain these goods. So, according to Althusius, politics is necessary for humans to attain the goods of a happy, comfortable, holy and just life.

Human society, what Althusius calls 'symbiotic life', is necessarily linked with politics.

The way that Althusius frames this symbiotic life is one of deep interdependence and fellowship. Althusius's symbiotes are co-workers (*sumboethoi* or συμβόηθοι).[75] They share the responsibility to communicate with each other the things necessary for a comfortable life. This resembles John Calvin's own thought about the 'neighbourly' society. Calvin held that the design of God for humans is they are to be neighbourly and serve one another.[76] God gave the first human a companion, therefore establishing the principle of what Nico Vorster has helpfully called 'the neighbourly nature of society'.[77] Calvin held that marriage is, in part, intended to show humans that they are obliged to serve and be in fellowship with their neighbours. Therefore, marriage is the basic pact, or covenant, upon which the neighbourly nature of society is established, and upon which society itself is founded.[78] Furthermore, Althusius cites Calvin's (from his *Institutes*) insight that God trains humans to be humble and ready to seek the help of others.[79] It is evident, then, that Althusius follows Calvin in his conception of the necessity and naturalness of human relationships, mutual interconnectedness, and, therefore, human society itself. The similarities between Calvin and Althusius on the nature of humanity and society are striking and go some way to showing that there was a level of consistency within the Reformed tradition on conceptions of the nature of society itself, along with conceptions of its origins, to which we will come shortly.

This distinctly Reformed view of political society is further developed by Althusius when he describes symbiotes as 'participants or partners' in community life.[80] There is, in Althusius's thought, a distinct mutuality, a give-and-take, in social relations. While this may seem obvious on one level, it is a pivotal point. Althusius's description of social symbiosis entails more than simply self-interest; symbiotes bear an inherent and natural responsibility towards one another to supply the goods of life.[81] Society, even political life itself, is entirely natural in Althusius's schema. The imparting of these goods meets the needs of the people in society and 'self-sufficiency and mutuality of life and human society are achieved'.[82] Althusius cites Cicero to support this point, when he says that 'a political community is a gathering of men associated by a consensus as to the right of sharing what is useful'.[83] Althusius's understanding of the nature of human life in society is, fundamentally, that it is an intertwined life which includes natural duties to provide for others.

The way that humans can share what is useful with one another is through participation in different kinds of political fellowships. The word Althusius uses here is *consociatio*. In fact, politics is, for Althusius, the art or skill (*ars*) of *consociandi*.[84] The term *consociatio* is fundamental to the thought of Althusius but has suffered from some mishandling by historians and political scientists. It appears to be something of a metaphorical wax nose, being shaped to contemporary use and interest regardless of the potential (and in some cases, actual) anachronism.[85] The most helpful way to render this key term in the context of Althusius's thought is 'political fellowship'.[86] This captures well the neighbourliness of Althusius's conception of political life, the theological nuances of the term, and emphasises Althusius's distinctive position that all aspects of social life, including the household, are political.[87] 'All symbiotic association and life is essentially, authentically, and generically political.'[88] For Althusius, *consociatio* is political fellowship.

There a number of categories of political fellowship in Althusius's political thought. At a very basic level, there are two kinds: 'simple and private', and 'mixed and public'.[89] That is, there are two kinds of locations of 'fellowship' for symbiotes. The first kind, simple and private, contains two kinds of political fellowship: the family and the collegium (which are similar to guilds). The second kind consists of the city, province and commonwealth. I will briefly explore how Althusius explains the basic nature of these to better understand his conception of political life. Private political fellowships are formed by symbiotes themselves and are constituted by a 'special pact' (*speciali pacto*).[90] This mechanism of 'pact' might appear to contradict my claim regarding Althusius's naturalist views, and the term is taken up by both Hobbes and Locke in their conventionalist framings of the origins of political life. However, I address this idea of *pactum* at some length below. The symbiotes form private political fellowships through pacts, according to Althusius, because they hold some interest in common.[91] Families and kinship political fellowships are natural and are described by Althusius as 'the school of public political fellowships'.[92] On the other hand, *collegia* are civil, voluntary, and can be disbanded.[93] Althusius describes the public political fellowship as a development from the private one: 'The public political fellowship exists when many private political fellowships are linked together.'[94] For example, the city is made up of families and *collegia* living in one place under civil laws.[95] It exists in perpetuity if there are one or more people living in it. The city is itself grounded in the 'law of nations' (*jus gentium*), which is, for Althusius, equivalent to the natural law.[96] In short, the private, natural political fellowship of the family is the basis for civil society in Althusius's thinking. All political life is built upon the natural fellowship of the family.

Althusius founds each of these forms of political fellowship upon the basic assumption that they serve symbiotic life. None of them exists for itself alone. The closest any of these political fellowships comes to being self-sufficient is the family, but even this serves the purpose of being a school of public political fellowships, and it is not independent of other families. Each public political fellowship is connected inherently to private political fellowships. Furthermore, each private political fellowship is unable to be self-sufficient without the larger public structures of city, province and commonwealth. There is evident in Althusius's thought regarding human political life a clear sense of interconnectedness with human symbiosis embedded in it. For him, political life is, at every level, natural. Althusius understands that people in society are bound up together and that they all share mutual responsibilities to ensure that each person in the society is enjoying the goods to which they are, in a sense, entitled. As Althusius himself says, participants in this common life are to impart to each other 'whatever is appropriate for a comfortable life of soul and body'.[97] This life of symbiosis and political fellowship has an inherent social interconnectedness, which comes with responsibilities. A key way this is expressed by Althusius is in his preference for the active life (*vita activa*) over the philosophical life (*vita contemplativa*). Humans are designed by God and impelled by Him through the natural law to love and serve their fellow human beings.

Althusius's preference for the active life over the contemplative is, as we shall now see, based on his symbiotic political anthropology. His reasoning is, in part, that humans have been commanded by God in His moral law (which is equated to the natural law) to 'love your neighbour as yourself'.[98] 'Of what use', asks Althusius rhetorically, 'is a hidden treasure, or a wise man who denies his services to the commonwealth?'[99] In an even stronger statement, Althusius questions the felicity of people living as hermits, for 'how can they promote the advantage of their neighbour unless they live in society?'[100] It is, therefore, a presupposition of Althusius's that people are required in some way to serve the common good, and that being in society is necessary to achieve this. According to Althusius, humans are meant to serve and give to others. Humanity is made by God fit for service to his or her fellow human. Indeed, according to Althusius, the highest end of the human's interaction with his fellow human is to love and serve him or her.[101]

This all gives us a clear understanding of how Althusius views the relationship between political community and human nature. Society is not an aberration for Althusius but is rather a positive good for the life of humans because they can serve each other and be in fellowship with one another. Having established these points in the relevant section of the *Politica*, Althusius next moves on to describe the origin of human society in some detail. It is the very points described above that drive humans into society, which he summarises as needs of the body, and the needs of, and seeds of virtue implanted in, the soul.[102] Althusius has expended effort on describing the natural dependence of the human on others for both physical and spiritual needs because he sees this aspect of human nature as a kind of ontological argument for the existence of human society.[103] These needs, according to Althusius, have been the cause of people joining into societies, and forming cities, villages, and, within them, schools, markets, guilds, and so on.[104] The highest good, the highest end, of human life is to seek the good of his or her fellow human. The only setting where that can be fulfilled, according to Althusius, is in human society, which must necessarily be a political society. Therefore, political life, as it is both natural and beneficial, is to be preferred over the non-political life. Humanity is necessarily political, for Althusius, and political life is natural. The final question we must answer to properly enunciate Althusius's role in the secularisation of ideas of political life is this: Did Althusius understand God or humanity to be the founder of political society? The answer should already be obvious after the analysis in the previous sections. However, it is the presence of the theoretical motif of *pactum* which complicates the picture.

### Natural *Pactum*: The Unintended Roots of the Reformed Social Contract Tradition

Althusius's utilisation of *pactum* is troubling for the conclusions of this chapter. Doesn't his use of the idea of pact, or covenant, place him in the same league as the social contract ideas of Hobbes and Locke? My answer is a firm 'no'. Althusius's idea of *pactum* was quite different to the later English thinkers in a number of respects. We will examine their views in the following chapters. But first, we must explore Althusius's political use of *pactum* in its own context and on its own terms. This process will help us to properly enunciate Althusius's role in the secularisation of ideas of political life.

In a sense, we started this chapter in the middle of the theoretical story by examining Althusius's natural law theory, before then returning to the beginning and examining his political anthropology in brief detail. This exercise has established that Althusius held to a theistic natural law theory, where God was the legislator and active enforcer of the natural law. It also showed that, consistent with this understanding of natural law, Althusius understood humans to be not only naturally suited to political life but designed by God to thrive in political community. It will, then, come as little surprise that Althusius was the same as Calvin and Hooker in his view of societal origins. Althusius believed that political society is founded, ultimately, by God rather than humanity, and this means that he had a sacral understanding of political life.

Althusius begins his explanation of the origins of society in his *Politica* by using Aristotle's explanatory model of four causes for the existence of a thing. The four causes are the material cause, the formal cause, the efficient cause, and the final cause. The efficient cause of political life, the source of the movement into human society, is, according to Althusius, 'consent [*consensum*] and agreement [*pactum*] amongst the communicating citizens'.[105] That is, the mechanism by which people make society occur is the making of a kind of agreement with one another. The formal cause of people joining into human society is the *vita activa*; that is, the active life of public good works and social interaction. This formal cause is the shape of human life in society, and the way in which people live.[106] The material cause, that is, the actual parts which make up society, is 'the aggregate of precepts', that is, the various laws and conventions of the society which ensure people will offer one another services and help which provide for the common advantage of social life.[107] The final cause, which is the most pivotal for both Aristotle and Althusius, is 'enjoyment' of life, 'the common welfare', and 'the conservation of a human society where you can worship God quietly and without error'.[108] The four causes all work together to make human society. So, initially, Althusius offers a typical Aristotelian explanation for the cause of human society, insofar as he utilises the four causes for his mode of discussion. Two of them will occupy the remainder of the discussion: the efficient cause and the final cause.

The efficient cause of political society is, according to Althusius, 'consent' and 'agreement'. The Latin word translated as 'agreement' by Frederick Carney, Althusius's English translator, is *pactum*, with the related term *pactio* also being used. This concept of *pactum* is the source of much confusion about Althusius's political thought. Some scholars brand him as a proto-liberal in his theory of society.[109] However, I believe this is a distortion. Considering his understanding of human nature and the natural law, his concept of *pactum* is less a form of social contract, and more a conception of the nature of social and political relations between individuals, natural social institutions, and formal political institutions and structures. Althusius does not see society as a contract in the way that later liberal theorists would understand it. Instead, Althusius understands people join together in political life by way of pact (*pactum*).[110] This pact is the efficient cause of political society in Althusius's thought and is perfectly compatible with his natural view of political life and natural law.

Rather than interpret him as a 'contractual' thinker, Althusius is to be read as a 'covenantal' thinker.[111] This is in line with ideas that are both chronologically and theologically antecedent to him, and makes more sense when one considers Althusius's historical context. We shall now examine the linkages between Althusius's use of *pactum* and some uses of related terms by thinkers related to him either by time, or by theoretical and theological framework.[112] One way of establishing what Althusius might have intended in his use of *pactum* is to examine how related thinkers used the same or similar terms. The term *pactum* is conceptually linked with, and sometimes overlaps, other Latin terms like *foedus* and *contractus*, and we might interpret these ideas as compact, pact, treaty, or even bargain or agreement.[113]

For example, John Calvin applied the idea of *pactum*, and the related *foedus*, to God's dealings with His people (both Israel and the Church) in a number of places. In his discussion of the continuities between the Old and New Covenants in the scriptures, Calvin used the term *foedus* to refer to the way that God related in a particular and conditional manner to his people. Two examples will suffice. In one case Calvin says that God related to Israel through a particular covenant before Christ's advent. He writes of 'the covenant [*foedus*] which the Lord made with the Israelites before the advent of Christ'.[114] A further example can be found in Calvin's discussion of the sacraments of baptism and the Lord's Supper, where he writes, 'Since the Lord calls his promises covenants [*foedera*] . . . sacraments are signs of the covenants [*foederum*], a resemblance is able to be adduced from the covenants [*foederibus*] of men themselves.'[115] So *foedus* is used by Calvin to describe God's dealings with humankind, and principally as a theological term. However, he also relates God's covenant signs to the way humans might use the covenant motif. It is, therefore, interesting that the idea of *foedus*, and the related *pactio*, were given common political-theological usage by Reformed thinkers just after Calvin's death, and in Althusius's time.[116]

The influential tract, *Vindiciae contra tyrannos* (1573, *Vindication against Tyrants*), attributed to 'Junius Brutus' and hailing from Huguenot hands (most likely those of Phillipe Du Plessis Mornay), provides an example of the political-theological use of the *foedus* word family.[117] Brutus writes:

> Now we read of two sorts of covenants [*foedus*] at the inaugurating of kings, the first between God, the King, and the People, that the people might be the people of God: The second, between the King, and the People, that the People shall obey faithfully, and the King command justly.[118]

Brutus is here establishing the principle of covenant (*foedus*) between both a people and God, a King and God, and (critically for Huguenot political theory) between a people and their King. He goes on to use both *pactio* and *foedus* in the same line of thought when he writes: 'Now after that kings were given unto the people, there was so little purpose of disannulling or disbanding the former contract [*pactio*] . . . We have formerly said at the inaugurating of kings, there was a double covenant [*duplex foedus*].'[119] This example from *Vindiciae* illustrates the seed of the *pactum* concept in the political thought of the Reformed stream to which Althusius belonged.

Althusius's ideas about *pactum* fit within this stream of thought which conceived of society as a kind of compact or pact. In the opening paragraph of the *Politica* Althusius writes that the symbiotes make a pact (*pacto*) each with the other.[120] Further on he says that they form a bond by way of a pact (*vinculo pacti*).[121] This pact is either expressly made, or tacit; there is no need to draw up a pact each time the conditions of the political fellowship change slightly.[122] People are participating, by general consensus, through this pact in the building of political life together, and they bind themselves to one another through this pact. The image Althusius uses here is a powerful one, giving social life a sense of seriousness and weight. People are in society together because of a kind of mutually binding oath. Althusius's *pactio* is not a loose agreement whereby some people can be disqualified if they transgress the conditions of said agreement, nor is it voluntary in nature and therefore easily dissoluble. The pact described by Althusius is also not based on individual people agreeing together to submit themselves to a ruler or a sovereign.[123] In this way, it is somewhat different from the character of the covenant in the *Vindiciae*. There are obligations attached to the act of joining into human society, both by nature and by the act of making a pact. It forms part of what Althusius calls the 'communion of right' (*juris communio*) in that it is the agreement, or pact, which, in part, defines the nature of social life.[124] As Althusius expounds in the rest of the *Politica*, his idea of a pact involves different elements of society, including the family, the guild, and local and provincial authorities. It also underpins the nature of society. How people join together, by way of this pact, illuminates the nature of the symbiosis and political fellowship, but also the efficient cause of that fellowship.

Having dealt with the efficient cause of political life, we move now to the 'final cause', which Althusius holds is 'the enjoyment of life' and 'the common welfare'. Althusius proceeds to offer a description of the conditions of humankind's move into society and the existential reasons for such a move. 'Aristotle', writes Althusius, 'teaches that man by his nature is brought into this social life and mutual sharing.'[125] Althusius references Aristotle's *Politics*, specifically the section where he writes about the natural-ness of all levels of human community, including the *polis*, which Aristotle holds is prior to the family and individual because the whole (that is, the *polis*) is prior to the part (that is, earlier forms like the family).[126] Aristotle also notes in this section that humans have 'a social instinct' implanted in them 'by nature'.[127] The impli-cation for Althusius's reference to Aristotle is clear: for Althusius, humans are naturally political and have social instincts implanted in them. In what virtually amounts to a quotation of Aristotle, Althusius notes that the human 'is a more civil animal than the bee or any other gregarious creature'.[128] God has made humans this way: 'God himself endowed each being with a natural capacity to maintain itself and to resist whatever is contrary to it.'[129] Althusius then states that it follows from this that humans cannot, in fact, survive apart from society with other humans. '[Since] dispersed men are not able to exercise this capacity' the natural instinct for joining into human society was also given by God to humankind.[130] Nature, in line with the natural law, is the final cause of political life for humankind, driving humans to the highest temporal pur-pose of a good life and common welfare.

It follows from this understanding that humans cannot 'live well' alone, and so Althusius writes that 'necessity induces one into political fellowship'.[131] The desire for the wants and goods of social life conserves political fellowship.[132] He shows further dependence on Aristotle when he writes that the commonwealth 'exists by nature' and that humanity is naturally a 'civil animal'.[133] This is a clear echo of the famous '*zoon politikon*' formula of Aristotle. Furthermore, according to Althusius, if someone does not consider himself in need of others, he is not to be considered part of civil society and must be either a 'beast or a god'.[134] People who were dispersed and living apart from one another could not protect themselves or provide for their basic needs. Althusius believes that they then joined together to form the first societies.[135] For Althusius, following Aristotle and others who imitate his political anthropology, humans are naturally joined into human society because of their basic needs, but also because of their desire for the good life. It is basically classic Aristotelian political naturalism.

### Conclusion

In summary, then, Althusius offers three key factors in his theory of societal origins. First, nature itself, as made by God, impels people to join together, both for teleological reasons and for practical reasons. Althusius combines both a natural final cause and, like Calvin and Hooker, a natural efficient cause in his explanation of societal origins. It is notable that the sources he relies on include Calvin, who we have established is a political naturalist, and Aristotle. Althusius's theory and the sources for it point to Althusius having a natural understanding of political life. This naturalist understanding means that he held that political society is sacred in origin: God is the one who founds human political life.

It was Otto von Gierke who resurrected scholarly interest in Johannes Althusius, dragging the obscure Reformed German from the doldrums of political thought. In doing so, Gierke gave Althusius something of a starring role in the emergence of what he described as the 'natural law theory of society'. In his own grand narrative, Gierke saw this natural law-based legal/political theory as undergirding the modern conceptions of political thought. 'Althusius', claims Gierke, 'proceeded . . . to erect the first complete system of political theory which was wholly based on Natural Law.'[136] In other words, Gierke claims that Althusius was the first to wrest political theory from the clutches of classical thought and medieval political theology, through his offering of a pure natural law political system.[137] In light of the above chapter, that description of Althusius should be rather jarring. His political theory was not at all 'wholly based on natural law'. It certainly did not have the characteristics of a secular account of politics and law. If Althusius had wanted to separate himself from medieval and classical thought, he failed miserably.

It was not my intention, in this chapter, to simply argue against Gierke. However, what I have argued demonstrates some misinterpretation on his part. My primary intention was to show two things: (1) Althusius's natural law theory had God as the legislator and enforcer of that law, and (2) his theory of societal origins shows that he held that God, through His natural law, is the founder of human society. In this way, Althusius continued the trend in early Reformed Protestant political thought of asserting the central role of God in the foundation of human political life. He joined both Calvin and Hooker in arguing, under the auspices of political naturalism, that civic life is not secular in nature or in origin. Even Althusius's use of *pactum* was consistent with this theistic political naturalism. However, this latter idea, that of covenant or pact, was taken up by Hobbes. As we will see in the next chapter, *pactum* was turned from being a natural bond for all social and political relationships into a contractual agreement whereby pre-political individuals agree to form political society to protect their rights. Along with a fundamental change in the understanding of natural law, this change in the role of the political covenant paved the way for a desacralised understanding of the origins of political life in the Reformed tradition.

## Notes

1. Otto von Gierke, *Johannes Althusius und die Entwicklung der naturrechtlichen Staatstheorien: zugleich ein Beitrag zur Geschichte der Rechtssystematik* appeared as the third volume in Gierke's *Das deutsche Genossenschaftsrecht* (Berlin: Wiedmann, 1868–1913), 4 vols. References to this volume will be to Otto von Gierke, *The Development of Political Theory*, trans. Bernard Freyd (New York: Howard Fertig, 1966). Parts of this chapter have been previously published in Simon P. Kennedy, 'Rethinking *consociatio* in Althusius's *Politica*', *Journal of Markets and Morality* 22.2 (2019): 305–16. These appear here with the gracious permission of the editors.

2. Many histories of political thought mention Althusius, but usually only in passing. For his non-canonicity, see Thomas O. Hueglin, *Early Modern Concepts for a Late Modern World: Althusius on Community and Federalism* (Waterloo: Wilfred Laurier University, 1999), 18–19.

3. Joachim Whaley, *Germany and the Holy Roman Empire*, vol. 1: *Maximilian I to the Peace of Westphalia, 1493–1648* (Oxford: Oxford University Press, 2011), 334.

4. See the account and accompanying references in Carl J. Friedrich, 'Introduction', in Johannes Althusius, *Politica methodice digesta of Johannes Althusius (Althaus) reprinted from the third edition of 1614*, ed. Carl J. Friedrich (Cambridge, MA: Harvard University Press, 1932), xxiv–xxv.

5. Frederick S. Carney, 'The Associational Theory of Johannes Althusius: A Study in Calvinist Constitutionalism' (PhD diss., University of Chicago, 1960), 12–13.

6. Stephen Grabill, 'Althusius in Context', in Althusius, *On Law and Power*, trans. Jeffrey J. Veenstra (Grand Rapids, MI: CLP Academic, 2013), xx.

7. Heinz Schilling, *Religion, Political Culture and the Emergence of Early Modern Society: Essays in German and Dutch History* (Leiden: Brill, 1992), 247–50. For an overview of the spread of Reformed Protestantism during this Reformation, see Henry Chadwick, *The Reformation* (Harmondsworth: Penguin, 1964), 148–9. On Johann VI's reforms in Nassau-Dillenburg, see Howard Hotson, *Johann Heinrich Alsted 1588–1638: Between Renaissance, Reformation, and Universal Reform* (Oxford: Clarendon Press, 2000), 18–24. On the role of Ramism in those reforms, see Howard Hotson, *Commonplace Learning: Ramism and Its German Ramifications 1543–1630* (Oxford: Oxford University Press, 2007), 101–26.

8. Whaley, *Holy Roman Empire*, 503.

9. Ian Hunter, 'The University Philosopher in Early Modern Germany', in *The Philosopher in Early Modern Europe: The Nature of a Contested Identity*, ed. Conal Condren, Stephen Gaukroger and Ian Hunter (Cambridge: Cambridge University Press, 2006), 50.

10. Howard Hotson, 'The Conservative Face of Contractual Theory: The *Monarchomach* Servants of the Count of Nassau-Dillenburg', in *Politische Begriffe und historisches Umfeld in der* Politica methodice digesta *des Johannes Althusius*, ed. Emilio Bonfatti, Giuseppe Duso and Merio Scattola (Wiesbaden: Harrassowitz Verlag, 2002), 260–1.

11. Ibid., 261.

12. On the Reformed context and influence, see Grabill, *Rediscovering the Natural Law*, 122–50; cf. Frederick S. Carney, 'Translator's Introduction', in Johannes Althusius, *Politica: an abridged translation of Politics Methodically Set Forth and Illustrated with Sacred*

*and Profane Examples*, trans. Frederick S. Carney (Indianapolis: Liberty Fund, 1995), xxvii. On Althusius's response to the confessional tensions, see John Witte, 'A Demonstrative Theory of Natural Law: Johannes Althusius and the Rise of Calvinist Jurisprudence', *Ecclesiastical Law Journal* 11.3 (2009): 264; cf. more generally John Witte, 'The Universal Rule of Natural Law and Written Constitutions in the Thought of Johannes Althusius', in *Morality and Responsibility of Rulers: European and Chinese Origins of a Rule of Law as Justice for World Order*, ed. Anthony Carty and Janne Nijman (Oxford: Oxford University Press, 2018), 167–86.

13. Johannes Althusius, *Politica methodice digesta et exemplis sacris et profanes illustrata* (Herborn in Nassovia: Christophorus Corvinus, 1603).

14. The following works provide a sample of the spread of scholarly interest in Althusius: Nicholas Aroney and Simon P. Kennedy, 'Johannes Althusius's Cosmopolitan Defense of Local Politics', in *Cosmopolitanism and Its Discontents: Rethinking Politics in the Age of Brexit and Trump*, ed. Lee Ward (Lanham, MD: Rowman & Littlefield, 2020), 19–36; Daniel J. Elazar, 'The Multi-faceted Covenant: The Biblical Approach to the Problem of Organizations, Constitutions, and Liberty as reflected in the thought of Johannes Althusius', *Constitutional Political Economy* 2.2 (1991): 194; Daniel J. Elazar, 'Althusius' Grand Design for a Federal Commonwealth', in *Politica: an abridged translation*, xl; Hueglin, *Early Modern Concepts*, 2; Alain De Benoist, 'The First Federalist: Johannes Althusius', *Telos* 118 (2000): 25–58; Thomas Hueglin, 'Johannes Althusius: Medieval Constitutionalist or Modern Federalist?', *Publius* 9 (1979): 41; Carl J. Friedrich, 'Preface', in *The Politics of Johannes Althusius*, ed. Carl J. Friedrich (Boston, MA: Beacon Press, 1964), ix–xi; Nicholas Aroney, 'Althusius at the Antipodes: The Politica and Australian Federalism', in *Jurisprudenz, Politische Theorie und Politische Theologie*, ed. Frederick Carney, Heinz Schilling, Dieter Wyduckel (Berlin: Duncker & Humblot, 2004), 529–46; John Witte Jr., *The Reformation of Rights* (Cambridge: Cambridge University Press, 2007), 158; Matt McCullock, 'The Culmination of Calvin's Right of Resistance', *The European Legacy* 11 (2006): 485–99; J. W. Baker, 'The Covenantal Basis for the Development of Swiss Political Federalism: 1291–1848', *Publius* 23.2 (1993): 38.

15. Robert von Friedeberg, '*Persona* and Office: Althusius on the Formation of Magistrates and Councillors', in *The Philosopher in Early Modern Europe*, ed. Condren, Gaukroger and Hunter, 161–73; cf. Hunter, 'The University Philosopher in Early Modern Germany', 35–65; Hotson, 'The Conservative Face', 251–90.

16. Hotson, 'The Conservative Face', 252–3.

17. Although, cf. David P. Henreckson, *The Immortal Commonwealth* (Cambridge: Cambridge University Press, 2019), 127–60.

18. Friedrich, 'Introduction', xxxii–xxxiii.

19. Johannes Althusius, *Politica methodice digesta atque exemplis sacris et profanes illustrata* (Arnheim: Johannes Janssonius, 1610); Johannes Althusius, *Politica methodice digesta atque exemplis sacris et profanes illustrata* (Herborn in Nassovia: Corvinus, 1614). Citations will be to the 1614 edition, as follows: *Politica* [chapter]:[section number]. English translation will be from Johannes Althusius, *Politica: an abridged translation*, unless otherwise noted. Citations will be to *Politica: an abridged translation*, [page]. Johannes Althusius, *Dicaeologicae libri tres, Totum et universum Jus, quo utimur, methodice complectentes* (Herborn in Nassovia: Corvinus, 1617). Edition cited here will be *Dicaeologicae libri tres, Totum & universum Jus, quo utimur, methodice complectentes* (Frankfurt: Corvinus, 1649). It will be cited as *Dic* [book].[chapter].[section]. English translations will be from Johannes Althusius, *On Law and Power*, unless otherwise noted, and will be cited as *On Law and Power*, [page].

20. Friedrich, 'Introduction', lxv; cf. Gierke, *The Development of Political Theory*, 56–8.

21. Friedrich, 'Introduction', lxvii–lxviii; Gierke, *The Development of Political Theory*, 70–6.

22. *Dic* 1.13.1; *On Law and Power*, 7.

23. *Dic* 1.13.1; *On Law and Power*, 7.

24. *Dic* 1.13.1; *On Law and Power*, 7.

25. *Politica* 21:18; *Politica: an abridged translation*, 139.

26. *Politica* 21:18; *Politica: an abridged translation*, 139.

27. *Politica* 21:16; *Politica: an abridged translation*, 139.

28. Grabill, *Rediscovering the Natural Law*, 130–42.

29. Zanchi, *De primi hominis lapsu*, cols. 190. 'Lex naturæ est voluntas Dei, eóque divina recte agendorum ac vitandorum ratio atque regula, omnium hominum mentibus à Deo ipso immediatè etiam post peccatum inscripta: qua generatim quid bonum & malum . . .' Translation from Girolamo Zanchi, *On the Law in General*, trans. Jeffrey J. Veenstra (Grand Rapids, MI: CLP Academic, 2012), 13.

30. Zanchi, *De primi hominis lapsu*, cols. 186; *Politica* 21:16; *Politica: an abridged translation*, 139.

31. Zanchi, *De primi hominis lapsu*, cols. 186. '. . . honestum faciendum sit & quid, ut vere malum sit vitandum'; *Politica* 21:16; *Politica: an abridged translation*, 139.

32. Cf. *Dic* 1.13.14. 'Docet autem & inscribit mentibus hominum Deus generalia principia boni & æqui, mali & iniqui.'

33. Witte, 'A Demonstrative Theory of Natural Law', 251.

34. *Dic* 1.13.18. Cf. see *Politica* 21:19.

35. *Dic* 1.13.6; *Politica* 21:19; ibid., 21:30. Also ibid., 1:11 and 1:19.

36. *Dic* 1.13.7; *On Law and Power*, 8; *Dic* 1.13.11; *On Law and Power*, 9; *Politica* 21:19; *Politica: an abridged translation*, 139.

37. *Dic* 1.13.8; ibid., 1.14.1; *Politica* 21:30.

38. *Dic* 1.13.11; *On Law and Power*, 9.

39. *Dic* 1.13.12; *Politica* 21:20.

40. *Politica*, 21:19; *Politica: an abridged translation*, 139.

41. *Dic* 1.13.12. Translation is my own. '. . . notitia, tum inclinatio naturalis'. Also 'impellitur arcano'.

42. *Politica* 21:19; *Politica: an abridged translation*, 139.

43. *Dic* 1.13.14; *On Law and Power*, 9.

44. *Dic* 1.13.14; *On Law and Power*, 9.

45. *Politica* 21:20; *Dic* 1.13.14.

46. Grabill, *Rediscovering the Natural Law*, 144.

47. Althusius, *Politica* 21.19; Calvin, *Institutes*, 2.2.22; Hooker, *Laws*, 3.9.3; Zanchi, *De primi hominis lapsu*, cols. 189; Franciscus Junius, *De Politiae Mosis Observatione*, 35–6.

48. *Politica* 21:20; *Politica: an abridged translation*, 140.

49. *Politica* 21:21; *Politica: an abridged translation*, 140.

50. Cf. *Dic* 1.13.15.

51. *Politica* 21:29; *Politica: an abridged translation*, 144.

52. Printed as an appendix in the 1614 edition of *Politica* as *De utilitate, necessitate et antiquitate scholarum: Admonitio panegyrica*, 969–1003. Translations from this are my own.

53. Althusius, *Admonitio*, 970. 'Nota etiam est humana imbecillitas, ignorantia, oblivio, & socordia.'

54. Althusius, *Admonitio*, 971. '. . . sed omne figmentum cogitationis & cordis humani, ab initio tantum ad malum sit propensum. Unde in reprobis etiamnum spiritus soporis, torporis efficacia, illusionum & tetra impuritas & sentina vitiorum, horror conscientiae, impotentia.'

55. *Politica* 23:21. 'Primo mobile, varium, inconstans & mutabile, pronum in affectus, quos ponit, vel sumit varios, imo contrarios sæpe & diversos, & plerunq.'; ibid., 23:25. 'Populus est præceps pavidus socors judicii expers nec delectu aut sapientia sed impetu temeritate suspicione . . .'; Friedrich, 'Introduction', lxx–lxxi.

56. *Dic* 1.13.16; *On Law and Power*, 10.

57. *Politica* 21:21; *Politica: an abridged translation*, 140; Cf. Zanchi, *De primi hominis lapsu*, cols. 191.

58. *Politica* 21:21; *Politica: an abridged translation*, 140.

59. *Dic* 1.13.14.

60. *Dic* 1.13.17.

61. *ST* Ia-IIae, Q. 90, art. 1; Tollefsen, 'Natural Law, Basic Goods', 133–4.

62. Calvin, Comm. Romans 2:14; CO 49:37–8; *Commentaries on Romans*, 96–7; Herdt, 'Calvin's Legacy', 435.

63. Junius, *De Politiae Mosis Observatione*, 20.

64. Zanchi, *De primi hominis lapsu*, cols. 191.

65. Ibid., cols. 191. 'Alterum est, quod non solum hoc doceat, verum etiam ad bonum faciendum obliget inclinetque . . .'

66. *Dic* 1.13.11; *On Law and Power*, 9.

67. *Dic* 1.13.11; *On Law and Power*, 9. Cf. *Politica* 9:21, which stipulates that positive civil law must not contradict the '*jus natural et divinium*'. Natural law forms the basis of civil law, both of which are directed towards the same goal.
68. For example, cf. *Politica* 21:15; ibid., 21:18; *Dic* 1.13.4; ibid., 1.13.19; ibid., 1.13.21.
69. *Politica* 1:3; *Politica: an abridged translation*, 17.
70. *Politica* 1:1.
71. Ibid., 1:1.
72. Ibid., 1:3; *Politica: an abridged translation*, 17.
73. *Politica* 1:4; *Politica: an abridged translation*, 17.
74. *Politica* 1:4; *Politica: an abridged translation*, 17.
75. *Politica* 1:6.
76. John Calvin, *Sermons on Genesis*, 180–1.
77. Vorster, 'Symbiotic Anthroplogy', 32.
78. For more examples of Calvin's view of society, see Comm. Eph. 5:21; CO 51:221–222; Comm. Gen. 2:18; CO 23:46.
79. *Politica* 1:26; Henreckson, *Immortal Commonwealth*, 142–3.
80. *Politica* 1:6.
81. *Politica* 1:7–8; cf. *Politica* 7:8.
82. Ibid., 1:7; *Politica: an abridged translation*, 19.
83. *Politica* 1.7; Carney cites Cicero, *De republica*, 1.25 at this point, but this seems to be a mistake. It appears more likely that Althusius is alluding to *De republica* 39a–42. Althusius's precise source is unclear, but it is most likely Augustine, *De civitate Dei*, 19:21.
84. *Politica* 1:1.
85. A point which Hueglin makes in *Early Modern Concepts*, 16. For a classic example of this anachronism, see Arend Lijphart, *Democracy in Plural Societies: A Comparative Exploration* (New Haven, CT: Yale University Press, 1977), 1.
86. Kennedy, 'Rethinking *consociatio*'; cf. Henreckson, *Immortal Commonwealth*, 135–7.
87. Henreckson, *Immortal Commonwealth*, 137.
88. *Politica* 2:42; *Politica: an abridged translation*, 32.
89. *Politica* 2:1, my own translation.
90. Ibid., 2:2, also 2:5 and 4:8. Carney translates this in 2:2 as 'special covenant'.
91. Ibid., 2:2.
92. Ibid., 2:42, my own translation.
93. Ibid., 4:2–3.
94. Ibid., 5:1, my own translation.
95. Ibid., 5:8.
96. Ibid., 5:3–4.
97. Ibid., 1:6; *Politica: an abridged translation*, 19.
98. *Politica* 1:23, *Politica: an abridged translation*, 22.
99. Ibid., 1:23; *Politica: an abridged translation*, 22.

100. *Politica* 1:25, my own translation.
101. Ibid., 1:23.
102. Ibid., 1.27. 'Corporis itaque; & animi necessitatis atque virtutum semina animis nostris infita.'
103. It is notable that he cites Franciscus Junius and Bartholomaeus Keckermann, two other Reformed Protestant jurists, on this very point. See ibid., 1:25.
104. Ibid., 1:27.
105. Ibid., 1:29; *Politica: an abridged translation*, 24.
106. *Politica* 1:29.
107. Ibid., 1:31.
108. Ibid., 1:30. My own translation.
109. The main examples are Hueglin, *Early Modern Concepts*, 86–7; Gierke, *The Development of Political Theory*, 58. Cf. Harro Höpfl and Martyn P. Thompson, 'The History of Contract as a Motif in Political Thought', *American Historical Review* 84.4 (1979): 935.
110. Carney translates *pactio* as 'agreement', but this is lacking illustrative force. Elazar uses 'covenant', which might be more useful. I prefer 'pact'.
111. Henreckson argues for both in his fine study on Reformed political thought and covenantal ideas, *Immortal Commonwealth*, 154.
112. Ibid., 927–44 provides a more fulsome overview of this question as related to early modern political thought.
113. Ibid., 927.
114. Calvin, *Institutes*, 2.10.1: '. . . quod olim cum Israelitis foedus ante Christi adventum Dominus pepigit'. Translation is my own.
115. Ibid., 4.14.6: 'Et quando Dominus promissiones suas foedera nuncupat . . . sacramenta, symbola foederum: ab ipsis hominum foederibus simile adduci potest.' Translation is my own.
116. Henreckson, *Immortal Commonwealth*, 135–7.
117. On authorship, cf. Skinner, *Foundations of Modern Political Thought*, vol. 2, 306, n3.
118. Junius Brutus, *Vindiciae contra tyrannos: sive, de Principis in Populum, Populique in Principem, legitima potestate* (Edimburgi: Thomas Gaurin, 1579), 11–12. 'Duplex autem foedus in Regum inauguratione legimus: primum, inter Deum & Regem & Populum, ut esset Populus, Dei Populus. Secundum vero, inter Regem & Populum, ut bene imperanti bene obtemperaretur.' Translations for this work are from Junius Brutus, *Vindiciæ contra Tyrannos: A Defence of Liberty against Tyrants* (London: Matthew Simmons and Robert Wilson, 1648). This quote from page 7.
119. Brutus, *Vindiciae*, 35–6. 'Iam ex quo Reges Populo dati sunt, no modo non desiit haec eadem Pactio . . . Diximus in Rege inaugurando duplex foedus initum suisse.' Translation from Brutus, *Defence of Liberty*, 21.
120. *Politica* 1:2.

121. Ibid., 1:6.
122. Cf. Ibid., 5:3.
123. In other words, it is not a 'social contract' in the modern sense of the word. For a good assessment of the social contract idea, see Patrick Riley, 'How Coherent is the Social Contract Tradition?', *Journal of the History of Ideas* 34.4 (1973): 543–8. Also see Michael Oakeshott, *Lectures*, 448–52.
124. *Politica* 1:10–12.
125. Ibid., 1:32; *Politica: an abridged translation*, 24.
126. Aristotle, *Politics*, 1253a25–27; translation from Aristotle, *The Politics*, ed. Stephen Everson (Cambridge: Cambridge University Press, 1988), 3–4.
127. Aristotle, *Politics*, 1253a30; *The Politics*, 4.
128. *Politica* 1:32. My own translation.
129. Ibid., 1:32; *Politica: an abridged translation*, 24.
130. *Politica* 1:32; *Politica: an abridged translation*, 24; cf. *Politica* 4:3.
131. *Politica* 1:33. My own translation.
132. Ibid., 1:33. Althusius cites Thomas Aquinas, from both his *Summa Theologica* and *De regimine principum*, on this point.
133. Ibid., 1:33; *Politica: an abridged translation*, 25.
134. *Politica* 1:33; *Politica: an abridged translation*, 25.
135. *Politica* 1:32.
136. Otto von Gierke, *Natural Law and the Theory of Society, 1500–1800*, trans. Ernst Barker (Boston, MA: Beacon Press), 37.
137. Cf. Ibid., 36.

# Chapter 4

# Thomas Hobbes: Reforming Nature, Profaning Politics

The *Journal* of the House of Commons shows that on the seventeenth day of October 1666, under the grim subject heading of 'Atheism', the House ordered 'That the Committee to which the Bill against Atheism and Profaneness is committed, be empowered to receive Information touching such books as tend to Atheism, Blasphemy, or Profaneness, or against the Essence or Attributes of God.'[1] Of particular interest to the House was the work of a certain Thomas Hobbes, written while he was exiled in Paris during the English Civil War. The work was titled *Leviathan* (published 1651). The *Journal* also records that the Committee was to 'report the Matter, with their Opinions, to the House', a charge they never fulfilled.[2]

The charge of 'atheism', if compared with the use of the term today, takes on something of a different form if understood in historical context.[3] When one considers that someone like Martin Luther could be accused of atheism for undermining mainstream theology, then the accusations against Hobbes are less alarming. The atheism that Hobbes was accused of indicates that some thought his ideas provoked beliefs that led to atheism. So, it is understandable that scholars are divided on the meaning of Hobbes's religious convictions for his political ideas. Perhaps they are divided over the meaning of his political ideas for his religious convictions? Whichever it is, I do not propose to resolve this ongoing debate. However, I will look to Hobbes as an exemplary character in the story of the secularisation of early modern political thought. Accusations of atheism directed towards Hobbes are not irrelevant. His understanding of nature, of natural law, and of the origins of society demonstrate that Hobbes desacralised political life, whether intentionally or not.

One central debate in Hobbes scholarship is over the relationship between Hobbes's theory of natural law and God. Indeed, the relationship has been under question ever since Hobbes began publishing his ideas on natural law, coming under sustained attack during his own time, and garnering him a reputation as a religiously subversive atheist.[4] In this, Hobbes was not dissimilar to his contemporary, Hugo Grotius (1583–1645), who made his provocative *etiamsi daremus* assertion in *De jure belli ac pacis* (1625).[5] This has been interpreted as indicative of the non-theistic tendencies in the Dutchman's natural law theory, despite his qualification that to grant the non-existence of God would be 'the greatest Wickedness' and that we 'ought to believe' in God's desire to reward those who obey Him.[6] Pufendorf, writing some decades later, did not fail to note the potential pitfalls of such an account.[7] As this chapter will show, Grotius was joined by Hobbes in positing a desacralised account of the law of nature.

Hobbes's theory of natural law will occupy us for much of this chapter. Fundamental to understanding his theory of natural law was his conception of 'nature', which was very different from the Aristotelian and scholastic conceptions evidenced in Calvin, Hooker and Althusius. I maintain that this means Hobbes deviated from the earlier natural law theories propounded by Reformed thinkers. In Hobbes's political writings, natural law became focused on the protection and promotion of pre-political natural rights.[8] These rights are threatened by the radical anti-sociability of humanity, and therefore humans must establish a political society to protect those rights. The central intention of political society is, for Hobbes, the protection of natural rights that are perpetually under threat because of human nature and its natural propensity towards social discord.

It is in this way – through the alteration of natural law – that Hobbes desacralised the idea of political society. Rather than political society being founded by God through created nature, society is a human artefact, created by way of a man-made covenant. Here, we see a very different deployment of the *pactum* motif which was central to Althusius's political theory. For Althusius, covenantal fellowship undergirded all social and political relationships but was not in any proper sense a *contract*. Hobbes's covenant was contractual in nature and undergirds his conventionalist theory of political society. I will address each of the above elements, in turn, showing Hobbes's ideas to be evidence that transcendent grounds of the social order were being undermined as early as the 1650s, with a turn in both natural law theories and the origins of political life.

## 'Nature' in the Thought of Hobbes

Biographers, including Hobbes himself, usually locate Hobbes's birth in relation to the attempted invasion of England by the Spanish Armada in 1588.[9] In doing so, they tend to focus on the presence of fear at the time of his birth. This geopolitical context is something of a harbinger for what would become a major theme in Hobbes's natural and political philosophies: disorder. But it is perhaps more notable that his birth near Malmesbury, in April of 1588, is only months before the arrival into the world of Marin Mersenne (1588–1648). Mersenne was a central figure, especially in his role as a networker, in the scientific and philosophical circle that Hobbes moved in during the mid-1530s. This circle, which included figures like René Descartes (1596–1650), Pierre Gassendi (1592–1655) and, more loosely, Galileo Galilei (1564–1642), contained many of the instigators of the philosophical and scientific revolution that would soon engulf Europe.[10] It was a revolution that would overturn many preconceptions about the order and governance of the universe. Hobbes's interest in natural philosophy (what we call 'science') grew in the 1630s.[11] His embrace of non-Ptolemaic cosmology and non-Aristotelian physics stems, in part, from his time on the European continent between 1634 and 1636.[12] Here we see the groundwork being laid for a new conception of 'nature' and the natural order.

Other roots of this are discernible in his response to his education at Magdalen Hall, Oxford. Hobbes himself states that he studied 'logic and Aristotelian physics', something he had an evident distaste for.[13] According to Sidney Hamilton, 'the tone of the Hall . . . was, on the whole, Puritan'.[14] The principal of Magdalen Hall when Hobbes began his studies was James Hussey, who was succeeded by John Wilkinson in 1605, a Puritan and Reformed man who ensured the ongoing influence of Puritan ideas at Magdalen stretched well into the seventeenth century.[15] We can gather from this that the general intellectual and theological milieu of Hobbes's years at Oxford were decidedly Reformed. Interestingly, there is no indication in his autobiographical material or otherwise that he resented the religious influence of the Hall. What we do know is that Hobbes disliked the curriculum of Aristotelian philosophy and methods.[16] With his rejection of Aristotle, he also rejected Aristotle's conception of nature.

We will now explore the meaning of this rejection, both for Hobbes's own ideas and for the wider trajectory of the role of the sacred in Reformed political thought. It is, of course, true that rejecting Aristotle did not necessarily mean rejecting the received understanding of nature. Calvin was not Aristotelian, per se, but he retained general continuity with the medieval concept of a God-governed natural order. Hooker and Althusius, on the other hand, were both self-consciously Aristotelian in their approach to natural law and nature itself. Considered in this context, Hobbes's departure from the received understanding of nature and natural law appears even more stark. So, what might Hobbes's new conception of nature mean for his political ideas? As we will see below, Hobbes's rejection of Aristotelian conceptions of nature deeply affected his cosmology, his physics and, ultimately, his political thought.

In *Leviathan*, Hobbes writes that 'Nature hath made men . . . equal',[17] and that 'Nature should thus dissociate, and render men apt to invade, and destroy one another.'[18] As disturbing as that description of humans is in the latter sentence, we must focus our attention on the first word: nature. What Hobbes meant by 'nature' was something quite different from what was meant by almost everyone prior to him, including Calvin, Hooker and Althusius. The dominant cosmological and physical worldview in Christendom, the Christian-Aristotelian view, was one of order and purpose. The universe was a unified whole. Everything that existed had an end, a *telos*. Each thing was moving towards that *telos*, straining to reach its natural goal. Indeed, things moved because they were moving towards their teleological goal. Once they reached that goal they could cease moving and rest. Rest had a primacy in the Aristotelian universe and was a sign that the thing had reached its goal. This ordered universe, with every element of it infused with purpose, meant that questions of right and wrong, of ethics and politics, could be derived in some sense from the order of nature. In the Aristotelian cosmos the 'is' could reap an 'ought'.[19]

Hobbes's universe is drastically different. It is a unified whole, to be sure, but it has no particular order. Hobbes's world is one of pure motion: bodies of matter moving without evident purpose or cessation.[20] These bodies will always move in the same direction, and at the same speed, except when they are interrupted by another body.[21] Contrary to the received Aristotelian physics, Hobbes sees the moving and the touching of bodies as offering no revelation of inherent value, purpose or order. Causation was simply bodies in motion diverting other bodies in motion. 'There can be no cause of motion', writes Hobbes, except when two moving bodies touch.[22] There is only motion and contrary motion. Here, Hobbes departs from the Aristotelian understanding that bodies move as they do because they have a purpose in doing so, a 'final cause'. Hobbes removes Aristotle's final cause as well as his formal cause, subsuming them into the material and efficient causes, thereby abolishing any sense of *telos* for bodies in motion.[23] 'The causes', states Hobbes, 'of universal things (of those, at least, that have any cause) are manifest of themselves . . . they have all but one universal cause, which is motion.'[24]

Hobbes puts this all in a rather understated way, but he has here, with one fell swoop, unravelled the prevailing Christian-Aristotelian cosmology. Bodies and motion were the things which made up Hobbes's universe. Bodies and motion were also all there was to Hobbes's concept of nature. Therefore, according to Hobbes, there is no teleology in nature at all. Indeed, Hobbes mocks the very idea of teleological reasoning.[25] So nature has been reduced from the purposeful movements of bodies towards their restful end in the world of Aristotle, to the mechanical, restless, purposeless movements of bodies in the world of Hobbes. However, this does not mean that Hobbes's world is meaningless and purposeless. Rather, Hobbes understands that there is no revelation of purpose or order accessible to human observation.[26] There is no moral or ethical meaning to draw out of how things actually are. For Hobbes, nature is not pregnant with causes which indicate ends but is pure mechanical motion with no discernible inherent purpose.

So, proceeding on this basis, Hobbes understands 'nature' as the condition of bodies when they are in the state of motion without any outside interference. Therefore, the natural condition is, according to Hobbes, inherently disorderly. The physics and geometry of nature are perfectly arranged and orderly, but the world therein is not. As Thomas A. Spragens writes, 'the new nature is exquisitely ordered – but the criteria of this order are purely and exhaustively geometric'.[27] This lack of teleology within nature itself obviously has implications for Hobbes's understanding of natural law.[28] His reformulation of natural law marks Hobbes out from the thinkers previously examined in this book. Whereas Calvin, Hooker and Althusius all understood the natural law to be linked to a transcendent purpose and design, Hobbes organises his theory of natural law around the necessity of sociability for the protection of humankind's natural rights. This lays the foundation for his desacralisation of the political.

## Nature and Natural Law

Hobbes's earliest writings on natural law and politics were composed during the troubled reign of Charles I. By the late 1630s, Charles found himself backed into a financial corner due to his engagement in expensive wars. Having not called Parliament for eleven years, Charles was, as Hobbes himself put it in his *Behemoth* (1680), forced to do so 'by the rebellion of the Scotch'.[29] A Parliament was called, infamous for its brief sitting between April and May 1640.[30] The events which followed the sitting of what he called 'that unlucky Parliament' most certainly shape Hobbes's political philosophy from this point, as his enunciation of the laws of nature becomes focused on the creation of a stable civic order.[31] Indeed, the fact that he completed his *Elements of Law, Natural and Politic* (1640) only days after the dissolution of the Short Parliament is pointed in itself.[32] While we will inspect Hobbes's later works in greater detail, it is in this work that we see the initial outlines of Hobbes's anthropocentric theory of natural law.[33]

The basis for Hobbes's natural law theory, as stated in *Elements*, is the idea that all people desire

> their own good, which is the work of reason: there can therefore be no other law of nature than reason, nor no other precepts of *natural law*, than those which declare unto us the ways of peace, where the same may be obtained, and of defence where it may not.[34]

Peace is the goal of the law of nature, according to Hobbes. The crisp definition found in *De cive*, published first in Latin in April 1642, one month after the outbreak of civil war in England, provides us with the clearest insight into the purpose of Hobbes's natural law: 'The *Natural law* ... is the Dictate of right reason about what should be done or not done for longest possible preservation of life and limb.'[35] Essentially the same definition, which is notably different from the scholastic definition of a participation in the eternal law of God by reason, is found in *Leviathan*.[36] The importance of self-preservation is, in itself, not a controversial part of adherence to the natural law, but using it as the foundation for the same marks a new turn. For Hobbes, something is a law of nature if it lends itself to the preservation of humanity. We will return to this desire for self-preservation in more detail when we consider Hobbes's anthropology below, including his state of nature (the 'state of warre'). But for now, we must emphasise that it is the connection between the natural law and self-preservation that marks out Hobbes from earlier natural law thinkers.[37] This connection informs Hobbes's understanding of the laws of nature themselves.

There are two 'fundamentall' laws of nature listed in *Leviathan*, Hobbes's greatest work of political philosophy. The first is *'to seek peace and follow it'*, while the second is:

> *That a man be willing, when others are so too, as farre-forth, as for Peace, and defence of himselfe he shall think it necessary, to lay down this right to all things; and be contented with so much liberty against other men, as he would allow other men against himselfe.*[38]

In what sense are these two precepts 'fundamentall'? Well, for Hobbes, the laws of nature do not function as a collection of broadly agreed-upon dictates, nor (as observed above) as a law built into human reason and connected to God's eternal law. Neither are they an unwritten reflection of God's divine moral law as expressed in the Decalogue. Rather, there is a universal principle being defended by Hobbes's enunciation of the laws of nature: self-preservation. To quote Perez Zagorin, Hobbes's laws of nature 'are the conclusion of a chain of reasoning that starts with what Hobbes insists is an empirically accurate description . . . of the propensities of human nature and its basic desire and passion for self-preservation'.[39] So, Hobbes says that 'every violation of Natural Laws consists in false reasoning or in stupidity, when men fail to see what duties are necessary to their own preservation'.[40] They are not a set of deductions available to rational minds set in the natural order of things, but are instead a set of pragmatic deductions based on the human desire to preserve human life.[41]

We can see even more clearly the radical departure Hobbes has made from the received tradition of natural law thinking if we compare his ideas to those of his contemporaries. For example, eminent English jurist Sir Edward Coke (1552–1634) defines the law of nature in his report (1608) on the famous case of the Scottish freeholder Robert Calvin.[42] Coke defines the natural law as 'that which God at the time of creation of the nature of man infused into his heart, for his preservation and direction' and he equates this with the eternal law and the moral law.[43] Coke further describes the natural law as 'written with the finger of God in the heart of man', and that Moses wrote down this law in his account of God's law.[44] Matthew Hale (1609–76) writes in his

*Some Chapters touching on the Law of Nature* (undated, though possibly written between 1668 and 1670),[45] under his discussion of divine law, that the natural law is 'contained in the two Tables of the Mosaic law'.[46] However, the 'Law of nature' has a twofold meaning for Hale. It refers, first, to the 'Order of the Universe' and how parts of nature itself are 'directed and governed to their severall Ends . . . suitable to their kinds and Natures'.[47] Note the heavily imbued Aristotelianism: all things are directed towards their ends according to their natures. The second meaning is this: the law which God has implanted into intellectual creatures, and is given to humans in their 'human Nature'.[48] Indeed, in what is a barely veiled swipe at Hobbes, Hale is critical of those who 'have made in effect self preservation the only Cardinall Law of human Nature' and deduce all laws of nature from this one principle.[49]

The final pertinent example comes from Richard Cumberland (1632–1718), who published his *Treatise of the Laws of Nature* in 1672 in part to respond to Hobbes. Cumberland defines the law of nature as 'certain Propositions of unchangeable Truth, which direct our voluntary actions, about choosing Good and refusing Evil', while also imposing positive obligations on people even prior to the existence of civil government.[50] Later, Cumberland defines the law of nature in more detail, describing it as a 'proposition' derived from the 'Nature of Things, from the will of God', which is accessible to the human mind and directs people towards actions which 'chiefly promote the common Good'.[51]

But it is not only Hobbes's fundamental understanding of the natural law which sets him apart from thinkers like Coke, Hale and Cumberland. Given the fundamental principle of the law of nature is different, the content is also different. Indeed, it is focused entirely on humanity and their self-preservation; it is now anthropocentric. This need for self-preservation, combined with the grim anthropology that Hobbes adhered to (to which we will turn soon), means humans must create a state of peace within an artificial civil society.[52] But before that is evident (and it must be rationally evident in Hobbes's mind), further laws of nature are necessary. Importantly, all the laws build towards the creation of political society. Indeed, the second law of nature (which is one of the two fundamental laws) is, in brief, that people should lay down their 'right to all things'. This law implies a distinction between a law and a 'right'. The 'right to all things' is, evidently, a natural and pre-political right which must be laid aside in order that human life may be preserved.[53] Precisely what the difference is between a right and a law, and why this particular natural law is so important for the protection of other pre-political rights, will be examined further in the next section.

We have examined the first two laws of nature in Hobbes's schema and will now outline the remainder to further show the centrality of self-preservation in his thought. The third law of nature is *'that men performe their Covenants made'*, which Hobbes says is the 'Fountain and Originall of JUSTICE'.[54] Here we witness the entry of the theologico-political motif of *pactum*, used so extensively by Althusius. However, as we shall see, Hobbes's idea of *pactum* is very different and is used to develop a desacralised theory of societal origins. Returning to Hobbes's third law of nature, he asserts that covenant-keeping is the very definition of justice. But covenant-keeping is not possible if the second law of nature is not kept. This is the situation in the state of 'Warre', which prompts people to form political society. The fourth law of nature is that *'a man which receiveth Benefit from another of meer Grace, Endeavour that he which giveth it, have no reasonable cause to repent him of his good will'*.[55] On the surface, this is a puzzling law of nature. However, it is related to making and keeping covenants. People make covenants with one another but, as discussed later, people make a free gift of their right to all things to the sovereign. Hobbes's fourth natural law is directed towards the prevention of a potentially disappointed, disenfranchised and possibly rebellious citizenry.[56] The fifth law of nature is *'That every man strive to accommodate himselfe to the rest'* – a pivotal law for living in a tolerable social situation.[57]

The sixth law of nature is similar to the fifth in that it seems unavoidable if one wants to live in social peace. It is *'That upon caution of the Future time, a man ought to pardon the offences past of them that repenting, desire it.'*[58] Forgiveness for past wrongs ends hostility. But those who 'persevere in their hostility' show 'an aversion to Peace'.[59] The seventh law of nature regards proportionality in the punishment of wrongs, encouraging that *'in Revenges . . . Men look not at the greatnesse of the evill past, but the greatnesse of the good to follow.'*[60] Punishment ('revenges') without a view to improvement for the future, be it for the person being punished or for society more generally, 'tendeth to the introduction of Warre'.[61] The eighth is *'That no man by deed, word, countenance, or gesture, declare Hatred, or Contempt of another.'*[62] It is self-evident that a breach of this law would work against the cause of social peace and, therefore, self-preservation. The ninth law is that *'every man acknowledge other for his Equall by Nature*'.[63] This law works against pride, but Hobbes also sees that people who do not view themselves as equal will not enter into covenant with those who they deem inferior. Likewise, covenants for social peace will not be possible if the law that '*no man require to reserve to himself any Right, which he is not content should be reserved to everyone of the rest*' is ignored.[64] People must, according to this law of nature, grant rights to others which they themselves require for life.

Hobbes does allow for differences to be worked out under the auspices of the law of nature. Anyone who is entrusted with the judgement of cases must '*deal Equally between them*' when doing so.[65] Partiality in judging tends, according to Hobbes, towards war. Thankfully, not everything needs a judge to decide use or ownership. Some things cannot be divided and therefore should, according to the law of nature, be '*enjoyed in Common*', or '*Proportionally to the number of them that have Right.*'[66] However, if the right to something cannot be divided proportionally (as in, ownership of property or money), then the law of nature requires '*That the Entire Right; or else, (making the use alternate,) the First Possession, be determined by Lot.*'[67] The laws of nature stipulate two kinds of lots: primogeniture and first possessor.[68] Those who are in a controversy requiring these or determinations of another kind must, according to Hobbes's law of nature, '*submit their Right to the judgement of an Arbitrator*'.[69] These Arbitrators must also '*be allowed safe conduct*' in order to intercede and keep the peace.[70] However, they must never be judge in cases involving themselves for, according to the law of nature, 'no man is a fit Arbitrator in his own cause'.[71] Finally, the nineteenth law of nature is that matters of fact must be decided upon by multiple witnesses.[72]

Hopefully, it is clear from this brief outline of Hobbes's laws of nature that they are founded upon what he perceives as the fundamental desire for self-preservation which is present in all people. They are, according to Hobbes, 'the Lawes of Nature, dictating Peace, for a means of the conservation of men in multitudes'.[73] These laws are not framed as the outworking of human participation in the eternal law by rational, practical reason. Rather, they are entirely anthropocentric 'laws', deduced from observation and from the fundamental need for social peace. It is true that Hobbes does maintain that the laws of nature are the laws of God, and it seems to me that Hobbes should be taken seriously when he states that this is his position, whether it is a coherent one or not.[74] However, what we have seen here is that the natural law of Hobbes is no longer the natural law of the scholastics and Aristotelians. His theory looks quite different from the thinkers we considered earlier. Rather, it is directed towards the problem that Hobbes saw right in front of him when he was formulating his natural law jurisprudence: disorder and war.

To resolve the difficulties of his day, Hobbes felt he needed to persuade people to obey a natural law which points them to social peace. It is a natural law that is directed towards human sociability, with the design of protecting pre-political rights possessed by wicked and antisocial human beings. For Hobbes, this is entirely necessary and leads to the human creation of political society and submission to a political sovereign who will enforce the laws of nature. But why are these laws of nature necessary? Is it not the case that people, as created by God, are naturally political? Hobbes abandons this premise and, as we will explore below, does so partially on the basis of a modified Reformed Protestant anthropology.

## Human Nature

The most detailed account of Hobbes's view of human nature and the pre-political state of humanity is found in *Leviathan*. That volume was composed during the later years of his self-exile in France. To use a phrase from his 'Preface' to *De cive*, England was 'seething' with political tension in the 1630s, and by the early 1640s the anti-royalist elements in England were beginning to set their focus on those defending absolute monarchy.[75] Hobbes fled in 1640 and found safety and company in Paris, remaining there for close to a decade.[76] He continued to mix with the Mersenne circle, as well as developing networks within the Reformed Protestant communities of France.[77] A royalist exile community began to grow in Paris, and soon included the Prince of Wales, Charles's son, whom Hobbes was to tutor in mathematics.[78]

During this Parisian period, Hobbes worked on what was to become his greatest work. It spoke indirectly, though still with undoubted pointedness, to the political situation back in his homeland. However, for our own purposes, it reveals two key things. First, it demonstrates his pessimistic anthropology, which I suggest is imbued with Reformed Protestant tones. Second, it shows the importance of pre-political rights in the formulation of Hobbes's theory of the origins of society and explains why the laws of nature were necessary for Hobbes in the first place. This issue links back, also, to his framing of the natural law. Both elements explain what we will address in the final section: the artificial, desacralised creation of political society.

In *De corpore*, Hobbes writes that 'Man's nature is the sum of his natural faculties and powers, as the faculties of nutrition, motion, generation, sense, reason, &c.'[79] In other words, humans are by nature a combination of mechanical bodily factors. The opening sections of *Leviathan* take their leave from this basic premise, emphasising the natural human. His description of human nature is less overtly theological than those anthropologies we have considered thus far, and he also differentiates himself from classical conceptions of anthropology by rejecting ideals like virtue to explain human nature, as well as the aforementioned rejection of teleology. What follows will be an all-too-brief account of the opening chapters of *Leviathan*, which will allow us to properly understand how he conceives of the human in the state of nature.

First and foremost, Hobbes sees that it is the imagination that drives action, not the external body of matter perceived by the human mind.[80] For Hobbes, sense experience is the basic cause of human action. 'Voluntary motions' are first begun by 'Imagination'; that is, the image of something that is in one's mind after seeing it. In other words, things appearing in the human mind are the first cause of voluntary motion.[81] Therefore, he credits actions like walking, speaking and striking to 'Endeavour'. He reasons that endeavour is a movement towards or away from something and is caused by appetite or desire. From here, Hobbes reasons that desire is the cause of 'Love', and its opposite 'Aversion' is the cause of 'Hate'. In his analysis, Hobbes makes a striking claim about the foundation of moral value. He says that 'whatsoever is the object of any mans Appetite or Desire; that is it, which for his part calleth *Good*'.[82] On the other hand, 'the object of his Hate, and Aversion, [is called] *Evil*'.[83] The reasoning here is that the basic motivations for human activity are caused by base feelings or experiences from within the human, not from outside of him or her. Here we see a rejection of Aristotle's final cause and the resulting loss of teleology. It is the very base desires and sensations which drive human behaviour, according to Hobbes, and he calls these desires 'Passions'. Hobbes's theory of human behaviour is a 'mechanistic psychology of the passions'.[84]

The outcome of this assessment of human sense and experience is not a happy one for Hobbes. These passions cause human conflict because humans do not act according to anyone else's interest but their own. Humans are selfish, and selfishness is what motivates them. They are moved by their passions to speak and act in ways which can have negative and positive outcomes for themselves and for others. However, in Hobbes's mind, the outcomes are ultimately negative. Indeed, in his 'Preface' to the *De cive*, he writes that all men know from experience that unless people are restrained by external, coercive power, every man 'will distrust and fear each other' and will ultimately be forced to use violence to protect themselves.[85] For Hobbes, the natural condition of humanity is one of conflict and strife, as man seeks his own interests, often at the expense of others. Humans will naturally make use of the strength they have to 'look out for himself'.[86] Hobbes here points to readily available evidence: even in times of peace nations build walls and set watches on neighbouring kingdoms; people travel with weapons for self-defence and lock their doors and their 'chests and boxes' at night. 'Can man express their universal distrust of one another more openly?'[87] Nor can humans trust each other's words. They are, according to Hobbes, inherently unstable in their use.[88] For 'the bonds of words are too weak to bridle men's ambition, avarice, anger, and other Passions'.[89] Indeed, Hobbes links this view of human nature to that of the Bible. He writes that 'all Men are evil (which perhaps, though harsh, should be conceded, since it is clearly said in holy Scripture)'.[90] Even if we concede that Hobbes does not think 'men are evil by nature', his description of human nature is strikingly similar to common formulations from Reformed theologians and confessional documents.[91]

For example, John Calvin's *Genevan Confession* (1536) states that 'by nature' humanity 'is only able to live in ignorance and be abandoned to all iniquity'.[92] The *Thirty-Nine Articles of the Church of England*, finalised in 1571, declares that humans are naturally 'inclined to evil'.[93] The *Westminster Confession of Faith* (1646), composed by an assembly of theologians and divines appointed by the House of Commons in 1643,[94] states that humanity is 'utterly indisposed, disabled, and made opposite to all good, and wholly inclined to all evil'.[95] The *Heidelberg Catechism* (1563) is similarly stark in its assessment of human sin. In response to the question 'But are we so perverted that we are altogether unable to do good and prone to do evil?' the answer comes 'Yes, unless we are born again through the Spirit of God.'[96] Indeed, the aforementioned *Thirty-Nine Articles* further maintain that this sinful nature 'doth remain . . . in them that are regenerated'.[97] Sin is inescapable in the anthropology of the Reformed tradition, resulting in a grim picture of human nature.

Even if Hobbes does not use the word 'sin' in the theological sense, Hobbes was in good, Reformed Protestant company in his assessment of human nature and the fallen, wicked condition of man.[98] This assessment colours how Hobbes sees humans in their natural state, which is their pre-political state.[99]

Returning, then, to *Leviathan*, Hobbes begins his explication of humanity's condition before the formation of society with the tenet that humans are equal.[100] Even inequalities of physical strength and faculty of the mind are 'not so considerable, as that one man can thereupon claim to himselfe any benefit, to which another may not pretend, as well as he'.[101] However, this natural equality is the source of trouble. For equal people also have equally strong desires and 'if any two men desire the same thing, which neverthelesse they cannot both enjoy, they become enemies'.[102] The starkest image of this equality leading to enmity is stated in *De cive*, where Hobbes notes 'how easy it is for even the weakest individual to kill someone stronger than himself'. Anyone can kill anyone. Equality leads to competition, which leads to what he calls 'diffidence'. Both of these, along with a desire for 'glory', are the cause of a condition as infamous as it is famous: the 'warre, as is of every man, against every man'.[103] Every person is an enemy of every other person, living in their own strength in a battle for self-preservation. This is such a dark situation that there is 'no place for Industry, . . . no Culture of the Earth, . . . no Arts; no Letters; no Society; and which is worst of all, continuall feare, and danger of violent death'.[104] Hobbes's pictures of nature itself, and then the state of nature for humanity, parallel one another. Both are conditions of disorder.[105]

Not only are humans wicked and naturally bent towards violence in self-defence but, according to Hobbes, they are also endowed with natural rights. This emphasis on pre-political natural rights is a key factor in the turn away from theistic political naturalism and towards a desacralised conventional account of the origins of political society. Hobbes says that a person possesses a natural right to 'use his power . . . for the preservation of his own Nature'. But also, anyone may '[do] any thing, which in his own Judgement, and Reason, hee shall conceive to be the aptest means thereunto'.[106] These rights are defined as a 'liberty' by Hobbes, which is in turn defined as 'an absence of externall Impediments'.[107] A law, on the other hand, 'determineth, and bindeth'.[108] These natural rights are obviously under constant threat in the state of nature. '[As] long as this natural Right of every man to everything [for purposes of self-preservation] endureth, there can be no security to any man.'

Everyone possesses these natural rights in the state of nature, and, although they do not have to exercise that right, they can do so by any means necessary.[109] The ability to forbear from exercising natural rights is important, as we have already seen in the law of nature which stipulates that people must put aside their rights to seek peace.[110] However, the main thrust of Hobbes's argument is that every person in the state of nature has a natural right to self-preservation, and that this situation is entirely untenable in that state because humans are profoundly wicked. Here is where the laws of nature fit into Hobbes's scheme.

The natural right to self-preservation leads 'consequently' (according to Hobbes) to the 'precept, or general rule of Reason, *That every man, ought to endeavour Peace*'.[111] The remainder of the laws of nature (outlined above) flow out logically from this point. It is the right of nature which leads to the existence of the laws of nature. The laws of nature exist to defend this pre-political natural right. However, there is a further problem, which the laws of nature do not resolve in Hobbes's mind. People in the state of nature, bearing natural rights, and having some kind of obligation under the laws of nature, are in conflict precisely *because they have natural rights whilst in the state of nature*. The problem is the state of nature. The vehicle for the problem is pre-political natural rights. The solution, as Hobbes himself states, is not the laws of nature, despite their very purpose being the protection of the right to self-preservation. On the contrary: 'the Lawes of Nature . . . of themselves, without the terrour of some Power, to cause them to be observed, are contrary to our natural Passions . . . [and] Covenants, without the Sword, are but Words'.[112] The defence of these pre-political rights must be taken up by someone or something imposed upon the natural order. Human wickedness is too great, and nature too disorderly. It is at this point in Hobbes's thought where anthropology becomes political anthropology. A great power is needed, and it must be erected by humans themselves.

## The Covenantal Formation of Society

The artificial nature of political society in Hobbes's writings is as important as it is striking. It is here that we see the role that God previously had in establishing political society being taken over by humans. As we have seen in earlier chapters, God was seen by Calvin, Hooker and Althusius as the creator of the naturally political person, a framework which I have termed 'theistic political naturalism'. In Hobbes's thought, God is understood as the creator of non-political humanity, and it is humans who create political society. Aristotle is, according to Hobbes, wrong to suggest that humans are naturally political, along with the bees and ants. Along with the temperament and disposition of humans towards anti-sociability outlined in his description of the state of war, they cannot agree to be in society naturally, according to Hobbes.[113] The way 'Men' will enter political life 'is by Covenant only, which is Artificiall'.[114]

We will address how this fleshes out in Hobbes's understanding of the origins of society presently. However, the question of 'covenant' is in the foreground. We saw in the previous chapter that Althusius's covenant, or pact, was basic to every political relationship in that it defined the nature of political fellowship. It was not an artificial voluntary agreement but was rather a natural, political bond between people, households, cities and provinces. Hobbes's and, as we will see, Locke's covenant is much closer to the idea of a contract. In fact, to frame his conception of covenant, Hobbes first defines a 'contract'. A contract is two people 'reciprocally *transferring* their *rights*'.[115] On the other hand, Hobbes's covenants, writes A. P. Martinich, 'look to the future for performance of the conditions specified in the present'.[116] A covenant is, according to Hobbes, where parties to the agreement 'leave the other to perform his part at some determinate time after', so the receiving party gains the given right, as promised, at some point in the future.[117] However, as we have noted above, the keeping of covenants is problematic in the state of nature. Hobbes is adamant that human nature, the law of nature, and the state of nature all conspire to require some overarching coercive power to compel people to keep their covenants. How can society, which is necessarily covenantal, be formed if people will not keep their covenants?

Hobbes frames the issue in terms of the ideal necessity of covenant-keeping for humanity rather than the actual inability for people to keep covenant in the state of nature. In other words, Hobbes focuses on humanity's need to be able to keep covenants and have others keep covenant. This need compels people to seek help. '[Before] the names Just, and Unjust can have place, there must be some coercive Power, to compel men equally to the performance of their Covenants . . . the Validity of Covenants begins not but with the Constitution of a Civill Power sufficient to compel men to keep them.'[118] The law of nature says that covenants must be kept, but the state of nature means that covenants will not be kept. The pre-political rights which humans possess cannot be protected in the state of nature under the juridical regime of the laws of nature. Civil government is necessary, according to Hobbes, because *'the natural laws* do not guarantee their own observance'.[119]

The solution is for people to create a political society wherein these rights (most fundamentally, the right to self-preservation) can be protected. To do this, Hobbes says that people must 'conferre all their power and strength upon one Man, or one Assembly of men', thereby reducing all of the individual wills to 'one Will'.[120] Indeed, they appoint this one man or assembly to 'beare their Person' so that this 'Soveraigne' will act on their behalf 'in those things which concerne the Common Peace and Safetie'.[121] But in order for the Sovereign to achieve this, the people must agree to give up their rights. The law of nature, which stipulates that people must be willing to renege on their right to all things, comes into play at this point. The people must make a covenant of 'every man with every man'. In this covenant, every person is promising something to every other person at some point in the future. It is 'as if every man should say to every man, *I Authorise and give up my Right of Governing my selfe, to* [the Sovereign], *on this condition, that thou give up thy Right to him, and Authorise all his Actions in like manner'*.[122] In order to protect their right to self-preservation, people must give up their right to everything that they are able to use for that self-preservation. But they do this at the expense of making a covenant, the observation of which sees that they will have their lives preserved.

This covenant is a 'COMMON-WEALTH' forming covenant. There are hints, here, of Reformed covenant theology, especially in the way that the multitude experience a kind of salvation from the consequences of their own wickedness.[123] Philosopher Michael Oakeshott is, perhaps, right to suggest that in *Leviathan* we see an attempt to 'reembody in a new myth the Augustinian epic of the Fall and Salvation of mankind'.[124] The multitude, which was before in a disordered and dangerous condition, have themselves now, according to Hobbes, caused 'the Generation of that great LEVIATHAN . . . to which we owe under the *Immortal God*, our peace and defence'.[125] The authority given to the Leviathan is given by 'every particular man', and in doing this the multitude have become '*The Author*' of the political society which will see an end to the state of nature.[126] Hobbes was, of course, distinctly concerned about the role of confessional conflict in the deterioration of civil order in England during the 1640s.[127] This concern is reflected in his *Behemoth* (published in 1679), where Hobbes lists 'ministers, as they called themselves, of Christ' as a guilty party in the stirring up of dissension leading to civil war.[128] We see in *Leviathan* that the worship of the 'Immortal God' is to be regulated and prescribed by the Sovereign, which is certainly one of Hobbes's guards against religious disorder.[129] The establishment of the Sovereign will also see the proper defence of individuals' rights. For the commonwealth is '*One Person*' who is authorised by the individuals to '*use the strength and means of them all . . . for their Peace and Common Defence*'.[130] The laws of nature lead us to understand that our rights can be best exercised by the Sovereign. Through the exercise of the individual's rights by the Sovereign, the right to self-preservation is protected.[131]

In sum, then, Hobbes has shaped a theory of societal origins which sees the key role given to humanity rather than God. The ingredient which is present in his scheme, and which is lacking in the accounts considered earlier in this book, is the presence of a pre-political condition in which people possess natural rights which require protection. The formation of political society only occurs because the natural law, which is in place to protect those natural rights, compels people to then form into political societies in which those natural rights are preserved. Natural law is, in this context, not the ground of natural rights as such, but is instead the guarantor of those rights. It now merely prescribes human behaviours and conditions which protect and encourage human sociability, which, in turn, protects pre-political natural rights.[132] The conventional (that is, artificial) response to this is the formation of political society. For Hobbes, and crucially for my larger argument, the political condition is an artefact made in response to the threat to pre-political natural rights. In Hobbes's political thought, the pre-political condition is divinely ordained (if disordered due to human wickedness), but political society is human-made.

## Conclusion

Returning to the House of Commons in 1666, we can reconsider whether Hobbes's writings 'tend to Atheism'. It is not clear from the above analysis that they did, even though they altered the role that God plays in the formation of human society. What Hobbes's political ideas did tend towards is the desacralisation of political society. This was an important marker in the trajectory of Reformed Protestant ideas in particular, but also western political thought more generally.[133] The received understanding of the role of God in the foundations of human political life, epitomised in this book by Calvin, Hooker and Althusius, was undergirded by a 'theistic political naturalism'. Humans were created by God to be in political society, and the natural order, shaped and governed by God through the natural law, undergirded this reality.

As we can now see, Hobbes's embracing of a new understanding of nature and natural law was part of the dismantling of the old consensus. Humans were not naturally political, for nature itself was pure motion, disordered and seemingly random. The natural human condition, what Hobbes called the 'state of nature', was similar to this, but the disorder was further punctuated by human wickedness. It is in this context, with an altered understanding of nature and anthropology, that Hobbes's natural laws fit in. Rather than being understood as eternal divine laws of natural order and rationality, Hobbes saw the natural law as a set of boundary markers governing disordered human behaviour. Civil governance was required, not for any teleological purpose, but for the purpose of protecting pre-political rights. For those rights to be adequately protected, humans had to improve the natural (dis-)order.

Political society was Hobbes's solution to the problem of vulnerable natural rights. These rights were founded by God as part of the natural order of His creation. However, ultimately, Hobbes purported an altered understanding of natural law resulting in a desacralised conception of the origins of political society. The foundations of the social order, the very idea of political life, had always been grounded upon the transcendent. But the transcendent grounds of the social order were being undermined. This pattern is further entrenched and developed through the political ideas of John Locke.

## Notes

1. *Journal of the House of Commons: Volume 8* (London: His Majesty's Stationery Office, 1802), 636.
2. The Committee is required to report in the lifetime of the Parliament by which it is appointed, and there is no record of them ever doing so in the recorded proceedings of the House.
3. A good overview can be found in Ada Palmer, *Reading Lucretius in the Renaissance* (Cambridge, MA: Harvard University Press, 2014), 21–5. For a more specific assessment of Hobbes's atheism, see Richard Tuck, 'The Christian Atheism of Thomas Hobbes', in *Atheism from the Reformation to the Enlightenment*, ed. Michael Hunter and

David Wootton (Oxford: Clarendon Press, 1992), 111–30. Also cf. A. P. Martinich, *The Two Gods of* Leviathan: *Thomas Hobbes on Religion and Politics* (Cambridge: Cambridge University Press, 1992), 19–21.

4. A good overview is found in Jon Parkin, 'Taming the Leviathan: Reading Hobbes in Seventeenth-Century Europe', in *Early Modern Natural Law Theories: Contexts and Strategies in the Early Enlightenment*, ed. Hochstrasser and Schroder, 39–46.

5. Hugo Grotius, 'Prolegomena', in *De jure belli ac pacis* (Paris: Nicolaum Buon, 1625), n.p. 'Et haec quidem quae iam diximus, locum haberent etiamsi daremus, quod sine summo scelere dari nequit, non esse Deum, aut non curari ab eo negotia humana . . .'.

6. I have used Richard Tuck's translation of the 'Prolegomena' from Hugo Grotius, *The Rights of War and Peace*, 3 vols, ed. Richard Tuck (Indianapolis: Liberty Fund, 2005), III: 1748. Good discussions of the implications of Grotius's natural law ideas for his Christian theism include: Ruben Alvarado, *Calvin and the Whigs: A Study in Historical Political Theology* (Aalten: Pantocrator, 2017), 95–110; Taylor, *A Secular Age*, 126–8; Richard Tuck, *Natural Rights Theories: Their Origin and Development* (Cambridge: Cambridge University Press, 1979), 76–7; Richard Tuck, *Philosophy and Government, 1572–1651* (Cambridge: Cambridge University Press, 1993), 197–8; Hochstrasser, *Natural Law Theories*, 4; Grabill, *Rediscovering the Natural Law*, 177–80.

7. Samuel Pufendorf, *De Jure Naturae et Gentium Libri Octo* (Londini Scanorum: Junghans, 1672), II.3.4; Pufendorf, *De Officio Hominis et Civis Juxta Legem Naturalem* (Londini Scanorum: Junghans, 1673), I.3.10–11.

8. For helpful discussions of Hobbes's natural law thought in relation to the broader sweep of 'modern natural law', see Knud Haakonssen, 'Early Modern Natural Law Theories', in *The Cambridge Companion to Natural Law Jurisprudence*, ed. George Duke and Robert P. George (Cambridge: Cambridge University Press, 2017), 76–102. Tuck, *Natural Rights Theories*, 58–142, appropriately emphasises other figures, including Grotius and Selden. Alvarado, *Calvin and the Whigs*, 75–110, also makes much of the role of Grotius. It is not my intention, here, to argue that Hobbes is *the* turning point. Rather, his ideas are symptomatic of a broader shift.

9. Thomas Hobbes, 'The Verse Life', in Thomas Hobbes, *The Elements of Law Natural and Politic*, ed. J. C. A. Gaskin (Oxford: Oxford University Press, 1999) 254; Aubrey, *Brief Lives*, 156; A. P. Martinich, *Hobbes: A Biography* (Cambridge: Cambridge University Press, 1999), 1–2; Miriam M. Reik, *The Golden Lands of Thomas Hobbes* (Detroit, MI: Wayne State University Press, 1977), 14.

10. Briefly on the Mersenne circle and Hobbes, see Martinich, *Hobbes: A Biography*, 90. Also see Thomas Hobbes, *The Correspondence*, vol. II, ed. Noel Malcolm (Oxford: Clarendon Press, 1994), 863.

11. Noel Malcolm, 'A Summary Biography of Hobbes', in Noel Malcolm, *Aspects of Hobbes* (Oxford: Clarendon Press, 2002), 21.

12. While not definitive, it is notable that his letters from Paris to William Cavendish, dated 1636, give some insight into his piquing interest in the physics of light, as well as showing him embracing the ideas of Galileo. See Thomas Hobbes, *The Correspondence*, vol. I, ed. Noel Malcolm (Oxford: Clarendon Press, 1994), 33–6 (Letter 19) & 37–8 (Letter 21); Reik, *The Golden Lands*, 53–54.

13. Hobbes, 'The Prose Life', in Hobbes, *The Elements of Law*, 245. For a description of Hobbes's education at Oxford, see Reik, *The Golden Lands*, 26–30.

14. Sidney G. Hamilton, *Hertford College* (London: F. E. Robinson & Co, 1903), 106.

15. See Hamilton, *Hertford College*, 106–12 for an account of Wilkinson's tenure; Martinich, *Hobbes: A Biography*, 18.

16. Aloysius Martinich, *Hobbes* (New York: Routledge, 2005), 4.

17. *Lev* XIII, 60:86.

18. *Lev* XIII, 62:89.

19. On the ancient and medieval idea of an ethical cosmos, see more generally Rémi Brague, *The Wisdom of the World*.

20. Thomas Hobbes, *The Collected Works of Thomas Hobbes*, vol. I, ed. William Molesworth (London: Routledge/Thoemmes, 1994), 109. Molesworth editions will herein be cited as EW, [volume number]:[page number]. The quotes here are from *De corpore* (1655). But the basic content of Hobbes's physics appears to have been developed in the 1630s. See Martinich, *Hobbes: A Biography*, 118–19. Also see Reik, *The Golden Lands*, 68–74; Hobbes, *Correspondence I*, 33–4 (Letter 19, dated 1636); Hobbes, *Correspondence I*, 62–86 (Letter 30, dated 1641); Hobbes, *Correspondence I*, 102–13 (Letter 34, dated 1641).

21. Hobbes, EW, 1:125.

22. Hobbes, EW, 1:124.

23. Hobbes, EW 1:131–2; Thomas A. Spragens, *Politics of Motion: The World of Thomas Hobbes* (London: Croom Helm, 1973), 64. Spragens's book is a good overview of this whole question of Hobbes's political philosophy and his adoption of the 'new science' and the non-Aristotelian cosmology.

24. Hobbes, EW, 1:69; For an overview of Hobbes's ideas on motion and science, see M. M. Goldsmith, *Hobbes's Science of Politics* (New York: Columbia University Press, 1966), 27–38; Tom Sorrell, *Hobbes* (London: Routledge, 1991), 55–67.

25. *Lev* LXVI, 374–5:467–8; EW 1:131–2.

26. Damrosch, 'Hobbes as Reformation Theologian', 349–50.

27. Spragens, *Politics of Motion*, 107.

28. Although cf. Jean Curthoys, 'Thomas Hobbes, the Taylor Thesis and Alasdair Macintyre', *British Journal for the History of Philosophy* 6.1 (1998): 20–5.

29. Hobbes, EW, 6:247.
30. Macauley, *The History of England*, 47–8; Ian Gentles, *The English Revolution and the Wars in the Three Kingdoms 1638–1652* (Harlow: Pearson Longman, 2007), 25.
31. Hobbes, EW, 6:247.
32. Martinich, *Hobbes*, 122.
33. A helpful volume which compares the texts of *Elements*, *De cive* and *Leviathan* is Deborah Baumgold (ed.), *Three-Text Edition of Thomas Hobbes's Political Theory*: Elements of Law, De Cive *and* Leviathan (Cambridge: Cambridge University Press, 2017).
34. Thomas Hobbes, *Elements of Law, Natural and Politic*, ed. Ferdinand Tönnies (London: Simpkin, Marshall and co., 1889), 15:1, 75. Citations of this work will be as follows: EL, [chapter]:[section], [page]. Also cf. EW, 4:87.
35. References to *De cive* are from Thomas Hobbes, *On the Citizen*, ed. Richard Tuck and Michael Silverthorne (Cambridge: Cambridge University Press, 1997). Citations will be as follows: DC, [chapter]:[section], [page number from Tuck]. So, DC, 2:1, 33.
36. *Lev* XIV, 64:91. On right reason (*recta ratio*), see Ernst-Wolfgang Böckenförde, 'Security and Self-Preservation before Justice: The Paradigm Shift and Transition from a Natural-Law to a Positive-Law Basis in Thomas Hobbes' System of Law', in *Constitutional and Political Theory: Selected Writings*, ed. Mirjam Künkler and Tine Stein (Oxford: Oxford University Press, 2017), 60.
37. Zagorin, *Hobbes and the Law of Nature*, 47. See also Noberto Bobbio, *Thomas Hobbes and the Natural Law Tradition*, trans. Daniela Gobetti (Chicago: University of Chicago Press, 1993), 149–71. Bobbio argues that Hobbes, rather than Grotius, is the first 'modern natural law theorist', in part due to his emphasis on self-preservation and his conventionalist account of the origins of society.
38. Both laws are found at *Lev* XIV, 64–5:92.
39. Zagorin, *Hobbes and the Law of Nature*, 46.
40. DC, 2:1, 33–4.
41. Zagorin, *Hobbes and the Law of Nature*, 48; cf. Bobbio, *Thomas Hobbes and the Natural Law Tradition*, 121–3, where he argues that Hobbes's natural laws 'do not prescribe actions that good in themselves', but rather prescribe actions which attain a certain end (self-preservation). Bobbio then proceeds to link this to legal positivism, which I think is mistaken. Cf. Samuel I. Mintz, *The Hunting of Leviathan* (Cambridge: Cambridge University Press), 26. Mintz claims that, for Hobbes, the laws of nature are 'eternal and immutable only as logical deductions, not as moral precepts', and are, thereby, 'stripped' of their 'absolute moral character' (35).
42. Edward Coke, 'Calvin's Case', *English Reports Full Reprint Vol. 77 – King's Bench*: 377–411, accessed at http://www.commonlii.org/uk/cases/EngR/1572/64.pdf (22 June 2018).

43. Ibid., 392.
44. Ibid.
45. See David S. Systma, 'Sir Matthew Hale (1609–1676) and Natural Law in the Seventeenth Century', *Journal of Markets and Morality* 17.1 (2014): 208.
46. Matthew Hale, 'Some Chapters touching on the Law of Nature', *Journal of Markets and Morality* 17.1 (2014): 286.
47. Ibid., 286.
48. Ibid., 287–8.
49. Ibid., 292–3.
50. Richard Cumberland, *Treatise of the Laws of Nature*, trans. John Maxwell, ed. Jon Parkin (Liberty Fund: Indianapolis, 2005), 289.
51. Ibid., 495–6.
52. This raises the questions of whether the laws of nature oblige, how they oblige, and what they oblige, which is the cause of much debate. These questions are not in purview, here. Readers should consult works such as Howard Warrender, *The Political Philosophy of Hobbes* (Oxford: Clarendon Press, 1970), 53–79, where he discusses the *in foro interno* and *externo* distinction. Tom Sorrell also discusses the same distinction, in 'Hobbes's Moral Philosophy', in *The Cambridge Companion to Hobbes's Leviathan*, ed. Patricia Springborg (Cambridge: Cambridge University Press, 2007), 132. Richard Tuck makes some important observations with regard to Warrender in *Natural Rights Theories*, 128–32. See also Martinich, *Two Gods*, 87–99; Quentin Skinner, 'The Context for Hobbes's Theory of Political Obligation', in Quentin Skinner, *Visions of Politics*, vol. 3: *Hobbes and Civil Science* (Cambridge: Cambridge University Press, 2002), 281–6; Bobbio, *Thomas Hobbes and the Natural Law Tradition*, 164–7; A. E. Taylor, 'The Ethical Doctrine of Hobbes', *Philosophy* 13 (52): 406–24.
53. See Richard Tuck's discussion in *Natural Rights Theories*, 107–18, for a discussion of Selden and the Great Tew circle's similar distinction.
54. *Lev* XV, 71:100.
55. Ibid., XV, 75:105.
56. Bernard Gert, 'The Law of Nature as the Moral Law', *Hobbes Studies* 1 (1988): 30–2.
57. *Lev* XV, 76:106.
58. Ibid.
59. Ibid.
60. Ibid.
61. Ibid., XV, 76:106–7.
62. Ibid., XV, 76:107.
63. Ibid., XV, 77:107.
64. Ibid.
65. Ibid., XV, 77:108.
66. Ibid.

67. Ibid.
68. Ibid., XV, 78:108.
69. Ibid., XV, 78:109.
70. Ibid., XV, 78:108.
71. Ibid., XV, 78:109.
72. Ibid.
73. Ibid.
74. *Lev* XV, 80:111; DC 3:33, 56; EL, 17:12, 93. Cf. Tuck, *Natural Rights Theories*, 126–7.
75. DC, 'Preface', s19, 13. References to this section of *De cive* will be as follows: DC(P), [section number]:[page number from the Tuck edition]. So DC(P), 19:13.
76. An account of his exile can be found in Martinich, *Hobbes: A Biography*, 161–215; cf. Jeffrey R. Collins, *The Allegiance of Thomas Hobbes* (Oxford: Oxford University Press, 2005), 60–1.
77. Conal Condren, *Thomas Hobbes* (New York: Twayne, 2000), 6.
78. Hobbes, *Correspondence I*, 136–41 (Letters 44 and 45); and ibid., 155–9 (Letter 52).
79. Hobbes, EW, 1:2.
80. Cf. F. S. McNeilly, *An Anatomy of Leviathan* (London: Macmillan 1968), 31; Goldsmith, *Hobbes's Science*, 50–1; Iain Hampsher-Monk, *A History of Modern Political Thought* (Oxford: Blackwell), 21.
81. *Lev*, especially chapters II and VI.
82. Ibid., VI, 24:39.
83. Ibid.
84. Laurence Berns, 'Thomas Hobbes', in *History of Political Philosophy*, ed. Leo Strauss and Joseph Cropsey (Chicago: Rand McNally, 1969), 356.
85. DC(P), 10:10.
86. Ibid.
87. Ibid., 11:10–11.
88. *Lev* V, 13:26, 17:30–1; ibid, VI, 29:45–6.
89. *Lev* XIV, 68:96.
90. Ibid., 12:11.
91. Ibid., 12:11. Cf. Kinch Hoekstra, 'Hobbes on the Natural Condition of Mankind', in *Cambridge Companion to Hobbes's Leviathan*, ed. Springborg, 112–13; Richard Ashcraft, 'Hobbes's Natural Man: A Study in Ideology Formation', *The Journal of Politics* 33.4 (1971): 1082–4. A discussion of Hobbes's view of the Fall would be interesting, here, but somewhat tangential. See *Lev* XX, 106:144; cf. Helen Thornton, *State of Nature or Eden?: Thomas Hobbes and His Contemporaries on the Natural Condition of Human Beings* (Rochester, NY: University of Rochester Press, 2005). In particular, see Chapter 1 for a discussion of the idea of good and evil in relation to Hobbes and the Fall. Also cf. Quentin Skinner, *Reason and Rhetoric in the Philosophy of Hobbes* (Cambridge: Cambridge University Press, 1996), 421.

92. John Calvin, 'The Genevan Confession', in *Calvin: Theological Treatises*, ed. J. K. Reid (London: SCM Press, 1954), 27.

93. Mark A. Noll, ed., *Confessions and Catechisms of the Reformation* (Leicester: Apollos, 1991), 216, article 9.

94. Robert Letham, *The Westminster Assembly: Reading Its Theology in Historical Context* (Phillipsburg, NJ: P & R, 2009), 30.

95. *Westminster Confession of Faith*, 6:4.

96. Noll, *Confessions and Catechisms*, 138, Question 8.

97. Ibid., 217, article 9.

98. Damrosch, 'Hobbes as Reformation Theologian', 347.

99. I think Glover is right to say of Hobbes's anthropology the following: 'A Christian interpretation of the predicament would relate it not to the nature of man per se, but to that defect in his nature which is sin and the result of sin.' See Willis B. Glover, 'God and Thomas Hobbes', *Church History* 29.3 (1960): 293; cf. Michael Oakeshott, *Hobbes on Civil Association* (Indianapolis: Liberty Fund, 1975), 62–4.

100. *Lev* XIII, 60:86; cf. DC, 1:3.

101. *Lev* XIII, 60:87.

102. Ibid., 61:87.

103. Ibid., 62:88.

104. Ibid., 62:89.

105. Spragens, *Politics of Motion*, 105–8.

106. *Lev* XIV, 64:91.

107. Ibid.

108. Ibid.

109. Ibid. Although, cf. John Finnis, 'Aquinas and Natural Law Jurisprudence', in *The Cambridge Companion to Natural Law Jurisprudence*, ed. Duke and George, 29.

110. Which, as Tuck points out, bring its status as a right into question. Cf. Tuck, *Natural Rights Theories*, 130.

111. *Lev* XIV, 64:91–2.

112. Ibid., XVII, 85:117.

113. Ibid., VII, 86–7:119–20.

114. Ibid., XVII, 87:120.

115. DC 2:9, 36; cf. *Lev* XIV, 66:96.

116. Martinich, *Two Gods*, 137–8.

117. *Lev* XIV, 66:96.

118. Ibid., XV, 71–2:100–1.

119. DC 5:1, 69.

120. *Lev* XVII, 87:120. The connection between covenant theology and 'public person' as a representative during the 1640s is drawn by Christopher Hill, 'Covenant Theology and the Concept of "A Public Person"', in Christopher Hill, *The Collected Essays of Christopher Hill,* vol. 3: *People and Ideas in 17th Century England* (Amherst: University of Massachusetts Press, 1985), 300–24. He focuses on Hobbes at 317–19.

121. On the idea of representation in Hobbes, see Mónica B. Vieira, *The Elements of Representation in Hobbes: Aesthetics, Theatre, Law, and Theology in the Construction of Hobbes's Theory of the State* (Leiden: Brill, 2009); Quentin Skinner, 'Hobbes on Representation', *European Journal of Philosophy* 13.2 (2005): 155–83.

122. *Lev* XVII, 87:120.

123. Franck Lessay does not draw the same parallels, but does address Hobbes's covenant theology, in 'Hobbes's Covenant Theology and Its Political Implications', in *The Cambridge Companion to Hobbes's Leviathan*, ed. Springborg, 243–70.

124. Oakeshott, *Hobbes on Civil Association*, 62.

125. *Lev* XVII, 87:120.

126. Ibid., XVII, 87–8:120–1.

127. Ibid., XVIII, 88–9:122.

128. Hobbes, EW, 6:167; ibid., 6:243–4. Martinich suggests a conflation in Hobbes's mind, though, between those seeking popular government and 'presbyterians'. A. P. Martinich, 'Presbyterians in 'Behemoth', in *Hobbes's Behemoth: Religion and Democracy*, ed. Tomaz Mastnak (Luton: Andrews UK, 2009), 183.

129. *Lev* XXXI, 192–3:252–4; ibid., XXXIII, 199:260; ibid., XXXIII, 205–6:268–9.

130. Ibid., XVII, 88:121.

131. Cf. Böckenförde, 'Security and Self-Preservation', 61–2.

132. Ruben Alvarado is very helpful on Hugo Grotius in this regard. See Alvarado, *Calvin and the Whigs*, 99–107.

133. Hobbes is, for good reason, linked to the modern natural law ideas seen in other settings, including the German Lutheran sphere. Thinkers like Samuel Pufendorf and Christian Thomasius are most important, here. See Knud Haakonssen, 'Early Modern Natural Law Theories', 84–5; Knud Haaksonssen and Michael J. Seidler, 'Natural Law: Law, Rights and Duties', in *A Companion to Intellectual History*, ed. Whatmore and Young, 383–94; Oakley, *Natural Law, Laws of Nature, Natural Rights*, 67; Hochstrasser, *Natural Law Theories*, 1–39.

# Chapter 5

# John Locke on Conventional Politics

Sometime before (or on) 8 February 1632, Robert Filmer (1588–1653) presented for the consideration of King Charles I a work entitled *A Discourse . . . of government in praise of Royaltie*. Filmer needed the crown's permission by way of a licence to proceed with the publication of his tract. Accordingly, the King's secretary, Georg Weckherlin, asked Charles whether the book ought to be published.[1] It seems likely that this work was an early version of what became known as *Patriarcha*, which posits that the divine origins of monarchical government are found in the patriarchal rulership of Adam. Why Filmer would have written such a work at this time is difficult to say with any precision, and Filmer's *Discourse* did not make it into the public eye for almost another fifty years.[2] When it finally did appear in 1680, it provoked responses from numerous Whig and anti-royalist figures, including Algernon Sidney (1623–83), who pejoratively labelled Filmer a 'servant' of the King.[3] James Tyrrell (1642–1718), in his 1681 *Patriarcha non Monarcha*, was more moderate in his criticism, suggesting that Filmer's arguments gave 'too much advantage to the Enemies of Kingship' by '[inflaming] Distemper'.[4] Another fierce response, and certainly the most famous, came from John Locke. In Locke's 1689 preface to his *Two Treatises of Government*, he wrote scathingly of his philosophical adversary: 'For if any one will be at the Pains himself', writes Locke, '. . . [to] endeavour to reduce his Words to direct, positive, intelligible Propositions . . . he will quickly be satisfied there was never so much glib Nonsense put together in well sounding English.'[5]

Filmer is almost exclusively remembered as the person whom Locke attacked in *Two Treatises*, whereas Locke secured a central place in the anglophone liberal tradition.[6] Adam Seligman and James Davison Hunter both point to Locke as a 'key transitional theorist' in the emergence of the Reformed–Enlightenment synthesis which held together the liberal democratic ideal.[7] The claim of this chapter is rather different, and it is not strictly related to the question of a putative synthesis between Reformed thought and Enlightenment ideals. I am focusing on the question of the connection between natural law ideas and the origins of political life, with a view to showing how these *loci* can inform our historical understanding of the emergence of secular conceptions of political life. Hobbes is the one example offered here of an earlier thinker who abandoned the transcendent grounds for political life. Locke further entrenches this pattern of political thought. This chapter essentially demonstrates that the desacralisation of political thought set in quite early in the Reformed tradition, and that this was linked to a change in theories of natural law.

As we will see, there are striking parallels between Hobbes's emphasis on self-preservation and Locke's. Likewise, Locke's use of the 'state of nature' also gestures towards Hobbes. In both of these instances, their ideas are also different in important ways. Locke's use of Hooker occupied us for some of Chapter 2. What follows below only adds to the claim that these two thinkers were actually very different. Hooker, along with Calvin and Althusius, carried on the old Reformed tradition of theistic political naturalism. This chapter will show that Locke entrenched the new pattern of desacralised conventionalism grounded on a new concept of natural law. Locke's legal and political writings evidence an anthropocentric natural law theory focused, like Hobbes's, on self-preservation, as well as a desacralised account of the origins of political life. Even if, as Davison Hunter rightly points out, Locke sees all political authority as derived from God, political life is established by humanity. Here, we see what Seligman calls the 'distancing of God from human affairs'.[8] Seligman places this change in the eighteenth century. However, as we will see, this was already occurring as early as the 1680s.

To show this trajectory in Reformed political thought, with Locke as our exemplary subject, we need to look at the historical and intellectual context for Locke's political writings. In particular, we will examine the patriarchal political theory of Robert Filmer, and also the context for Locke's jurisprudential and political writing up until the composition of his *Two Treatises*.[9] Filmer was a political naturalist, admittedly of a different kind to Calvin, Hooker and Althusius. This fact of Filmer's naturalism almost certainly affected Locke's positive presentation of his own political ideas. We will then investigate Locke's theory of natural law. His natural law thought cohered with a traditional scholastic natural law (which rightly includes both the intellectualist/voluntarist and realist/nominalist variations), but only to an extent. Ultimately, like Hobbes's, it was a natural law theory centred on the desire for self-preservation. From there, we will examine Locke's political anthropology, which will then be linked to his account of the origins of political life. In the end, Locke will be shown to have continued the trajectory away from a transcendent foundation for the social order, instead embracing a conventionalist account of political life.

## The Context for Locke's Theory of Political Life

John Locke was born in 1632, the year in which the aforementioned *Discourse* by Robert Filmer was rejected by the royal censor.[10] Filmer's argument, a curious one to our ears today, was not without its allies during his and Locke's lifetime. Filmer wrote the bulk of *Patriarcha* during the early years of the constitutional crisis that culminated in the English Civil War.[11] His theory of the origin of civil government was that Adam was the first head of his family and was also a political monarch. This original monarchy, grounded upon Adam's patriarchal headship, is forever the model for all political authority. According to patriarchal theory, the commonwealth is analogous to the family, and the king is the father, the head of that family. James I (1566–1625) argued for a kind of royal absolutism based on divine right, tinged with the idea that kings are *pater patriæ* (father of the fatherland).[12] However, as Cesare Cuttica notes, James I's 'monarchist discourse did not correspond *tout court* to Filmer's'.[13] Sir Edward Coke wrote in 1608 that it was according to the natural law that we ought to obey kings, for the moral law of God says '*honora patrem* (honour your father), which doubtless doth extend to him that is *pater patriæ*'.[14] The basic terms of this political theory were readily available in Filmer's (and Locke's) context.[15] However, Filmer's argument stands apart from the mere analogy of fatherly rule to political rule.[16] His was a patriarchal political theory, one which put forward an argument about the patriarchal origins and foundations of monarchical authority.

Filmer argued that people are born in subjection to their fathers. 'Adam', says Filmer, '[and] the succeeding patriarchs had, by right of fatherhood, royal authority over their children.'[17] Fatherhood is itself a form of political rule, according to Filmer, and is, furthermore, monarchical rule. This rule is given by God through natural means to the eldest son. Therefore, any idea of a social contract is defunct, and people are not themselves to be understood as creating political life. Rather, people are naturally political and are naturally in submission to political (patriarchal) authority. Political rule is given to kings in the framework of theistic natural law; subjection to fathers and to kings is according to the law of nature.[18] Filmer acknowledges that kings are not literally the fathers of their subjects, but instead are fathers by way of primogeniture of the king and are indeed called '*pater patriae* (father of the fatherland)'.[19] The king has a duty of 'universal fatherly care of his people'.[20] These ideas of Filmer's were not without recent precedent in the English context. Most notably, Hadrian Saravia (1532–1612) and a 1606 Convocation of the Church of England had expressed virtually the same theory of political authority as Filmer.[21]

The composers of the latter work (known as *The Convocation Book*) state that God gave Adam and all 'chief Fathers successively before the Flood, Authority, Power and Dominion over their Children, and Offspring, to rule and govern them'.[22] This rule was 'called either Patriarchal, Regal or Imperial', and can be called either '*Potestas Patria*' or '*Potestas Regia*', for, as the authors held, they are effectively the same thing.[23] Filmer himself further reasoned from this that civil rule is designated by God and by nature to the 'eldest parent', leaving no room for 'such imaginary pactions between kings and their people as many dream of'.[24] This is corroborated by the *Convocation Book*. The authors of that work write that Noah ruled his family after the Flood with 'Patriarchal, or, in effect, Regal Government', which was then passed to his three sons for them to carry on.[25] To their mind, this is inconsistent with the idea of government by contractual consent, and those who hold to this 'doth greatly erre'.[26]

Rather than a contract undergirding political legitimacy, Filmer holds that kings are chosen by God, but set up by the people. In fact, according to Filmer, this form of government is the only one deemed worthy of consideration.[27] This is because it is unnatural for the people to govern themselves or to choose their rulers. Instead, they are to submit to whomever God sets over them. War and strife, according to Filmer, are usually caused by illegitimate rebellion against a monarchy, and not caused by the illegitimacy of the monarchy.[28] Far from being a road to ruin, monarchy is a path to peace and stability.[29] Kings are also the makers and keepers of laws but are not bound by them in a positive sense. Instead, they are under the 'natural law of a father' which gives them a responsibility to act 'for the public good of their subjects'.[30] Therefore, parliaments are not lawmaking bodies. Instead, they are courts of appeal and petition, as well as assemblies of consent to the laws the king makes.[31] 'Filmerism', writes Peter Laslett, 'was above all things the exaltation of the family', turning the principles of the household 'into the principles of political science'.[32] Filmer was not alone in this, as evidenced by the eventual publication of *Patriarcha* in 1680 by royalists. Indeed, John Locke was combating a political theory which issued much wider than Filmer's writings, and it was threatening to undermine a cause he held dear; government according to the will of the people.[33]

Filmer died in 1653, one year before Locke was granted a studentship at Christ Church, Oxford. Having grown up in a Puritan home, it would have been somewhat comforting for Locke to have had Puritan theologian John Owen (1616–83) presiding over both Christ Church and the University as a whole.[34] After graduating, Locke secured a series of teaching posts at Christ Church, culminating in his appointment as a college tutor. It was during this phase of his career that he composed the *Essays on the Law of Nature* (1663–4), originally delivered as lectures at the College.[35] Along with this, he wrote two tracts on politics (1661 and 1662), which, as Laslett notes, displayed a marked contrast to the thought later expressed in *Two Treatises* and propagated traditionalist and Hobbesian tendencies.[36] This points to something changing rather dramatically in his ideas between the early 1660s and late 1670s, with the most obvious explanation being his coming into the service of Lord Ashley, who was to become the Earl of Shaftesbury.[37] His association with Shaftesbury meant Locke was caught up in the world of Whiggish ideas and politics and, as Laslett has established, it was the Exclusion Crisis, driven by Shaftesbury and the Whigs, which triggered Locke's writing of the *Two Treatises of Government*.[38]

Simply put, the Exclusion Crisis revolved around the possibility of an avowed Roman Catholic ascending to the English throne. The question became one of either God-ordained hereditary monarchy, or the guaranteeing of a monarch loyal to the Church of which he would be the head, as well as the guaranteeing of parliamentary control of executive policy.[39] Not only this; it also led to the pre-liminary question of whether a parliament could rightly alter the line of succession, thereby giving the parliament a kind of consti-tutional ascendency over the crown.[40] A natural royalist response to this scenario was, in Pocock's words, 'a denial of the antiquity of the commons', an important implication of Filmer's argument in *Patriarcha*.[41] Shaftesbury and his fellow Whigs had a bill pass the House of Commons in 1680 which mandated the passing over of the Roman Catholic James Stuart in the royal succession, but the bill was stopped in the Lords.[42] A general election was held to break this impasse, with the same outcome: after the election, the Lords blocked the bill again.

What were Locke's role and response in all of this? He was trav-elling in France during the later 1670s but was summoned home by Shaftesbury in mid-1679.[43] From what we can gather, it was then that Locke and Shaftesbury worked together on justifying the alter-ation of the so-called 'ancient constitution'. And it was during this period of exertion that Locke began working on his greatest work of political thought. Laslett puts the beginnings of what would become the *Second Treatise* as early as 1679. Filmer's *Patriarcha* was published in 1680.[44] Locke's mind was already turned towards the refutation of patriarchalism, *jure Divino* hereditary kingship, and absolutism. It seems that at the point that Filmer's work entered the public eye, Locke set about the almost line-by-line dismantling of *Patriarcha* which we see in the *First Treatise*.[45] The wider context for the *Two Treatises*, as Mark Goldie has pointed out, was a repres-sive, absolutist 'Restoration Royalism'. The narrower context is the *Patriarcha* of Robert Filmer.[46] Both, most certainly, go together, as Filmer's tract was 'very nearly official Royalist ideology'.[47]

What Locke eventually published (a decade later) was ulti-mately a justification for the necessity of popular legitimacy for any government, as well as a refutation of patriarchalist political theory in particular, and 'absolutism' in general.[48] It also consti-tuted an implicit justification for the overthrow of the Stuart mon-archy. Rather than follow the method of most other anti-royalists by appealing to a mythical and historical 'ancient constitution', Locke used biblical exegesis and then a purely normative politi-cal theory to refute Filmer and argue for revolution.[49] However, there is more to Locke's thought than revolution. Contrary to the patriarchal political naturalism of Filmer, and contrary to the the-istic political naturalism of Calvin, Hooker and Althusius, we see Locke rejecting any idea of divine origins for political life. In fact, in order to provide a theoretical basis for revolution, Locke propagates a conventionalist understanding of the origins of political life, in part driven by a reshaping of natural law towards the socialisation and self-preservation of humanity. Locke was not answering the ideas of Calvin, Hooker or Althusius. Rather, it was Filmer's posthumous publication, arguing for the natural, but the *jure Divino* political rule of Adam and his patriarchal successors, which prompted Locke's resolute affirmation of a desacralised conception of the origins of political life. Filmer's *Patriarcha*, Richard Ashcraft points out, 'acted as a catalyst in forcing the ideological battle onto the terrain of natural law'.[50] This, as we shall see, is one of Locke's key focal points in his refutation. As Laslett writes, 'it was [Filmer], and not Locke . . . who set the terms of the argument'.[51]

## Natural Law

The most fundamental statement of Filmer's political theory is that no one is born free.[52] In stark contrast, Locke held that everyone, in the natural (pre-political) condition, is free.[53] Filmer, in *Patriarcha*, made the crude characterisation that this fundamental liberty implied an unhinged social morality, where anyone might have power over anyone else.[54] If he was referring to Hobbes's state of nature, then there is some ground for such a characterisation. However, Locke refutes Filmer on this basic point. Rather than people being untrammelled in the state of nature, the 'State of Nature has a Law of Nature to govern it, which obliges everyone'.[55] This raises important questions, explored in earlier chapters regarding other thinkers. We will examine below Locke's understanding of natural law, and how it had some continuities with medieval natural law theories and earlier Reformed natural law. We will also see how Locke's natural law ideas had some common ground with the position of Thomas Hobbes. The role of self-preservation is the vexed element in this conversation. I will argue that the role of self-preservation in Locke's thought creates conditions for the introduction of pre-political rights which, as in Hobbes's conception of the state of nature, need protection by way of the artificial creation of a politics. In this way, Locke continued the pattern of undermining the transcendent grounds for the political order.

As we saw above, Hobbes's natural law ideas constituted a significant break from the earlier tradition of natural law thinking. Some scholars argue that Locke is essentially a Hobbesian in this regard.[56] These scholars invariably focus on self-preservation and, perhaps in reaction to certain (especially Straussian) approaches to Locke, this can mean that the issue is sidelined. I say sidelined because self-preservation has not been totally overlooked in the literature.[57] I will argue below that Locke's treatment of natural law, focusing as he does on self-preservation, means he does depart from previous natural law thinking, albeit not entirely. That is why James O. Hancey is partly correct to suggest that Locke may be viewed 'as one of the last defenders of traditional natural law' rather 'than as its first corrupter'.[58] I would prefer to qualify that rather pithy statement by saying that Locke may be viewed as both a defender and corrupter of 'traditional natural law'. Before we examine why this is so in more detail, we must acknowledge what has been commonly discussed regarding Locke's natural law thought.

There are two aspects that are often considered in relation to Locke's natural law theory: his theism, and whether he is a voluntarist or a realist. Francis Oakley (along with Elliot W. Urdang) has addressed both of these questions. According to Oakley and Urdang, the centrality of the Christian God for Locke's natural law theory is well established, and so is his coherence with scholastic voluntarism.[59] Locke is, as Oakley argues, 'a voluntarist of the late medieval stamp . . . [with a] firm commitment to the existence of an order'.[60] Yolton agrees with this, stating that 'Locke was seeking to justify a system of morality by grounding the moral law on something objective . . . [that is,] God's will.'[61] Leyden also argues for a level of continuity with medieval thought, stating that Locke's understanding of how people come to know the natural law is entirely unoriginal and is 'derived from the scholastics'.[62] This is rather understated, of course, and Leyden makes a qualification that the exception to this rule is 'perhaps' Locke's view of the 'part played by sense-perception'.[63]

Sense-perception is key for Locke in his epistemology of natural law. Indeed, how we come to know the natural law occupies much of Locke's energy as he considers the law of nature more generally in his *Essays on the Law of Nature*. These *Essays* were likely delivered as lectures (or disquisitions) at Oxford. They offer a reasonable, if incomplete, picture of Locke's early natural law thought and, as we shall see, he carries some of the key principles through to his use of the natural law in the *Two Treatises*. But the epistemological question, that is, how we can know the natural law, clearly vexes Locke. The question for Locke and his interpreters is not whether God has given us the natural law; almost every reader of Locke accepts that God is central to his natural law thought.[64] The question is, rather: how does God reveal this law to us?[65] In the first of the essays, Locke writes that the natural law is 'the decree of the divine will . . . indicating what is and what is not in conformity with rational nature', and that this decree 'is discernible by the light of nature'.[66] The 'light of nature' is, according to Locke, how a human can get 'some sort of truth or knowledge . . . by himself and without the help of another'.[67] It is knowledge attained without the help of divine revelation.[68] This still leaves the question of how that knowledge is attained, and Locke eliminates two common possibilities.

First, he rejects the idea that we can know the natural law by observing the 'general consent' of humans.[69] Richard Hooker himself emphasised this method of ascertaining the natural law.[70] Locke argues, contra Hooker, that the recent experience of civil war and the Interregnum demonstrate that human consent is no way to establish the dictates of the natural law.[71] As J. W. Gough pithily notes, for Locke, 'Vox populi vox Dei is false'.[72] Locke also rejects the common Reformed and, indeed, medieval idea that the natural law is written on the heart or mind of humanity.[73] Indeed, Locke rejects innate ideas entirely, instead advocating the theory that the human mind is a *tabula rasa*; an 'empty tablet' or a blank slate.[74] In a 1671 draft of what would become the *Essay Concerning Human Understanding*, Locke writes that it is 'probable to me that there is noe notion, Idea or knowledg of any thing originaly in the soule, but that at first it is perfectly rasa tabula'.[75] Further, 'no principles, either practical or speculative, are written in the minds of men by nature'.[76] Even the idea of God himself is not present in the natural person, according to Locke, although knowledge of God and his law is attainable, as we will soon see.[77]

This leaves open the question, then, of how the 'rasa tabula' ascertains knowledge of the natural law, and what role human reason has in the same. Locke deals with human reason at the beginning of Essay I, when he argues that the scholastic, specifically Thomistic, understanding of natural law as a 'dictate of reason' (*recta ratio*) is incorrect; for 'reason does not so much establish and pronounce this law of nature as search for it and discover it'.[78] Reason is not, itself, the source of knowledge of the law of nature. Locke understands that sense-perception is the foundation for knowledge of the natural law. He writes that the 'foundations . . . on which rests the whole of that knowledge which reason builds up . . . are the objects of sense-experience'.[79] However, for humans to bring rational order out of their sense experience, reason must play a role also. Locke writes that 'sensation furnishing reason' and reason 'guiding the faculty of sense' means that 'there is nothing so obscure, so concealed, so removed from any meaning that the mind ... could not apprehend it by reflection and reasoning'.[80] This includes knowledge of God, and knowledge that 'he intends man to do something' and requires something of humanity.[81] This leads to the consideration of what precisely God might require, which takes us to the content of the natural law.

It is here that we can see how Locke's epistemology impacts his understanding of the content of natural law. If the content of the natural law is restricted to things evident to sense-perception, within the broader category of the 'light of nature', then certain moral precepts could be difficult to justify as dictates of that law. Indeed, Locke is evasive on the content of natural law, seemingly unable or unwilling to expand much upon the matter.[82] This may, in part, come down to the restrictions attached to his epistemology.[83] In his earliest writings, Locke embraced Hooker's division of laws out of a single 'divine law', and into 'natural and positive law'.[84] But his clarity and precision diminished by the time of the *Essays*. Yolton lists a range of rules 'derivable from the law of nature' in Locke's writings, and correctly points out that it is 'clearly impossible to derive these precepts from any single principle, whether it be innate, the light of reason, or a standard agreed upon by men'.[85] There are, without question, ambiguities if one starts connecting his epistemology with statements in *Two Treatises* that assume the rational accessibility of the law of nature. However, my intention is not to critique Locke so much as illuminate the element of his natural law thought which looms quite large, and which impacts so much of his political thought, including his conception of the origins of politics. Regardless of Locke's consistency or cogency on the question of natural law and epistemology, self-preservation seems the irresistible focus for him.

In his early work, such as the *Essays on the Law of Nature*, Locke shows a hesitation to embrace self-preservation as fundamental or primary. However, he still concedes that 'if any law of nature would seem to be established among all as sacred in the highest degree ... surely this is self-preservation', which 'some lay ... down as the chief and fundamental law of nature'.[86] The latter part of this statement hints at Locke's hesitancy to embrace self-preservation as a 'fundamental law of nature', and it is close to certain that he has Hobbes's thought in mind when he talks of 'some' focusing unduly on self-preservation. This scepticism of the importance of self-preservation is corroborated to an extent by Essay VIII, where Locke answers the question 'Is Every Man's Own Interest the Basis of the Law of Nature?' in the negative.[87] Self-interest is, to be sure, different to self-preservation. However, it is related in that self-preservation would seem to be a key out-working of the principle of self-interest. An even more profound rejection of self-preservation is found in what Locke writes in a 1677 journal entry just prior to his drafting of the *Two Treatises*. In it, Locke is discussing false opinions and how people might come to them, whether 'by education time out of mind' or 'the municipal laws of the country'.[88] These false opinions are then maintained to further their own interests and pride, according to Locke, and such opinions block out the testimony of 'scripture and reason'.[89] One such opinion is, interestingly, that of the 'Hobbist, with his principle of self-preservation, whereof himself is to be judge, will not easily admit a great many plain duties of morality'.[90] Hardly a glowing endorsement of Hobbesian self-preservation.[91]

Ultimately, Locke does turn to self-preservation as the defining doctrine for his natural law theory, which, in turn, then feeds into his natural rights theory and his understanding of the origins of political life. We will come to natural rights and political origins soon. Here, we must tackle the emphasis on self-preservation in Locke's *Two Treatises of Government*. This emphasis, it should be pointed out, is not quite like Hobbes's. Hobbes, as we saw in the previous chapter, worked out his moral philosophy (and his natural law theory) deductively and logically from the foundation of the law that humans desire to preserve themselves. Locke does not do this. Rather, like Hobbes, Locke does work out a theory of pre-political natural rights from this idea of preservation, and the protection of those natural rights becomes the justification for the formation of political life. Further, like Hobbes's, Locke's 'political society' is desacralised because the agents who are forming society are humans, rather than God.

## Anthropology and Self-Preservation

If God is *not* the primary agent in the creation of political life, then the starting point for Locke's anthropology becomes all the more interesting. This starting point is God. It is not merely the generic God; as John Dunn has pointed out, it is the God of Calvinists. He is a God who has made humankind and has called him (using Locke's language) to 'do something'.[92] Locke's political anthropology is an expression of Reformed Protestant anthropology more generally, with God as maker, humans as His creation, and those humans being given (by the very fact of their creation) a distinct purpose. In the language of Dunn, the existence of humans means they have a 'calling' from God.[93] Not only this but, according to Locke, humans are God's property by virtue of their being made by him.[94] Furthermore, the natural law is designed to protect His property. Out of this logic comes the fundamental natural law of self-preservation. We will see below, in the penultimate section of this chapter, that this scheme of the 'creator' protecting his 'property' is followed through in Locke's theory of political origins, where humanity creates political life. But, the argument being rehearsed, we can now establish the basic structure of Locke's political anthropology.

Locke lays the foundations for the more complete, positive explanation of the role of self-preservation for his political theory in the *First Treatise of Government*, where he deals most directly with Robert Filmer's patriarchal political theory. In the midst of a discussion of Filmer's assertion that Adam had sovereignty over his children due to his role as father, Locke observes that, contra the claim that the ancient practice of exposure proves the sovereignty of fathers, parents often altruistically preserve their children.[95] Locke argues that God has 'taken a peculiar care' to ensure that the 'several Species of Creatures' are able to continue because individuals 'neglect their own private good' and 'seem to forget that general Rule which Nature teaches all things of self Preservation'.[96] Whilst, in this case, Locke is pointing out an exception to 'the general rule', this 'rule' of self-preservation stands out. Locke points out that this exception is unusual; the 'Preservation of their Young . . . over rules the Constitution of their particular Natures'.[97] That is, the desire to ensure the survival of their children makes creatures neglect the 'Rule of Nature' to preserve themselves, even if temporarily.

Locke further stipulates that self-preservation is fundamental to human nature in a discussion of property inheritance in the wider context of a critique of Filmer's theory of monarchical inheritance. The 'first and strongest desire God planted in Men', a desire built into 'the very Principles of their Nature', is 'Self-preservation'.[98] Here, Locke is arguing that people have a 'right' to use animals and other creatures in order 'to take care of, and provide for their Subsistence', a right all people have 'in common'.[99] The grounds for his stipulation is that people are, by nature, first and foremost concerned with self-preservation. Filmer argues for a kind of 'donation' of monarchical rule from Adam to his sons, which is itself founded upon God's donation of dominion to Adam (cf. Genesis 1:28).[100] Locke argues that the donation by God to Adam was not a donation of regal sovereignty, but a donation of 'a right to a use of the Creatures' in order to '[pursue] that natural Inclination he had to preserve his Being'.[101] 'Man', writes Locke, has a 'Right . . . to use any of the Inferior Creatures, for the subsistence and comfort of his Life', as animals which are used by him are his possession and to be used for his good.[102] The desire for self-preservation is, then, a basic fact of human nature; indeed, it is a foundational one.[103]

As God's creation, Locke sees humankind as God's possession as well.[104] It is true that at one point in the *Second Treatise* he indicates a theory of self-ownership.[105] However, the importance of divine workmanship and possession for his political anthropology is difficult to dispute.[106] According to Locke, the natural state of human beings is not a function of anything innate in them. Rather, their natural condition as God's property is conferred upon them by their status as created beings. 'Men', asserts Locke, are 'the Workmanship of one Omnipotent, and infinitely wise Maker.'[107] Humans are a 'curious and wonderful . . . piece of Workmanship'.[108] Being God's workmanship they are also owned by God. People 'are his Property, whose Workmanship they are, made to last during his, not one anothers Pleasure'.[109] Men are owned by God because they were made by Him.[110] As an example of how this idea functions for Locke, he uses it to refute Filmer's claim that fathers own their children.[111] Locke argues that children are not the workmanship of their parents, but rather are 'the Workmanship of their own Maker, the Almighty'.[112] Jeremy Waldron puts it well when he says that, for Locke, the parents' role is 'governed by the equality that is grounded on God's vision for their offspring' rather than a vision of rulership.[113] People are, as Waldron also points out, equal in Locke's state of nature.[114] The pre-political state is one of '*Equality*, wherein all the Power and Jurisdiction is reciprocal, no one having more than any other'.[115] In the *First Treatise* Locke writes that 'all that share in the same common Nature, Faculties and Powers, are in Nature equal, and ought to partake in the same common Rights and Priviledges'.[116] Indeed, Locke quotes the 'Judicious *Hooker*' on this equality, stating that Hooker makes ontological equality the 'Foundation of that Obligation to mutual Love amongst Men'.[117] Whether Hooker does this or not is a different question, but it is

obvious that Locke sees that equality brings with it moral obligations. So, too, as we shall see next, does the fact of God's creation of
humankind. This will link back to Locke's understanding of natural
law and forward to the law of self-preservation.

In Essay IV (from *Essays on the Law of Nature*), Locke, referring back to his assertion that humans can only ascertain certain
knowledge through sense-perception and reason together, writes
that 'since on the evidence of the senses it must be concluded that
there is some maker of all these things . . . it follows from this that
he has not created this world for nothing and without purpose'.[118]

Here, we see Locke pointing to a teleological view of existence.
This varies significantly from Hobbes, who, of course, abandoned
such a notion and states that humans have no *finis ultimus* or *sum-
mum bonum*.[119] Locke, on the other hand, embraces the notion of a
'great design of God', which Ian Harris notes is directly related to the
mandate in Genesis 1 to '*Increase* and *Multiply*'.[120] John Dunn, too,
points to Locke's underlying understanding of a purposeful design in
God's creation. 'The entire cosmos', according to Dunn's Locke, 'is
the work of God . . . [who] created every part of it for his own purposes.'[121] Humans are fitted with certain faculties ('an agile, capable
mind, versatile and ready for anything') for a reason. 'We can', purports Locke, 'infer the principle and a definite rule of our duty from
man's own constitution.'[122] In the *Essays*, the 'great design' is partly
directed God-ward ('to assign and render praise') and partly directed
towards humanity.[123] Even here, the early Locke pushes the reader
towards the conclusion that God requires humankind to preserve
himself in political community: '[H]e [that is, humankind] feels himself not only to be impelled by life's experience and pressing needs
to procure and preserve a life in society with other men, but also to
be urged to enter into society by a certain propensity of nature.'[124]
It is sense experience that tells us this and, as we shall now see, it
is the cardinal rule of human nature, and of natural law itself, that
humans should preserve God's property, their own selves. They do
so by creating political life.

As noted above, Locke holds that the state of nature, which
is the pre-political state, has a law of nature 'to govern it'. It is,
as Dunn says, 'a jural condition and the law which covers it is
the theologically-based law of nature'.[125] In a paradigmatic section of the *Second Treatise*, Locke states that this law is 'Reason',
which 'teaches all Mankind . . . that being all equal and independent, no one ought to harm another in his Life, Health, Liberty, or Possessions'. Each person is '*bound*' by this law of nature

'to preserve himself' and 'to preserve the rest of Mankind'.[126] Why is this the case, though, that people are obliged to not harm others or themselves? It is because humans are 'the Workmanship of one . . . infinitely wise Maker . . . [who are] his Property'.[127] The logic of Locke's anthropology is laid out so clearly in this passage, it is almost startling, and he goes on repeatedly to outline the place of self-preservation in the operations of the law of nature.

Self-preservation is both a law and right, according to Locke. Indeed, the right to self-preservation is one of several rights which Locke believes need protecting, and protection is had by observing the law of nature. The law of nature 'willeth the Peace and *Preservation of all Mankind*'.[128] The '*Fundamental Law of Nature*' is that '*Man being to be preserved*'.[129] In another place, Locke says that 'Reason, *which was the Voice of God in him*, could not but teach him and assure him, that pursuing that natural Inclination he had to preserve his Being, he followed the Will of Maker.'[130] Humans, in general, have, according to Locke, a '*Right to Self-preservation*' as well as a '*Right . . . of Preserving all Mankind*'.[131] The difference between a law and a right is defined by Locke in the same way as Hobbes: 'right is grounded in the fact that we have the free use of a thing, whereas law is that which enjoins or forbids the doing of a thing'.[132] It would seem, then, that rights are derived from the law of nature. Any trespass on these rights, which constitutes a transgression of the law of nature, means that people have '*a Right to punish the Offender, and to be Executioner of the Law of Nature*'.[133] Further, people also have a right to reparations, and have a right to their own property 'in his own *Person*' and in the '*Work* of his Hands'.[134] Recall Locke's basic catalogue of things that are protected by the law of nature: life, health, liberty and possessions. One could say, following Richard Tuck's analysis of theories of *ius naturale*, that life, health and liberty are themselves under the rubric of possessions for Locke, and all these rights drive towards the preservation of the self and others.[135] Locke's rights are property rights grounded in the natural law.[136] These property rights allow Locke to rebut Filmer's sacred, *jure Divino* theory of political origins. He does this by way of a desacralised, conventionalist understanding of the origins of politics.

## The Artificial Origins of Political Life

We have seen that Locke understands that God protects His property by the natural law. However, humans must protect their rights, their property, by civil law.[137] So, they create political life. My suggestion is that the way Locke frames his conventionalist account of the origins of politics places him further outside of the Reformed and Aristotelian traditions. At times, Locke seems to be aligning himself with these streams of political thought. Since the implications of his repeated references to Hooker have been dealt with in Chapter 2, suffice to reinforce here that one needed to be seen as with Hooker to be taken seriously by any royalist Anglican during Locke's time. This Hookerian rhetorical strategy suited Locke's polemical purposes very well.[138] So, too, his reference to aligning himself with 'the old way' of government 'being made by contrivance, and the consent of Men'.[139] Despite Locke's biblical quote early in the *First Treatise*, from 1 Peter 2:13, about submitting to manmade ordinances, this 'old way' is not the one held up by the earlier Reformed Aristotelian tradition.[140] It is couched in a very different understanding of the law of nature and led, I will argue, to a desacralisation of theories of political life.

The fundamental law of nature, that '*Man* [be] *preserved*', is a guard for property rights. The natural law is meant to protect natural rights in Locke's state of nature, hence why people themselves can act as an '*Executioner of the Law of Nature*'. A human naturally has 'a Power, not only to preserve his Property, that is, his Life, Liberty and Estate against Injuries and Attempts of other men', but also to be a judge and executioner of the natural law.[141] However, the problem is that people inevitably put themselves in a '*State of War*' with others by threatening their basic rights. As soon as someone uses 'force, or a declared design of force upon the Person of another, where there is no common superior on Earth to appeal to for relief', this situation is '*the State of War*'.[142] The absence of a '*common Judge with Authority*' is Locke's basic definition of the state of nature.[143] Locke has already acknowledged the role of the natural law in this situation. But here we see that the natural law is not sufficient, in Locke's mind, to combat these adversarial conditions. Indeed, Locke admits that, with people themselves wielding the right to protect their own property by the personal executive power, we should expect to see partiality in judgement, as well as acts of 'Ill Nature, Passion and Revenge'.[144] The solution, for Locke, is relatively simple. '*Civil Government* is the proper Remedy for the Inconveniences of the State of Nature.'[145] The avoidance of the State of War 'is one great *reason of Mens putting themselves into Society* and quitting the State of Nature'.[146] People 'quit' their 'Executive Power of the

Law of Nature, and . . . resign it to the publick', thereby creating a '*Commonwealth*'.[147] Note that it is humans that do this. God 'appoints' civil government in general, but it is humankind who acts to create political life.[148]

Locke's understanding of the artificial nature of politics, and the parallel between God's protection of His property and humanity's, is illuminated by a brief passage from the *First Treatise*. Locke argues that 'Property . . . is for the benefit and sole Advantage of the Proprietor, so that he may even destroy the thing, that he has Property in by his use of it, where need requires.'[149] It is not clear from this that Locke understands God to 'benefit' as such from his proprietorship of humans. Rather, the parallel between God's proprietorship and humankind's is established if one recalls Locke's statement that humans 'are his [that is, God's] Property [and] Workmanship . . . made to last during his, not one anothers Pleasure'.[150] We can see, here, Locke's idea that the maker and owner of a thing can do away with his property as necessary; that God himself 'may even destroy the thing . . . where need requires', assuming that doing so will be for his 'benefit and sole Advantage'.[151] Government is slightly different, but the parallel to property is striking. It is a parallel which Locke himself draws. He writes that 'Government being for the Preservation of every Mans Right and Property, *by preserving him from the Violence or Injury of others*, is for the good of the Governed.'[152] In other words, to refute Filmer's absolutism, Locke states that government is always driven by the common good: 'the Sword is not given the Magistrate for his own good alone'.[153] However, it seems that the right to the use and benefit of a thing is determined by its creator: 'the workmanship model', as James Tully would have it.[154] Importantly, the creator, in the case of civil government, is, according to Locke, humanity.

The vulnerability of humanity in the state of war is the reason for humans to move into political life. Humans are, according to Locke, bound to preserve themselves, and also have 'a Power . . . to preserve his Property, that is, his Life, Liberty and Estate'.[155] But they cannot properly do so in the state of war. Filmer would have it that man is never in a state of war, because all political right is directly from God and He is the creator of political life. Locke disagrees. '*Political Society*' is 'where every one of the Members hath quitted this natural Power' and 'resign'd it up into the hands of the Community'.[156] People, by a consensual and '*original Compact*', '*put on the bonds of Civil Society*', and 'by consenting with others to make one Body Politick under one Government' place themselves under the laws of that political society.[157] Civil government is created by way of pact, a motif which recalls both Althusius and Hobbes. However, Locke's *pactum* is not Althusius's. Rather, it resembles Hobbes's covenant, being an agreement between individuals in the state of war to end that state and create political life. The artificial Commonwealth, that most important institution in Locke's anti-Filmerian polemic, then becomes the executor of the natural law on behalf of the willing populace, who have, themselves, set up 'a Judge on Earth, with Authority to determine all the Controversies, and redress the Injuries, that may happen to any Member of the Commonwealth'.[158]

## Conclusion

If Filmer's position on the origins of political life was, as Locke himself wrote, 'so much glib Nonsense put together in well sounding English', it obviously required a sophisticated refutation. The manuscript presented to Charles I by Filmer, which later became *Patriarcha*, was more formidable than Locke lets on. To combat Filmer's establishment royalism – his absolutism – Locke saw that a refutation of his theistic political naturalism was required. Unlike that of many of Locke's allies, his was not a refutation on historical grounds. Locke had to convince his allies and opponents alike that the English polity was not *de jure Divino*. Rather, it had to be artificial, or conventional. Locke's artificial Commonwealth is created by humans for protection of their property: their lives, their liberties and their estates. The possession of rights in the pre-political state of nature, and the danger to those rights in the state of war, served as justification for the artificial formation of political society.[159] The *jure Divino* political naturalism of Filmer, which served to justify monarchical absolutism, was rebutted by Locke with a conventionalist account of the origins of politics based primarily on a natural law of self-preservation, and the necessity of protecting pre-political rights.

The polemical context for Locke's work somewhat explains his approach to the question of the origins of politics. However, it does not diminish the significance of the approach in light of the argument maintained throughout this thesis. Richard Ashcraft has shown, quite conclusively, that Locke's polemic fits within the broader context of late seventeenth-century Whiggism.[160] As did Locke himself, that political ideology (for want of a better word) grew, in part, out of a Reformed Protestant context. Moreover, the fact that Locke's political theory became an accepted expression of Whiggish thought demonstrates that Reformed Protestant ideas about the origins of political life had shifted most decidedly from the theistic naturalism of Calvin, Hooker and Althusius to the conventionalism of Hobbes and Locke. Locke is no way the source or root of the secularisation of early modern political thought; the connections to Hobbes's ideas proved this much, although Hobbes can hardly be blamed either. Nevertheless, Locke was an unwitting populariser of desacralisation, entrenching the removal of God from conceptions of political origins in the Reformed Protestant tradition.

## Notes

1. Anthony B. Thompson, 'Licensing the Press: The Career of G. R. Weckherlin during the Personal Rule of Charles I', *The Historical Journal* 41.3 (1998): 668. Thompson cites the following manuscript: Weckherlin memo, 8 Feb. 1632, BL, Trumbull MSS., Misc. Corr., XLII, fo. 35: 'Sir Robert Filmer brought me a Discours to bee licensed for printing written of Governement and in praise of Royaltie and the supreme authority thereof & c.'

2. See Peter Laslett, 'Sir Robert Filmer: The Man versus the Whig Myth', *The William and Mary Quarterly* 5.4 (1948): 529, where Laslett notes that the circulation of manuscripts 'for many years' before publication was 'typical of the literary activity of these Kentish gentlemen, and particularly of Filmer'.

3. Algernon Sidney, *Discourses Concerning Government* (London: Booksellers of London and Westminster, 1698); reproduced in Algernon Sidney, *Discourses Concerning Government*, ed. Thomas G. West (Indianapolis: Liberty Fund, 1996), 7. Cf. Cesare Cuttica, 'Sir Robert Filmer (1588–1653) and the Condescension of Posterity: Historiographical Interpretations', *Intellectual History Review* 21.2 (2011): 196. Also see J. G. A. Pocock, *The Ancient Constitution and the Feudal Law: A Study of English Historical Thought in the Seventeenth Century* (Cambridge: Cambridge University Press, 1987), 187, where he points out that Filmer's *The Freeholder's Grand Inquest* was also used by the royalists. The *Freeholder's Inquest* contains many of the same arguments found in *Patriarcha*.

4. James Tyrrell, *Patriarcha non monarcha. The Patriarch unmonarch'd: Being Observations on a late treatise and divers other miscellanies, published under the name of Sir Robert Filmer Baronet. In which the falseness of those opinions that would make monarchy Jure Divino are laid open: and the true Principles of Government and Property (especially in our Kingdom) asserted. By a Lover of Truth and of his*

*Country* (London: Richard Janeway, 1681), n.p. Quotes are from the 'Preface'. Pocock has also identified William Petyt's (1636–1707) 1680 book as a response, in part to Filmer. See William Petyt, *The antient right of the Commons of England asserted, or, A discourse proving by records and the best historians that the Commons of England were ever an essential part of Parliament* (London: F. Smith, T. Bassett, J. Wright, R. Chiswell and S. Heyrick, 1680). Cf. Pocock, *Ancient Constitution*, 187–8.

5. John Locke, 'The Preface', in John Locke, *Two Treatises of Government* (London: Awnsham Churchill, 1698), ss.25–6.

6. Cuttica, 'Sir Robert Filmer', 195.

7. Hunter, 'Liberal Democracy', 27; Seligman, *The Idea of Civil Society*, 21–5.

8. Seligman, *The Idea of Civil Society*, 29.

9. Peter Laslett claims that, apart from the preface mentioned above, the *Two Treatises* was composed before 1681. See Peter Laslett, 'Introduction', in John Locke, *Two Treatises of Government* (Cambridge: Cambridge University Press, 1994), 3–126; cf. Dunn, *The Political Thought of John Locke*, 47–8.

10. The dating of the composition of *Patriarcha* has been the subject of debate. John M. Wallace, 'The Date of Robert Filmer's *Patriarcha*', *The Historical Journal* 23.1 (1980): 155–65, argues that the earliest manuscript (the 'Chicago') was written in 1648. Peter Laslett, 'Introduction', in Robert Filmer, *Patriarcha and other political works of Sir Robert Filmer* (Oxford: Blackwell, 1949), 3, argues that it is dated before 1642 but after 1635. Cf. Laslett, 'Sir Robert Filmer', 531–2. James Daly, 'Some Problems in the Authorship of Sir Robert Filmer's Works', *The English Historical Review* 98.389 (1983): 761, argues for an early version by 1641. Richard Tuck, 'A New Date for Filmer's *Patriarcha*', *The Historical Journal* 29.1 (1986): 183–6, proposes a pre-1631 date, which Johann P. Sommerville follows in 'The Authorship and Dating of Some Works Attributed to Filmer', in Robert Filmer, *Patriarcha and Other Writings*, ed. Johann P. Sommerville (Cambridge: Cambridge University Press, 1991), xxxiv.

11. On Filmer's originality and wider intellectual context, see J. P. Sommerville, 'From Suarez to Filmer: A Reappraisal', *The Historical Journal* 25.3 (1982): 525–40. Cf. Cesare Cuttica, *Sir Robert Filmer (1588–1653) and the Patriotic Monarch* (Manchester: Manchester University Press, 2012), 104–29.

12. E.g. James I, *The Trew Law of Free Monarchies: or The Reciprock and Mutuall Duetie Betwixt a Free King, and His naturall Subjects* (1598), in King James VI and I, *Political Writings*, ed. Johann P. Sommerville (Cambridge: Cambridge University Press, 2006), 76–7. For an excellent account of James VI/I and his divine right theory, see Oakley, *The Watershed of Modern Politics*, 162–71.

13. Cuttica, *Sir Robert Filmer*, 109.

14. Coke, 'Calvin's Case', 392. Cf. Johannes Althusius, *Politica*, 1:12.

15. Cuttica, *Sir Robert Filmer*, 104–42.

16. Gordon J. Schochet, *Patriarchalism in Political Thought: The Authoritarian Family and Political Speculation and Attitudes Especially in Seventeenth-Century England* (Oxford: Basil Blackwell, 1975), 146.

17. Robert Filmer, *Patriarcha: The Naturall Power of Kinges Defended against the Unnatural Liberty of the People: by Arguments Theological, Rational, Historical, Legall*, 1.3, in Filmer, *Patriarcha and Other Writings*, 6. References will appear as follows: Filmer, *Patriarcha*, [chapter]:[section], [page number in Sommerville].

18. Filmer, *Patriarcha*, 1:1, 3; *Patriarcha*, 1:10, 12; *Patriarcha*, 2:6, 21; Richard Ashcraft, *Revolutionary Politics & Locke's Two Treatises of Government* (Princeton, NJ: Princeton University Press, 1986), 186–9. As an important and interesting side note, William Cavanaugh notes that, for Filmer, the Fall of Adam seems to have 'little practical effect on his political theory'. See Cavanaugh's discussion in 'The Fall of the Fall', 484–6.

19. Filmer, *Patriarcha*, 1:8, 10.

20. Ibid., 1:10, 11.

21. Hadrian Saravia, *De Imperandi Authoritate, et Christiania Obedientia, Libri Quatuor* (London, Excudebant Reg. typog., 1593). On the relationship between the ideas of Saravia and Richard Hooker, as well as an outline of Saravia's patriarchalism, see J. P. Sommerville, 'Richard Hooker, Hadrian Saravia, and the Advent of the Divine Right of Kings', *History of Political Thought* 4.2 (1983), 229–45.

22. *Bishop Overall's Convocation Book, M DC VI: Concerning the Government of God's Catholick Church and the Kingdoms of the Whole World* (London: Walter Kettilby, 1690), section 1.1, 2.

23. *Convocation Book*, 1.2, 3.

24. *Patriarcha*, 1:3, 7.

25. *Convocation Book*, 1.6, 7–8.

26. *Convocation Book*, 1.6, 8. Cf. Oliver O'Donovan's analysis in *The Desire of the Nations*, 163–5.

27. *Patriarcha*, 2:1–18, 12–34.

28. *Patriarcha*, 2:19, 34.

29. Schochet, *Patriarchalism*, 132.

30. *Patriarcha*, 3:6, 42.

31. *Patriarcha*, 3:12, 52–3; cf. the discussion of medieval parliaments in Oakeshott, *Lectures in the History of Political Thought*, 305–21.

32. Laslett, 'Whig Myth', 544; Alvarado, *Calvin and the Whigs*, 117.

33. Cf. Sommerville, 'Absolutism and Royalism in the Seventeenth Century', in *Cambridge History of Political Thought 1450–1700*, ed. J. H. Burns and Mark Goldie (Cambridge, Cambridge University Press, 1991) 360–1, where he discusses the relative absence of patriarchal ideas in France.

34. J. R. Milton, 'Locke's Life and Times', in *The Cambridge Companion to John Locke*, ed. Vere Chappell (Cambridge: Cambridge University Press, 1994), 5.

35. John Locke, *Political Essays*, ed. Mark Goldie (Cambridge: Cambridge University Press, 1997), 79.

36. Peter Laslett, 'Introduction', 7–8. The *Two Tracts* argue that the civil magistrate can, rightly, rule on all things that are 'indifferent' (*adiaphora*) without encroaching upon the Christian liberty of their subjects, an argument reminiscent of both Hooker and Hobbes. This is a striking contrast to what he would later argue, of course. The tracts are reproduced in Locke, *Political Essays*, 3–78. For an interesting analysis and critique of various characterisations of the differences between the *Two Tracts* and *Two Treatises*, see Timothy Stanton, 'Authority and Freedom in the Interpretation of Locke's Political Theory', *Political Theory* 39.1 (2011): 6–30.

37. John Dunn, *Locke* (Oxford: Oxford University Press, 1984), 4–6; Ashcraft, *Revolutionary Politics*, 78–87ff.

38. Laslett, 'Introduction', 3–126.

39. Dunn, *The Political Thought of John Locke*, 44.

40. Ian Harris, *The Mind of John Locke: A Study of Political Theory in Its Intellectual Setting* (Cambridge: Cambridge University Press, 1994), 205.

41. Pocock, *Ancient Constitution*, 348. Cf. Michael Lobban, *A History of the Philosophy of Law in the Common Law World, 1600–1900* (Dordrecht: Springer, 2007), 91–2.

42. Macauley, *The History of England*, 127.

43. Locke was still sending and receiving letters in Paris in April 1679, and in Calais as late as 8 May 1679. By late May, he was receiving letters in London. See letters 465, 466, 467 and 469 in *The Correspondence of John Locke,* vol. 2: *letters nos 462–848*, ed. E. S. de Beer (Oxford: Clarendon Press, 1976), 6–19. Laslett is of the same mind and provides further evidence. See Laslett, 'Introduction', 31, and accompanying footnote. Cf. Ashcraft, *Revolutionary Politics*, 137.

44. On *Patriarcha*'s reception, see Cuttica, *Sir Robert Filmer*, 187–224; Pocock, *Ancient Constitution*, 187–91. Cf. ibid, 344–53.

45. Laslett, 'Introduction', 59. Dunn is less sure, but puts it at 1681 at the latest. See Dunn, *The Political Thought of John Locke*, 47–8.

46. Mark Goldie, 'John Locke and Anglican Royalism', *Political Studies* 31 (1983): 61–85, especially p. 65.

47. Gordon J. Schochet, 'Sir Robert Filmer: Some New Bibliographical Discoveries', *The Library* 26.2 (1971): 159; Goldie, 'John Locke', 66.

48. Harris, *The Mind of John Locke*, 192–4.

49. Cf. Pocock, *Ancient Constitution*, 184–228. Pocock notes how 'exceptional' Locke was in 'omitting any discussion of English legal or constitutional history from the *Two Treatises of Civil Government*' (188). Why he might have done this is discussed in ibid., 354–6.

50. Ashcraft, *Revolutionary Politics*, 189.
51. Laslett, 'Introduction', 68; cf. Gordon J. Schochet, 'The Family and the Origins of the State in Locke's Political Philosophy', in *John Locke: Problems and Perspectives*, ed. John W. Yolton (Cambridge: Cambridge University Press, 1969), 81–2; Schochet, *Patriarchalism*, 244.
52. Cf. *Patriarcha*, 1:3, 2.
53. TT, 2:4, 269.
54. Filmer, *Patriarcha*, 1:1, 2.
55. TT, 2:6, 271.
56. Strauss, *Natural Right and History*, 221–7; Leo Strauss, 'Locke's Doctrine of Natural Law', *The American Political Science Review* 52.2 (1958): 490–501, where Strauss defends his reading of Locke against charges that Wolfgang von Leyden's publication of Locke's *Essays on the Law of Nature* (Oxford: Clarendon Press, 1954) undermined his claims. See especially page 499, where he addresses self-preservation. Cf. Michael P. Zuckert and Catherine H. Zuckert, *Leo Strauss and the Problem of Political Philosophy* (Chicago: University of Chicago Press, 2014), 196–214; Michael S. Rabieh, 'The Reasonableness of Locke, or the Questionableness of Christianity', *The Journal of Politics* 53.4 (1991): 933–57. Robert Horwitz makes a moderate case for Locke's similarities to Hobbes. See Robert Horwitz, 'John Locke's *Questions Concerning the Law of Nature*: A Commentary', *Interpretation* 19.3 (1992): 251–306; Thomas G. West, 'The Ground of Locke's Law of Nature', *Social Philosophy and Policy* 29.2 (2012): 1–50. The Straussian interpretation has, rightly, been sharply critiqued. Most relevantly, see John W. Yolton, 'Locke on the Law of Nature', *The Philosophical Review* 67.4 (1958): 478.
57. A few examples include the following: S. Adam Seagrave, 'Locke on the Law of Nature and Natural Rights', in *A Companion to Locke*, ed. Matthew Stuart (Chichester: Wiley-Blackwell, 2015), 388–9; Alex Tuckness, 'The Coherence of a Mind: John Locke and the Law of Nature', *Journal of the History of Philosophy* 37.1 (1999): 83–6; Rickless, *Locke*, 172–4; Alvarado, *Calvin and the Whigs*, 139–40.
58. James O. Hancey, 'John Locke and the Law of Nature', *Political Theory* 4.4 (1976): 448.
59. Francis Oakley and Elliot W. Urdang, 'Locke, Natural Law, and God', *Natural Law Forum* 11 (1966): 92–109; cf. J. W. Gough, *John Locke's Political Philosophy* (Oxford: Clarendon Press, 1973), 10–11. See W. M. Spellman, *John Locke and the Problem of Depravity* (Oxford: Clarendon Press, 1988), 56, where he argues that Locke 'was unwilling to follow the [Reformed] voluntarist argument' all the way through.
60. Francis Oakley, 'Locke, Natural Law, and God – Again', *History of Political Thought* 38.4 (1997): 649.
61. Yolton, 'Locke on the Law of Nature', 483.
62. Wolfgang von Leyden, 'John Locke and Natural Law', *Philosophy* 31.116 (1956): 30; Harris, *The Mind of John Locke*, 97–8.

63. Leyden, 'John Locke and Natural Law', 30. For a discussion of the historical and intellectual context for Locke's *Essays*, especially related to theological anthropology, see Spellman, *John Locke and the Problem of Depravity*, 49–62.

64. One significant exception being those who follow Strauss in his interpretation. They seem to find grounds for an atheistic natural law theory in Locke.

65. Dunn, *The Political Thought of John Locke*, 25.

66. References to the *Essays* will be from John Locke, *Political Essays*, edited by Mark Goldie (Cambridge: Cambridge University Press, 1997), 79–133. I will use the form ELN, [page number from Goldie edition]. So, ELN, 82.

67. Ibid., 89; cf. *Westminster Confession of Faith*, 21:4: 'The light of nature sheweth that there is a God . . .'

68. Gough, *John Locke's Political Philosophy*, 12.

69. ELN, 106–16. Tradition is also dealt with as a way of attaining an understanding of the law of nature: ibid., 90–4. This is similar to the method described in Essay V on consent. On the similarities between this and Locke's assertions along these lines in *Essay Concerning Human Understanding*, see Neal Wood, *The Politics of Locke's Philosophy: A Social Study of 'An Essay Concerning Human Understanding'* (Berkeley: University of California Press, 1983), 151–2.

70. LEP 1.8.3; Harris, *The Mind of John Locke*, 91. Also cf. Thomas Aquinas, *ST* Ia-IIae, Q. 94, art. 4. It is interesting that in Locke's early *Second Tract on Government* his definition of law and his categorising of the different laws is explicitly Hookerian: see John Locke, 'Second Tract on Government', in Locke, *Political Essays*, 62–3.

71. ELN, 106; cf. John Locke, 'Draft B', section 5, page 16<h> of original manuscript. See John Locke, *Draft for the* Essay Concerning Human Understanding, *and Other Philosophical Writings*, vol. 1, ed. Peter H. Nidditch and G. A. J. Rogers (Oxford: Clarendon Press, 1990), 110–11. Note that I am citing 'Draft B' (1671), rather than the final *Essay*, because my chronological end point is the writing of the *Two Treatises*. References to Draft B will be in the following form: 'Draft B', [section]:[manuscript page], [page in Nidditch and Rogers]. So, 'Draft B', 5:16<h>, 110–11; Harris, *The Mind of John Locke*, 92–3; Spellman, *John Locke and the Problem of Depravity*, 47–9.

72. Gough, *John Locke's Political Philosophy*, 18.

73. ELN, 95–6; cf. Hans Aarsleff, 'The State of Nature and the Nature of Man in Locke', in *John Locke: Problems and Perspectives*, ed. John W. Yolton (Cambridge: Cambridge University Press, 1969), 129–32. On the contemporary reactions to Locke's rejection of the traditional Christian understanding, see Wood, *The Politics of Locke's Philosophy*, 56.

74. ELN, 96: 'rasae tabulae'. Interestingly, this is not without precedent in the broader Reformed tradition. Cf. Johann Heinrich Alsted, *Cursus philosophici encyclopaedia* (Herborn: 1620), vol. 1, 2768. Cited in Hotson, *Johann Heinrich Alsted*, 76.

75. 'Draft B', 17:70, 128.

76. ELN, 100. Cf. Tuckness, 'The Coherence of a Mind', 89, where he argues that Locke does not reject innate inclinations along with his rejection of innate ideas.

77. 'Draft B', 5:16<c>–16<d>, 108.

78. ELN, 82.

79. Ibid., 101.

80. Ibid., 100–1; 'Draft B', 14:47–9, 123. This well explained in Horwitz, 'John Locke's *Questions Concerning the Law of Nature*', 270–1.

81. ELN, 105; cf. 'Draft B', 5:16<c>–16<e>, 108–9; Yolton, 'Locke on the Law of Nature', 487.

82. TT, 2:12, 275; cf. Hancey, 'John Locke and the Law of Nature', 440; Dunn, *The Political Thought of John Locke*, 21.

83. Cf. Dunn, *The Political Thought of John Locke*, 188–9.

84. Locke, *Political Essays*, 62–3.

85. Yolton, 'Locke on the Law of Nature', 487–8. Yolton lists the following as derivable from ELN and the *Two Treatises*:
    a. Love and respect and worship God.
    b. Obey your superiors.
    c. Tell the truth and keep your promises.
    d. Be mild and pure of character and be friendly.
    e. Do not offend or injure, without cause, any person's health, or possession.
    f. Be candid and friendly in talking about other people.
    g. Do not kill or steal.
    h. Love your neighbor and your parents.
    i. Console a distressed neighbour.
    j. Feed the hungry.
    k. 'Whoso sheddeth man's blood, by man shall his blood be shed.'
    l. That property is mine which I have acquired through my labor so long as I can use it before it spoils.
    m. Parents are to preserve, nourish, and educate their children.

86. ELN, 112. Locke goes on to say that some societies' customs are so powerful as to even contradict self-preservation as a principle. Cf. 'Draft B', 6:17, 111, which is almost identical.

87. ELN, 127–33. Cf. ibid., 116, where, at the beginning of Essay VI, Locke writes about 'some who trace the whole law of nature back to each person's self-preservation', objecting to this that 'if the source and origin of all this law is the care and preservation of oneself, virtue would seem to be not so much man's duty as his convenience'.

88. Recorded in Lord Peter King, *The life of John Locke: with extracts from his correspondence, journals, and common-place books* (London: H. Colburn, 1829), 100.
89. Ibid., 101.
90. Ibid., 102.
91. Aarsleff, 'The State of Nature', 136.
92. See more generally Dunn, *The Political Thought of John Locke*, 214–42. The phrase of Locke's is from ELN, 105.
93. Dunn, *The Political Thought of John Locke*, 222.
94. Jeremy Waldron, *God, Locke, and Equality: Christian Foundations in Locke's Political Thought* (Cambridge: Cambridge University Press, 2002), 162; James Tully, *A Discourse on Property: John Locke and His Adversaries* (Cambridge: Cambridge University Press, 1980), 62; A. John Simmons, *The Lockean Theory of Rights* (Princeton, NJ: Princeton University Press, 1992), 30–1.
95. TT, 1:56, 180–1; Cf. *Patriarcha* 1:4, 7; *Patriarcha* 2:4, 18–19.
96. TT, 1:56, 181.
97. Ibid., 1:56, 181.
98. Ibid., 1:88, 206.
99. Ibid., 1:87, 206.
100. It is unclear what precise portion of Filmer Locke is critiquing. However, *Patriarcha* 1:9, 10–11 discusses this idea, as does Filmer's discussion of John Selden in *Observations concerning the Originall of Government, upon Mr Hobs Leviathan, Mr Milton against Salmasius, H. Grotius De Jure Belli* (1652). See Filmer, *Patriarcha and Other Writings*, 216–17.
101. TT, 1:86, 205.
102. Ibid., 1:92, 209. For a helpful account of the context for Locke's theory of property, both colonial and political-theological, see Tom Pye, 'Property, Space and Sacred History in John Locke's *Two Treatises of Government*', *Modern Intellectual History* 15.2 (2018): 327–52.
103. My emphasis on self-preservation should not be confused with that of Leo Strauss. I am arguing that self-preservation affects Locke's political anthropology in such a way as to emphasise the role of pre-political rights, whilst rejecting the idea that Locke is a 'Hobbist'. Cf. Strauss, *Natural Right and History*, 247. Laslett's critique is found in the footnote on lines 18–27 at TT, 1:56, 181.
104. TT, 1:30, 1:53–4.
105. TT, 2:27.
106. While aspects of the 'self-ownership' reading of Locke are adopted here, I cannot see past the workmanship theme, which is particularly prevalent in the *First Treatise*. Advocates of the self-ownership reading include Michael Zuckert, *Launching Liberalism: On Lockean Political Philosophy* (Lawrence: University of Kansas Press, 2002);

C. Bradley Thompson, *America's Revolutionary Mind: A Moral History of the American Revolution and the Declaration That Defined It* (New York: Encounter Books, 2019). A summary of the contention is found in S. Adam Seagrave, 'Self-Ownership vs. Divine Ownership: A Lockean Solution to a Liberal Dilemma', *American Journal of Political Science* 55.3 (2011): 712. For a *via media*, see also Johan Olsthoorn, 'Self-Ownership and Despotism: Locke on Property in the Person, Divine *Dominium* of Human Life, and Rights-Forfeiture', *Social Philosophy and Policy* 36.2 (2020): 242–63.

107. TT, 2:6, 271.
108. Ibid., 1:86, 205.
109. Ibid., 2:6, 271.
110. Dunn, *The Political Thought of John Locke*, 252; Tully, *A Discourse on Property*, 40–1.
111. On the role of the family in Locke's political thought, see Schochet, 'The Family and the Origins of the State', 81–98.
112. TT, 2:56, 305; cf. Ibid., 1:52; Waldron, *God, Locke, and Equality*, 113–14.
113. Waldron, *God, Locke, and Equality*, 114.
114. Also see Dunn, *The Political Thought of John Locke*, 106–7. 'The reason why men are equal is their shared position in a normative order, the order of creation.'
115. TT, 2:4, 269.
116. Ibid., 1:67, 190; Simmons, *The Lockean Theory of Rights*, 80.
117. TT, 2:5, 270; cf. Hooker, *LEP* 1.8.7.
118. ELN, 105.
119. Hobbes, *Lev* XI, 47:70.
120. TT, 1:41, 170; Harris, *The Mind of John Locke*, 214.
121. Dunn, *The Political Thought of John Locke*, 87; also see Tully, *A Discourse on Property*, 38–9.
122. ELN, 105.
123. Ibid., 105–6.
124. Ibid., 106.
125. Dunn, *The Political Thought of John Locke*, 106.
126. TT, 2:6, 271.
127. Ibid., 2:6, 271.
128. Ibid., 2:7, 271.
129. Ibid., 2:16, 278–9.
130. Ibid., 1:86, 205.
131. Ibid., 2:11, 274; cf. ibid., 2:8, 272.
132. ELN, 82.
133. TT, 2:8, 272. Cf. Ashcraft, *Revolutionary Politics*, 190–1 on Whiggish natural law theory, which Locke certainly resembles here.
134. TT, 2:9, 273; ibid., 2:26, 287; Tully, *A Discourse on Property*, 105.
135. Tuck, *Natural Rights Theories*, 171–3.

136. Alvarado, *Calvin and the Whigs*, 140.
137. Cf. Simmons, *The Lockean Theory of Rights*, 256–7.
138. See more in Kennedy, 'Richard Hooker as Political Naturalist'.
139. TT, 1:6, 144.
140. Ibid.
141. TT, 2:87, 323–4.
142. Ibid., 2:19, 280.
143. Ibid., 2:19, 281.
144. Ibid., 2:13, 275.
145. Ibid., 2:13, 276.
146. Ibid., 2:21, 282. For a summary of Whiggish political discourse around the purpose of civil government and natural law at the time of the drafting of the *Two Treatises*, see Ashcraft, *Revolutionary Politics*, 197.
147. TT, 2:89, 325.
148. Ibid., 2:13, 275–6; cf. Edmund S. Morgan, *Inventing the People: The Rise of Popular Sovereignty in England and America* (New York: W. W. Norton, 1988), 56.
149. TT, 1:92, 209.
150. Ibid., 2:6, 271.
151. Ibid., 1:92, 209.
152. Ibid., 1:92, 209–10. Emphasis is my own.
153. Ibid., 1:92, 210.
154. Tully, *A Discourse on Property*, 4.
155. TT, 2:87, 323
156. Ibid., 2:87, 324.
157. Ibid., 2:95, 331; ibid., 2:97, 332; ibid., 2:87, 324.
158. Ibid., 2:89, 325.
159. Tuck, *Natural Rights Theories*, 173.
160. See more generally, Ashcraft, *Revolutionary Politics*.

# Conclusion

American public intellectual Yuval Levin once stated that 'politics is really rooted in political philosophy', and that political discourse will 'make much more sense if you see that people are arguing about [different] ways of understanding what the human person is, what human society is, and especially what liberal society is'.[1] In other words, disagreements about political ideology stem from disagreements about political anthropology and about the nature of nature. The history of these conceptions has been the focus of this investigation into various Reformed Protestant thinkers. We have seen that two of them, namely Hobbes and Locke, decoupled the transcendent from their theories of political life. The question that naturally follows is this: what is the consequence of this decoupling? We will address this question more directly soon. First, we should recapitulate the main lines of my argument in order to feel its full force.

This book has pursued one particular argument concerning how the transcendent came to be disconnected from ideas about human political life. I have argued that the way this happened in the Reformed tradition was through changes in both natural law theories and in conceptions of the origins of political life. In the opening chapters, I argued that early Reformed thought held to a sacralised conception of both natural law and the origins of political life. The chapter on Calvin demonstrated Calvin's continuity with his medieval forebears in his basic understanding of natural law and in his theistic political naturalism. The natural law was, first and foremost, a law given by God himself to undergird the *mundi fabrica*, the fabric of the universe. According to Calvin, this natural law also governed human social relations both before and after the Fall. Calvin thought there was potential for a 'natural', prelapsarian political condition, and the same holds true after the Fall. Richard Hooker's position was much the same, although he adhered much more closely to a classic Thomist account of natural law and the origins of politics. For Hooker, also, God is the founder of human political life under the auspices of the natural law.

The opening chapters also established that both early continental and early anglophone Reformed Protestants adhered to the same sacralised understanding of political life. Johannes Althusius, writing after Hooker, took an even more firmly Aristotelian approach to political anthropology. His natural law theory was Thomist, and his understanding of political life was sacralised. However, Althusius also made substantial use of a politico-theological motif which would later be used in the desacralised accounts of Thomas Hobbes and John Locke. For Althusius, the motif of pact (or covenant) underwrote his whole social and political theory and yet was far from a social contract. Althusius, then, demonstrates both a Reformed theistic political naturalism, but also the early roots of the political use of *foedus* and *pactum*, motifs that would be utilised in secularising political theories.

Thomas Hobbes's political theory was one example of this. He took up the covenantal idea and turned it towards a conventionalist, desacralised theory of the origins of politics based on a social contract. Accompanying, and ultimately undergirding this, was an entirely new theory of natural law. For Hobbes, the laws of nature were derived from the basic law of human self-preservation, and they drove logically towards the necessity of political life for the existence of sociability. This shift in focus at the level of natural law informed Hobbes's shift in focus at the level of his theory of the origins of political life. The *pactum* of Althusius was a theologically rich account of the tapestry of social and political relations. However, it was transformed by Hobbes into a covenant between every person in the pre-political condition to submit to one absolute authority to protect their pre-political rights. Even if Hobbes's account was informed by Reformed theology in some respects, he clearly undermined the transcendent rendering of political life by disconnecting political life from nature itself. God becomes inactive in the creation of political life because, on Hobbes's account, humans create it in spite of nature. Locke entrenched this secularised account of political life. Like Hobbes, he focused his theory of the laws of nature on the idea of human self-preservation and sociability. Locke taught that political life was formed by people, rather than God, in order to protect God-given natural rights. The idea that the creature, rather than the Creator, was responsible for the making of political life was plausible and increasingly dominant from that point on.

John Dunn, in his authoritative account of Locke's political thought, writes that he 'simply cannot conceive of constructing an analysis of any issue in contemporary political theory around the affirmation or negation of anything which Locke says about political matters'.[2] It is tempting to take the same approach here, and only suggest implications for historical disciplines. However, there are ways that my findings may bear upon contemporary socio-political concerns. Before addressing these, I shall indicate how the findings in this book might alter the landscape of historical, political and theological scholarship.

I began by reviewing different attempts to locate the origins of a secular conception of political life. Some overlook or minimise the significance of natural law ideas in relation to secularisation. For example, Oliver O'Donovan and Charles Taylor both look to the broader framework of early modern political thinking for insights into why God was removed from conceptions of political life. They locate the root of the secularisation of political life in a shift in human self-perception: humans came to see themselves as the primary agents in the shaping of their political existence. O'Donovan identifies the concept of legislation as a fulcrum upon which political thought turned towards the secular. The key question is: who was the legislator? For a long time, this was understood to be God. In O'Donovan's account, even a *de jure Divino* monarch did not propagate artificial law, per se. Rather, law preceded him in the sense that the pre-existing transcendent law defined the nature of kingship and who were to be his successors.[3] However, the early modern period saw a distinct anthropocentric turn in the basic understanding of law and political legitimacy.[4] '[The] ruler's primary responsibility', writes O'Donovan, 'ceased to be thought of as being to divine law, but rather to the people whose supposed act constituted him.'[5] The *demos* became the font of law and the political order. Therefore, it seems quite natural that, flowing from this, more radical notions of a pre-political, artificial, contractual basis for political life became prevalent. My account adds a focus on anthropology, both theological and political, to this narrative. The underlying plausibility of O'Donovan's account is weakened unless the role of God (through the natural law) and of humanity (through pre-political pacts or contracts) is recast in the way described here. The anthropocentric turn in the understanding of civil law and the political order was undergirded by an anthropocentric turn in theories of natural law.

Similarly, Taylor identifies the emergence of a 'reconstructivist' conception of the world, with humans coming to understand that they were the builders of their own political existence.[6] Taylor calls this the 'Locke–Grotius idealization', in which political life is an 'instrument' that is wielded by the self-made political collective.[7] My account of this shift in early modern political thought emphasises an element that is not present in Taylor: anthropological beliefs underlie the change in human self-perception. I have shown that there was an entirely new understanding of nature, human nature, and humanity's place in nature undergirding these changes in self-perception, which then led to anthropocentric theories of societal origins. Taylor does, indeed, go some way along this path in his examination of 'social imaginaries'[8] and 'the buffered self'.[9] We can now add to his picture of the reshaping of natural law as connected to the formation of political life, a change that fundamentally alters political anthropology.[10] The move from theistic naturalism to conventionalism, where politics becomes an artefact, is a fruit of this change. So is the disappearance of God from theories of political life.

In contrast to O'Donovan and Taylor, Francis Oakley and Quentin Skinner both acknowledge the role played by the underlying theories of natural law and anthropology in the emergence of secularisation. Skinner takes the view that the widespread adoption of Aristotelian naturalism, especially as mediated through Marsilius, Bartolus and the early Italian humanists, laid the foundation for a desacralisation of conceptions of political life. Skinner claims that these thinkers eschewed Augustinian indifference towards political matters. In place of this, they emphasised the importance of civic liberty, active citizenship and the supremacy of the civil magistrate over temporal matters.[11] Political life was, thereafter, understood to be devoid of eternal *telos*, and was seen as a self-sustaining good in and of itself.[12] This secularised conception of political life led to a reconfiguration of the concept of the good citizen and good ruler around the purely temporal concerns of active civic citizenship and the maintenance of republican liberty.[13] According to Skinner's narrative, this 'naturalisation' of the role of civil government was further embedded in the European mind by the post-Reformation inter-confessional conflicts, which served to confirm that 'the powers of the State would have to be divorced from the duty to uphold any particular faith'.[14] The 'upheavals of the Reformation', according to Skinner, contributed 'to the crystallising of the modern, secularised conception of the State'.[15] Skinner's claim that political naturalism undergirded these seismic, secularising, shifts seems quite opposed to my own. However, it is probably the generalisation of his claim rather than accuracy of it that my account challenges. Perhaps Skinner is right to say that the Aristotelian turn in the thirteenth century paved the way for a non-transcendent *telos* for political life in the minds of later political thinkers. My suggestion here is that political naturalism was not simply a secularising force; paradoxically, it also played a sacralising role in the mind of certain thinkers in the sixteenth and seventeenth centuries, a fact which must be considered in future histories of early modern political thought.

The question of the desacralising role of political naturalism is considered in more depth by Francis Oakley, who characterises the results of the medieval adoption of Aristotle's idea of *physis* as one which mitigated against *de jure Divino* kingship. Christian thinkers adopted Aristotle's concept of nature, but did so with a 'disenchanted' understanding of the natural world.[16] Oakley, who focuses his energies at this point on Thomas, Aegidius Romanus and James of Viterbo, suggests that no matter the extent to which these thinkers 'appeal beyond [the naturalism of Aristotle's political vision] to a supernaturally revealed divine law and . . . divine structure of governance', they ended up transforming Aristotle's enchanted naturalism and desacralising it.[17] Whereas my suggestion here is that political naturalism maintains the sacrality of political life, Oakley suggests that the same idea had the opposite effect on these medieval thinkers. For them, 'the divine is drained from nature, the natural end which the political community exists to serve becomes . . . a sadly restricted and diminished one', leading political life to be cast as a 'secondary and merely *secular* organism'.[18] Like Skinner, Oakley conceives of this appropriation of political naturalism as providing the grounds upon which later desacralised accounts of political life could then be built. My account suggests a more nuanced outcome to this process, one which maintains both the idea of natural causation for political existence, and also God's concurrence in its founding and operation.[19] Rather than naturalism being opposed to the supernatural, it is conventionalism that pits itself against a sacral understanding of political life.

Histories of early modern and Enlightenment natural law theory are also impacted by my analysis. Stephen Grabill and

T. J. Hochstrasser have both dealt with historical developments in Reformed Protestant natural law thought.[20] However, neither of them attempts what I do, here, in arguing that natural law ideas changed across the sixteenth and seventeenth centuries whilst trying to show how and why they may have done so. Scholarship on 'pre-Enlightenment' natural law thought remains split off from the scholarship focused on 'Enlightenment' thought. Traversing these entrenched periodisations in investigating the Reformed tradition will no doubt bear further fruit and build on my own work, as well as that of scholars like Grabill and Hochstrasser. I have explained here, in a narrower sense, the context for, and the emergence of, the natural law theories and societal theories of Hobbes and Locke, whom I have located in a Reformed Protestant genealogy. Therefore, my findings are also relevant to the literature on other confessional cultures in the Protestant tradition. Hobbes and Locke are forerunners or interlocutors in Lutheran-focused natural law histories. In one sense, then, this book is a kind of pre-history of the inter- and intra-confessional philosophical jousting that occurs in the German academies and universities during the eighteenth century. My account of pre-Enlightenment Reformed natural law and political thought provides some important context for these Lutheran developments, whilst shedding light on the Reformed tradition more generally.

The final, and perhaps the most wide-reaching, implication flowing from the above chapters is the fact that the early Reformed thinkers, rather than breaking sharply on first principle issues in political thought, actually retained significant continuity with medieval thinkers. On the questions of political anthropology, the relationship between God, political life and natural law, I have shown that Calvin, Hooker and Althusius shared considerable common ground with those who came before them. This should hardly be surprising, but it belies many accounts of the impact of the Reformation on the western mind. The Weberian thesis that the rending of the sacred–secular divide by Calvin and others caused a desacralisation of all of life does not look quite as neat in light of the above.[21] Indeed, it appears to take over a century for Reformed thinkers to render God a mere spectator in the creation of political life.

Francis Oakley has written about 'the political [being] extruded . . . from the order of redemption' through the 'desacralisation of the political' in western thought.[22] He argues that most of this was achieved by those in the medieval era. I am inclined to think he is right. Therefore, if multiple generations of Reformed thinkers held on to the idea of a sacred origin for political life, as has been shown here, then any historical explanation that attributes the blame for secularisation to Reformed Protestantism must account for this fact. The representatives of Reformed Protestantism surveyed here stubbornly retain a sacralised view of the political until the middle of the seventeenth century when Hobbes provides evidence of a substantial breach in that dam. The persistence of a more medieval view of natural law and political life in the first century and a half of the Reformed tradition suggests the causes of this desacralisation were less to do with Reformed thought than might be otherwise assumed. There must have been other factors at play. Oakley's work shows there was groundwork laid prior to the European reformations. No doubt there are more contributing factors that emerged after the reformations. It is clear, then, that what is presented here must be carefully considered by scholars of early modern religious and political thought, be they historians, theologians or political theorists.

Regardless of whether the Reformed, or Protestants more generally, were responsible for the desacralisation and secularisation of the west, scholars must still wrestle with the nature and impact of this desacralisation. I said earlier that I would contest the early John Dunn's methodological judgement and address why this question still matters. I will do so because, as Nederman says, ideas in history can have a substantial impact on our own self-understanding. He writes that 'the very "otherness", the foreignness' of the now distant past 'may have salutary decentering effects upon our complaisant contemporary assumptions about political life and its relation to a whole host of other philosophical questions'.[23] This is, I think, quite true. It is also true that the past tells us about ourselves and our own situations if we only allow it to do so. This way of thinking permits us to return to a question raised at the beginning of this volume: liberalism and its 'discontents'.

How does this account square with other genealogies of liberalism? This book had no pretence to achieving the end of providing a genealogy of liberalism. However, it speaks to the issue quite closely if one considers the parallel questions underlying this study and the questions being asked of liberalism in other venues. Historian and political theorist Larry Siedentop takes a long view of secular liberalism, and argues that secularism, rather than being an invention of the Enlightenment, is an idea stemming from the medieval Christian conception of the individual. 'Christianity', writes Siedentop, 'changed the ground of human identity', leading to an embrace of the individual as the basic social unit, the emergence of constitutional conceptions of government, and the shaping of the secular nation-state.[24] All of this groundwork is laid before the European reformations. Secular liberalism is, according to Siedentop, a medieval, and Christian, 'gift'.[25] So, while Siedentop is not especially concerned with the instability of liberalism, his genealogy does imply that the roots of the 'secular' element lie earlier than what I suggest. Oliver O'Donovan is in substantial agreement with Siedentop with regard, at least, to the method of looking much earlier than the early modern period for the roots of liberalism: 'the roots of this new organisation of political priorities run deep into the centuries that preceded it'.[26]

John Rawls offers a genealogy of liberalism in order to place his own work refining the liberal system in something of a historical context. But rather than comment on its vulnerabilities, he assumes its validity as a political framework based on its place in history. Rawls does not address liberalism as a problem, but rather is interested in the difficulty spawned by the existence of a plurality of 'incompatible yet reasonable comprehensive doctrines' within a purported democratic society.[27] According to Rawls, liberalism exists because this difficulty exists. Why are there multiple incompatible comprehensive doctrines? Rawls's answer is 'The Reformation . . . [which] fragmented religious unity . . . and led to religious pluralism, with all its consequences for later centuries.'[28] It resulted in 'the appearance within the same society of a rival authoritative and salvationist religion'.[29] This brought about the necessity of managing religious pluralism, argues Rawls, with the emergence of 'long controversies over religious toleration in the sixteenth and seventeenth centuries'.[30] Liberal, secular constitutionalism was, writes Rawls, a 'success' because Europe discovered, through wrestling with religious pluralism, 'the possibility of a reasonably harmonious and stable pluralist society'.[31] Hence, it seems, Rawls himself takes up this mantle and proceeds to try to prise out a more coherent framework for 'political liberalism'. Rawls's story of the origins of liberalism, then, serves to justify his own project rather than to understand how liberalism came to be what it was and is. It skirts around the complex history of the pre-Reformation era which Siedentop unravels, and simplifies the Reformation and post-Reformation era whilst overlooking nuances of the kind I have addressed. The Enlightenment is then framed as a refining towards the optimal conditions of the twentieth century. For Rawls, the trouble for liberalism is not its roots or its history. The problem to be identified is a present concern: the existence of incompatible comprehensive accounts of life.

Patrick Deneen, writing from the quarter of political theory, suggests a different source of trouble for liberalism. He argues that the instability is due to the overturning of 'classical and Christian' assumptions about anthropology and 'social norms that had come to be believed as sources of pathology'.[32] These sources included traditional conceptions of political and individual virtue, and a reshaping of these led to the reimagining of long-standing social structures and customs, from which the resulting conception of (enlarged) individual liberty required a new understanding of natural science and civil science to allow for humans to act on their new-found liberty.[33] However, Deneen argues that these elements are, in fact, the sources of the problems embedded in liberalism; they make liberalism inherently self-destructive and 'largely impervious to discerning its deepest weaknesses and even self-inflicted decline'.[34] Whereas Rawls seems almost naively optimistic in his account of the emergence of the liberal ideal, focusing as he does on the logical need for liberalism as a result of historical events, Deneen is almost dismissively critical of the liberal ideal, both today and as a historical phenomenon. He mournfully concludes that 'liberalism has drawn down on a preliberal inheritance and resources that at once sustained liberalism but which it cannot replenish'.[35] The things which have sustained liberalism, Deneen argues, are now out of its reach and lost in a bygone era. Better public policy will not fix the problem; the demon is in too deep.[36] The tensions are too old and too fraught to be resolved with quick fixes.

My own account offers a fresh perspective on the origins of what many have identified as tensions in the contemporary liberal order. James Davison Hunter writes that the 'procedural republic', in the form of liberal civic institutions, 'can address certain matters of power'. However;

> The cultural logic of the Enlightenment project has lost credibility, and the liberal – genuinely liberal – regime it inspired is collapsing . . . [The procedural republic] cannot tell a compelling story that binds a community in common purpose. The cultural logic that underwrote liberalism exists only in fragments, and it is not likely to come together again in any coherent way.[37]

Davison Hunter asserts that the liberal regime is collapsing because of this fragmenting of the 'cultural logic' of the Enlightenment. The 'shared epistemology of transcendence', grounded in the 'Reformed–Enlightenment synthesis', was the ground upon which the anglophone west originally imagined the liberal political order. Davison Hunter, along with Adam Seligman, argues that this cultural logic began to come apart during the eighteenth century when the sense of transcendence at the foundation of the moral order was replaced by the ideas of moral sentiments and 'natural sympathy'.[38] Indeed, Seligman suggests that the way people in the anglophone west came to answer normative questions about human nature and natural law shifted; since that time, our cultural logic has been fragmented. My argument here bears directly on Davison Hunter's idea of the cultural logic of the Reformed–Enlightenment synthesis. However, *contra* Seligman and Davison Hunter, we have seen that it was the fundamental, seventeenth-century ideas of nature and human nature that changed in the Reformed mind, rather than the later shifts in Scottish moral philosophy that Seligman describes. It was these changes that desacralised conceptions of political life.

I previously mentioned Levin's contention that political discourse can be basically summarised as a debate over differences in ideas about anthropology and the nature of human society. Human nature, nature itself, and the foundation of political life have been the foci of this book. We have seen the ways the Reformed tradition approached these important concepts during the early modern period. Hobbes and Locke were shown to have decoupled God from their theories of political life, and the question that naturally follows this is: why does this matter? Perhaps it is the case that disjuncts and tensions in our current public discourse stem from a collapse of the consensus around a previously shared understanding of human nature, and the relationship between political life and the transcendent. The very debates and difficulties we are witnessing in our own societies today might stem, in part, from discord in our (often unconscious) political philosophies, starting with first principles: nature, human nature, and the nature of political life.

How one answers these normative, first principle questions will affect the way one addresses the putative unravelling of liberalism we are witnessing today. For example, Richard Rorty suggests that we should abandon the idea that we can have 'religious and philosophical accounts of a suprahistorical ground [combined] with a historical narrative about the rise of liberal institutions and customs'.[39] He further claims that the grounds for the liberal order should not be found beyond 'contingent historical circumstance', and that people ought to believe that an historically contingent belief 'can still regulate action' and 'be worth dying for'.[40] In other words, Rorty holds that a belief that has no objective basis must still be seen to offer motivation to citizens of the liberal polity towards ethical and political activity.[41] The very idea of the transcendent is contrary to Rorty's 'liberal utopia'; a place where 'the notion of "something that stands behind history" has become unintelligible, but in which a sense of human solidarity remains intact'.[42] It seems that we might be living in Rorty's liberal 'utopia', where there is no transcendental, suprahistorical ground for the liberal democratic order. This 'utopia' has, perhaps, at least some of its roots in the seventeenth-century decoupling of God from conceptions of natural law and political origins.

However, appearances seem to belie the utopian vision, with many identifying it as a dystopia. According to thinkers like Seligman, Davison Hunter and Deneen, the modern liberal project of a transcendence-free grounding for a liberal society seems inherently unstable. This is also the concern of German jurist Ernst Wolfgang Böckenförde. He states that *the liberal, secularized state is sustained by conditions it cannot itself guarantee*'.[43] The liberal state, he writes, 'can only survive if the freedom it grants its citizens is regulated from within, out of the moral substance of the individual and the homogeneity of society'.[44] However, Böckenförde also laments that the secular liberal state cannot ensure that the regulation of liberty remains sound 'without abandoning its liberalness' and resorting to totalising claims.[45] Böckenförde seems to be arguing that Rorty's utopia is not possible because some universal claim is necessary to retain the liberal order.[46] Liberalism cannot remain liberal without a shared epistemology of transcendence.

Peter E. Gordon summarises Böckenförde's account of the dilemma that lies at the heart of the liberal project:

> [Liberal] democracy finds its sources of both morality and cohesion in the pre-political grounds of the Christian religion . . . if secularization is allowed to progress unchecked, democracy will lack any unifying moral substance whatsoever and it will disintegrate into . . . norm free materialism.[47]

For Böckenförde, as Mirjam Künkler and Tine Stein note, the modern liberal state, 'as a necessarily secular state, cannot resort to imposing certain values or worldviews on its citizens without undermining the very liberalism on which it is founded'.[48] Tine Stein has shown elsewhere that Böckenförde's dictum, and the context for his posing of the dilemma, is fundamentally liberal.[49] Böckenförde wants to retain liberal democracy. However, he acknowledges that there remains a problem at the heart of the liberal conception of the civil order. We can go with Rorty and abandon transcendent, suprahistorical grounds for our liberal order. However, we are left with Böckenförde's dilemma, that liberalism cannot function without some kind of totalising claim at its core. Following Böckenförde, this apparent vacuum at the core of liberal democracy is, perhaps, one of the root causes of the rise of anti-liberal political leaders, who claim the moral and political high ground in liberal democratic polities on the basis of totalising cultural and religious claims. It seems this dilemma is not merely theoretical.

How does the history contained in these pages help us understand this dilemma? It is not clear that returning to theistic political naturalism would resolve this problem; in any case, the thinkers examined here who held this view could hardly be considered liberal. The moral vision of Locke and those who followed after him in shaping western political life was, fundamentally speaking, a Christian vision. I have shown here that the seed of the liberal order's undoing may have been buried in Locke's ideas, and Hobbes's before him. The reshaping of natural law around human self-preservation removed the natural basis for political life, which, in turn, abolished the connection between God and the political sphere. In other words, the separation of a transcendent *telos* from the natural law meant that political life was no longer directed towards a vertical relationship with the divine. Instead, political life was only concerned with the horizontal.

Perhaps this lies at the heart of the contemporary crisis of western liberal democracy today, as perceived by scholars like Legutko, Deneen, Milbank and Pabst. We see from the above chapters that thinkers in the Reformed tradition initially understood God to be the foundation of political life. By the end of the seventeenth century, this had changed and humanity was seen as the maker of its own political existence. At the very beginning of the anglophone liberal project, the theistic presuppositions that nourished it were taken away and construction could begin on Rorty's liberal dystopia. This is, of course, only a diagnosis of the problem. History can only provide diagnoses, not cures or imperatives to self-betterment. However, if the abandonment of a totalising claim at the foundation of the liberal order is one major cause of the illness, a totalising claim may be necessary to uphold the liberal ideal into the future.

## Notes

1. Yuval Levin, 'Interview with Bill Kristol', accessed at http://conversationswithbillkristol.org/transcript/yuval-levin-transcript/ (7 November 2017).
2. Dunn, *The Political Thought of John Locke*, x.
3. O'Donovan, *The Desire of the Nations*, 236.
4. O'Donovan, 'Government as Judgement'; O'Donovan, *The Desire of the Nations*, 236–42.
5. O'Donovan, *The Desire of the Nations*, 241.
6. Taylor, *A Secular Age*, 125–6.
7. Ibid., 188.
8. Charles Taylor, *Modern Social Imaginaries* (Durham: Duke University Press, 2004), 23–48.
9. Taylor, *A Secular Age*, 29–41.
10. See Taylor, *Modern Social Imaginaries*, 8–12, where he goes some way towards this conclusion.
11. More generally, see Skinner, *Foundations of Modern Political Thought*, vol. 1, chapters 3 and 4.
12. Ibid., 50.
13. Ibid., chapters 5 and 6.
14. Skinner, *Foundations of Modern Political Thought*, vol. 2, 352.
15. Ibid., 352.
16. Oakley, *Mortgage of the Past*, 136.
17. Ibid., 137.
18. Ibid.
19. Cf. Freddoso, 'God's General Concurrence.'
20. Grabill, *Rediscovering the Natural Law*, 175–91; T. J. Hochstrasser, 'Conscience and Reason: The Natural Law Theory of Jean Barbeyrac', *The Historical Journal* 36.2 (1993), 289–308; T. J. Hochstrasser, 'The Claims of Conscience: Natural Law Theory, Obligation, and Resistance in the Huguenot Diaspora', in *New Essays on the Political Thought of the Huguenots of the Refuge*, ed. John Christian Laursen (Leiden: Brill, 1995), 15–52.
21. For example, see Max Weber, *The Protestant Ethic and the Spirit of Capitalism*, trans. Talcott Parsons (Abingdon: Routledge, 2001), 71–80; Taylor, *A Secular Age*, 179; more generally, see Gregory, *The Unintended Reformation*. For a helpful summary of Weber, see Anthony J. Carroll, 'The Importance of Protestantism in Max Weber's Theory of Secularisation', *European Journal of Sociology* 50.1 (2009): 67–70.
22. Oakley, *The Watershed of Modern Politics*, 292.
23. Nederman, *Lineages*, xv.
24. Larry Siedentop, *Inventing the Individual: The Origins of Western Liberalism* (Cambridge, MA: Belknap Press, 2014), 352ff. This summarises his entire argument.

25. Ibid., 360.
26. O'Donovan, *The Desire of the Nations*, 226; James K. A. Smith, *Awaiting the King: Reforming Public Theology* (Grand Rapids, MI: Baker Academic, 2017), 100–12.
27. John Rawls, *Political Liberalism: Expanded Edition* (New York: Columbia University Press, 2005), xvi.
28. Ibid., xxii.
29. Ibid., xxiii.
30. Ibid., xiv.
31. Ibid., xxv.
32. Deneen, *Why Liberalism Failed*, 23–4.
33. Ibid., 24–6.
34. Ibid., 28–9.
35. Ibid., 29–30.
36. Ibid., 42.
37. Davison Hunter, 'Liberal Democracy', 35.
38. Ibid., 28; Seligman, *The Idea of Civil Society*, 17–36.
39. Richard Rorty, *Contingency, Irony, and Solidarity* (Cambridge: Cambridge University Press, 1988), 68.
40. Ibid., 189.
41. Rorty vehemently rejects the charge of relativism.
42. Ibid., 190.
43. Ernst-Wolfgang Böckenförde, *Der säkularisierte Staat: Sein Charakter, seine Rechtfertigung und seine Probleme im 21. Jahrhundert* (Munich: Carl Friedrich von Siemens Stiftung, 2007), 71; translation from Ernst-Wolfgang Böckenförde, 'The Rise of the State as a Process of Secularization', in Ernst-Wolfgang Böckenförde, *Religion, Law, and Democracy: Selected Writings*, ed. Mirjam Künkler and Tine Stein (Oxford: Oxford University Press, 2021), 167. Emphasis is original.
44. Böckenförde, *Der säkularisierte Staat*, 71; Böckenförde, 'The Rise of the State', 167.
45. Böckenförde, *Der säkularisierte Staat*, 71; Böckenförde, 'The Rise of the State', 167.
46. Although, cf. Tine Stein, 'The Böckenförde Dictum – On the Topicality of a Liberal Formula', *Oxford Journal of Law and Religion* 7.1 (2018), 102–3. Also cf. Jan-Werner Müller, 'What the Dictum Really Meant – And What It Could Mean for Us', *Constellations* 25.2 (2018): 196–206, who discusses the historical context for the dictum, framing it as a plea to Catholics to embrace the liberal state.
47. Peter E. Gordon, 'Between Christian Democracy and Critical Theory: Habermas, Böckenforde, and the Dialectics of Secularization in Postwar Germany', *Social Research: An International Quarterly* 80.1 (2013): 186–7.

48. Mirjam Künkler and Tine Stein, 'State, Law, and Constitution', in Ernst-Wolfgang Böckenförde, *Constitutional and Political Theory: Selected Writings*, ed. Mirjam Künkler and Tine Stein (Oxford: Oxford University Press, 2017), 1.

49. Stein, 'The Böckenförde Dictum'; Müller, 'What the Dictum Really Meant.'

# Select Bibliography

**Primary Sources**

Althusius, Johannes. 1603. *Politica methodice digesta et exemplis sacris et profanes illustrata*. Herborn in Nassovia: Christophorus Corvinus.

Althusius, Johannes. 1610. *Politica methodice digesta atque exemplis sacris et profanes illustrata*. Arnheim: Johannes Janssonius.

Althusius, Johannes. 1614. *Politica methodice digesta atque exemplis sacris et profanes illustrata*. Herborn in Nassovia: Corvinus.

Althusius, Johannes. 1649. *Dicaeologicae libri tres, Totum & universum Jus, quo utimur methodice complectentes*. Frankfurt: Corvinus.

Althusius, Johannes. 1995. *Politica: an abridged translation of Politics Methodically Set Forth and Illustrated with Sacred and Profane Examples*. Trans. Frederick S. Carney. Indianapolis: Liberty Fund.

Althusius, Johannes. 2013. *On Law and Power*. Trans. Jeffrey J. Veenstra. Grand Rapids, MI: CLP Academic.

Ambrosiaster. 2009. *Commentaries on Romans and 1–2 Corinthians*. Ed. Gerald L. Bray. Downers Grove, IL: IVP Academic.

Aquinas, Thomas. 1952. *Summa Theologica*. Trans. Fathers of the English Dominican Province. Chicago: Encyclopedia Britannica.

Aquinas, Thomas. 2002. *Political Writings*. Ed. R. W. Dyson. Cambridge: Cambridge University Press.

Aristotle. 1988. *The Politics*. Ed. Stephen Everson, trans. Benjamin Jowett. Cambridge: Cambridge University Press.

Aristotle. 1992. *Physics*. In *Aristotle: The Complete Works, Electronic Edition*. Trans. Jonathan Barnes. Charlottesville, VA: InteLex Corp.

Aristotle. 2014. *Nicomachean Ethics*. Ed. Roger Crisp, trans. Roger Crisp. Cambridge: Cambridge University Press.

Augustine of Hippo. 1956. *De bono coniugali*. In *Nicene and Post-Nicene Fathers*, vol. 3: *On the Holy Trinity, Doctrinal Treatises, Moral Treatises*. Ed. Philip Schaff. Grand Rapids, MI: Eerdmans.

Augustine of Hippo. 1956. *Nicene and Post-Nicene Fathers*, vol. 3: *On the Holy Trinity, Doctrinal Treatises, Moral Treatises*. Ed. Philip Schaff. Grand Rapids, MI: Eerdmans.

Augustine of Hippo. 1990. *De Genesi ad litterum liber imperfectus*. Translation from Saint Augustine, *On Genesis: Two Books on Genesis: Against the Manichees and on the Literal Interpretation of Genesis: An Unfinished Book*. Trans. Roland J. Teske. Washington, DC: The Catholic University of America Press.

Augustine of Hippo. 1998. *De civitate Dei*. Translation from Augustine of Hippo, *The City of God against the Pagans*. Ed. R. W. Dyson. Cambridge: Cambridge University Press.

Augustine of Hippo. 2003. *City of God*. Trans. Henry Bettenson. London: Penguin.

Augustine of Hippo. 2010. *Letters: Volume 3 (131–164)*. Trans. Sister Wilfrid Parsons. Washington, DC: The Catholic University of America Press.

Beza, Theodore. 1958. 'Life of Calvin'. In John Calvin, *Tracts and Treatises on the Reformation of the Church*, lv– cxxxviii. Grand Rapids, MI: Eerdmans.

1690. *Bishop Overall's Convocation Book, M DC VI: Concerning the Government of God's Catholick Church and the Kingdoms of the Whole World*. London: Walter Kettilby.

Calvin, John. 1559. *Institutio christianae religionis, in libros quatuor nunc primum digesta, certisque distincta capitibus, ad aptissimam methodum: aucta etiam tam magna accessione ut propemodum opus novum haberi possit*. Geneva: Robert I. Estienne.

Calvin, John. 1544. *Brieve instruction, pour armer tous bons fideles contre les erreurs de la secte commune des anabaptistes*. Geneva: Iehan Girard.

Calvin, John. 1863–1900. *Joannis Calvini opera quae supersunt omnia*. Ed. Guilielmus Baum, Eduardus Cunitz and Eduardus Reuss. 59 vols. Brunsvigae: C. A. Schwetschke.

Calvin, John. 1948–59. *Calvin's Commentaries*. Trans. John King et al. 45 vols. Grand Rapids, MI: Eerdmans.

Calvin, John. 1954. *Calvin: Theological Treatises*. Ed. J. K. Reid. London: SCM Press.

Calvin, John. 1969. *Commentary on Seneca's De Clementia*. Trans. Ford Lewis Battles and Andre Malan Hugo. Leiden: Brill.

Calvin, John. 1982. *Treatises Against the Anabaptists and Against the Libertines*. Trans. Benjamin Wirt Farley. Grand Rapids, MI: Baker Book House.

Calvin, John. 1993. *Sermons on Job*. Trans. Arthur Golding. Edinburgh: Banner of Truth.

Calvin, John. 2009. *John Calvin's Sermons on Genesis: Chapters 1:1–11:4*. Trans. Rob Roy McGregor. Carlisle, PA: Banner of Truth.

Calvin, John. 2011. *Institutes of the Christian Religion*. Ed. John T. McNeill, trans. Ford Lewis Battles. 2 vols. Louisville, KY: Westminster/John Knox Press.

Chrysostom, John. 1999. *Homilies on Genesis, 1–17*. Trans. Robert C. Hill. Washington, DC: The Catholic University Press of America.

Cicero. 1991. *On Duties*. Ed. M. T. Griffin and E. M. Atkins. Cambridge: Cambridge University Press.

Cicero. 1999. *On the Commonwealth and On the Laws*. Ed. James E. G. Zetzel. Cambridge: Cambridge University Press.

Coke, Edward. 1907. *Calvin's Case*. Vol. 77, in *English Reports King's Bench (1378–1865)*, 377–411. London: Stevens & Sons, Limited. http://www.commonlii.org/uk/cases/EngR/1572/64.pdf.

Cumberland, Richard. 2005. *Treatise on the Laws of Nature*. Ed. Jon Parkin, trans. John Maxwell. Indianapolis: Liberty Fund.

Filmer, Robert. 1991. *Patriarcha and Other Writings*. Ed. Johann P. Sommerville. Cambridge: Cambridge University Press.

Gratian. 2012. *The Treatise on Laws (Decretum DD. 1–20) with the Ordinary Gloss*. Trans. Augustine Thompson and James Gordley. Washington, DC: The Catholic University of America Press.

Grotius, Hugo 1625. *De jure belli ac pacis libri tres*. Paris: Nicolaum Buon.

Grotius, Hugo. 2005. *The Rights of War and Peace*. Ed. Richard Tuck, trans. Jean Barberyrac. Indianapolis: Liberty Fund.

Hale, Matthew. 2014. 'Some Chapters Touching on the Law of Nature'. Ed. David S. Systma. *Journal of Markets and Morality* 17 (1): 257–346.

Hobbes, Thomas. 1656. *The questions concerning liberty, necessity, and chance*. London: Andrew Cook.

Hobbes, Thomas. 1889. *Elements of Law, Natural and Politic*. Ed. Ferdinand Tönnies. London: Simpkin, Marshall, and Co.

Hobbes, Thomas. 1991. *Leviathan*. Ed. Richard Tuck. Cambridge: Cambridge University Press.

Hobbes, Thomas. 1994. *The Correspondence*. Ed. Noel Malcolm. 2 vols. Oxford: Clarendon Press.

Hobbes, Thomas. 1994. *The Collected Works of Thomas Hobbes*. Ed. William Molesworth. 9 vols. London: Routledge/Thoemmes.

Hobbes, Thomas. 1997. *On the Citizen*. Ed. Richard Tuck. Cambridge: Cambridge University Press.

Hobbes, Thomas. 1999. *The Elements of Law Natural and Politic*. Ed. J. C. A. Gaskin. Oxford: Oxford University Press.

Hobbes, Thomas. 2017. *Three Text Edition of Thomas Hobbes's Political Theory:* Elements of Law, De Cive *and* Leviathan. Ed. Deborah Baumgold. Cambridge: Cambridge University Press.

Hooker, Richard. 1845. *The Works of Richard Hooker*. 3 vols. Ed. John Keble. Oxford: Oxford University Press.

Hooker, Richard. 1977–93. *The Folger Library Edition of the Works of Richard Hooker*. 6 vols. Ed. W. Speed Hill et al. Cambridge, MA/Binghamton: Belknap Press/Medieval & Renaissance Texts & Studies.

Irenaeus. 1956. *Against Heresies*. In *The Ante-Nicene Fathers*, vol. 1: *The Apostolic Fathers, with Justin Martyr and Irenaeus*. Ed. and trans. Alexander Roberts, James Donaldson and Philip Schaff. Grand Rapids, MI: Eerdmans.

Isidore. 1999. *Etymologies*. In *From Irenaeus to Grotius: A Sourcebook in Christian Political Thought*. Ed. and trans. Oliver O'Donovan and Joan Lockwood O'Donovan. Grand Rapids, MI: Eerdmans.

James I. 2006. *Political Writings*. Ed. Johann P. Sommerville. Cambridge: Cambridge University Press.

John of Salisbury. 1955. *Metalogicon*. Trans. Daniel D. McGarry. Los Angeles: University of California Press.

John of Salisbury. 1990. *Policraticus*. Trans. Cary J. Nederman. Cambridge: Cambridge University Press.

1802. *Journal of the House of Commons*. London: His Majesty's Stationery Office.

Junius, Franciscus. 1593. *De Politiae Mosis Observatione: Quid in populo Dei obseruari, quid non obseruari ex ea oporteat, postquàm gratia & veritas per Christum facta est, & Euangelio promulgata*. Lugduni Batavorum: Officiana Plantiniana Raphelengius.

Junius, Franciscus. 2015. *The Mosaic Polity*. Trans. Todd M. Rester. Grand Rapids, MI: CLP Academic.

Locke, John. 1976. *The Correspondence of John Locke: Vol. 2, letters nos 462–848*. Ed. E. S. de Beer. Oxford: Clarendon Press.

Locke, John. 1990. *Draft for the* Essay Concerning Human *Understanding, and Other Philosophical Writings*. Ed. Peter H. Nidditch and G. A. J. Rogers. Vol. 1. Oxford: Clarendon Press.

Locke, John. 1994. *Two Treatises of Government*. Ed. Peter Laslett. Cambridge: Cambridge University Press.

Locke, John. 1997. *Political Essays*. Ed. Mark Goldie. Cambridge: Cambridge University Press.

Marsilius of Padua. 1324. *Defensor Pacis*. Translation from Marsilius of Padua. 2005. *The Defender of the Peace*. Trans. Annabel Brett. Cambridge: Cambridge University Press.

Philo. 1953. *Questions on Genesis*. Trans. Ralph Marcus. Cambridge, MA: Harvard University Press.

Plato. 1993. *The Republic*. Trans. Robin Waterfield. Oxford: Oxford University Press.

Plato. 1997. *Plato's Cosmology: The Timaeus of Plato*. Trans. Francis McDonald Cornford. Indianapolis: Hackett.

Pufendorf, Samuel. 2003. *The Whole Duty of Man According to the Law of Nature*. Indianapolis: Liberty Fund.

Saravia, Hadrian. 1593. *De Imperandi Authoritate, et Christiana Obedientia, Libri Quatuor*. London: Excudebante Reg. typog.

Seneca. 2009. *De clementia*. Ed. Susanna Braund. Oxford: Oxford University Press.

Seneca. 2010. *Naturales quaestiones*. Translation from Lucius Annaeus Seneca, *Natural Questions*. Trans. Harry M. Hine. Chicago: University of Chicago Press.

Sidney, Algernon. 1698. *Discourses Concerning Government*. London: Booksellers of London and Westminster.

Sidney, Algernon. 1996. *Discourses Concerning Government*. Ed. Thomas G. West. Indianapolis: Liberty Fund.

Thomasius, Christian. 2011. *Institutes of Divine Jurisprudence: with selections from Foundations of the Law of Nature and Nations*. Indianapolis: Liberty Fund.

Tyrell, James. 1681. *Patriarcha non monarcha: The Patriarch unmonarch'd: Being Observations on a late treatise and divers other miscellanies, published under the name of Sir Robert Filmer Baronet . . .* London: Richard Janeway.

Westminster Assembly. 1985. *The Confession of Faith*. Glasgow: Free Presbyterian Publications.

Wyclif, John. 1375–6. *De civili dominio*. In *From Irenaeus to Grotius: A Sourcebook in Christian Political Thought*, 1999. Ed. and trans. Oliver O'Donovan and Joan Lockwood O'Donovan. Grand Rapids, MI: Eerdmans.

Zanchi, Girolamo. 1617. *Operum theologicorum*, vol. 4: *De primi hominis lapsu, de peccato, & de lege Dei*. Geneva: Samuelis Crispini.

Zanchi, Girolamo. 2012. *On the Law in General*. Trans. Jeffrey J. Veenstra. Grand Rapids, MI: CLP Academic.

Zwingli, Huldrych. 1953. 'On the Education of the Youth'. In *Zwingli and Bullinger: Selected Translations*, ed. G. W. Bromiley, 102–18. London: SCM Press.

## Secondary Sources

Aarsleff, Hans. 1969. 'The State of Nature and the Nature of Man in Locke'. In *John Locke: Problems and Perspectives*, ed. John W. Yolton, 99–136. Cambridge: Cambridge University Press.

Ahnert, Thomas. 2011. 'Introduction'. In Christian Thomasius, *Institutes of Divine Jurisprudence: with selections from Foundations of the Law of Nature and Nations*, ed. Thomas Ahnert, trans. Thomas Ahnert, xi–xxiv. Indianapolis: Liberty Fund.

Allese, Francesca. 2008. *Philo of Alexandria and Post-Aristotelian Philosophy*. Leiden: Brill.

Alonso, Fernando H. Llano. 2012. 'Cicero and Natural Law'. *Archives for Philosophy of Law and Social Philosophy* 98 (2): 157–68.

Alvarado, Ruben. 2017. *Calvin and the Whigs: A Study in Historical Political Theology*. Aalten: Pantocrator.

Aroney, Nicholas. 2004. 'Althusius at the Antipodes: The *Politica* and Australian Federalism'. In *Jurisprudenz, Politische Theorie und Politische Theologie*, ed. Frederick Carney, Heinz Schilling and Dieter Wyduckel, 529–46. Berlin: Duncker & Humblot.

Ashcraft, Richard. 1971. 'Hobbes's Natural Man: A Study in Ideology Formation'. *The Journal of Politics* 33 (4): 1076–117.

Ashcraft, Richard. 1986. *Revolutionary Politics & Locke's Two Treatises of Government*. Princeton, NJ: Princeton University Press.

Asselt, Willem J. van. 2013. 'Calvinism as a Problematic Concept in Historiography'. *International Journal of Philosophy and Theology* 72 (2): 144–50.

Atkinson, Nigel. 1997. *Richard Hooker and the Authority of Scripture, Tradition and Reason: Reformed Theologian of the Church of England?* Carlisle: Paternoster.

Aubrey, John. 1975. *Brief Lives*. London: The Folio Society.

Avis, Paul D. 1981. *The Church in the Theology of the Reformers*. London: Marshall Morgan & Scott.

Backus, Irena. 2003. 'Calvin's Concept of Natural and Roman Law'. *Calvin Theological Journal* 26 (3): 7–26.

Baker, J. W. 1993. 'The Covenantal Basis for the Development of Swiss Political Federalism: 1291–1848'. *Publius: The Journal of Federalism* 23 (2): 19–42.

Baltes, John. 2016. *The Empire of Habit: John Locke, Discipline, and the Origins of Liberalism*. Rochester, NY: University of Rochester Press.

Bell, Duncan. 2014. 'What is Liberalism?' *Political Theory* 42 (6): 682–715.

Benedict, Philip. 2002. *Christ's Churches Purely Reformed*. New Haven, CT: Yale University Press.

Berns, Laurence. 1969. 'Thomas Hobbes'. In *History of Political Philosophy*, ed. Leo Strauss and Joseph Cropsey, 354–78. Chicago: University of Chicago Press.

Biéler, André. 2005. *Calvin's Economic and Social Thought*. Geneva: World Council of Reformed Churches.

Blumenberg, Hans. 1983. *The Legitimacy of the Modern Age*. Trans. Robert M. Wallace. Cambridge, MA: MIT Press.

Böckenförde, Ernst-Wolfgang. 1991. 'The Rise of the State as a Process of Secularisation'. In Ernst-Wolfgang Böckenförde, *State, Society and Liberty: Studies in Political Theory and Constitutional Law*, trans. J. A. Underwood, 26–46. New York: Berg.

Böckenförde, Ernst-Wolfgang. 2007. *Der säkularisierte Staat: Sein Charakter, seine Rechtfertigung und seine Probleme im 21. Jahrhundert*. Munich: Carl Friedrich von Siemens Stiftung.

Böckenförde, Ernst-Wolfgang. 2017. *Constitutional and Political Theory: Selected Writings*. Ed. Mirjam Künkler and Tine Stein. Oxford: Oxford University Press.

Böckenförde, Ernst-Wolfgang. 2017. 'Security and Self-Preservation before Justice: The Paradigm Shift and Transition from a Natural-Law to a Positive-Law Basis in Thomas Hobbes' System of Law'. In Ernst-Wolfgang Böckenförde, *Constitutional and Political Theory: Selected Writings*, ed. Mirjam Künkler and Tine Stein, 55–68. Oxford: Oxford University Press.

Böckenförde, Ernst-Wolfgang. 2021. *Religion, Law, and Democracy: Selected Writings*. Ed. Mirjam Künkler and Tine Stein. Oxford: Oxford University Press.

Böckenförde, Ernst-Wolfgang. 2021. 'The Rise of the State as a Process of Secularization'. In Ernst-Wolfgang Böckenförde, *Religion, Law, and Democracy: Selected Writings*, ed. Mirjam Künkler and Tine Stein, 152–68. Oxford: Oxford University Press.

Bohatec, Josef. 1934. *Calvin und das Recht*. Feudingen in Westfalen: Buchdruckererei u. verlagsanstalt.

Bou-Habib, Paul. 2015. 'Locke Tracts and the Anarchy of the Religious Conscience.' *European Journal of Political Theory* 14 (1): 3–18.

Bourke, Richard. 2018. 'Revising the Cambridge School: Republicanism Revisited'. *Political Theory* 46 (3): 467–77.

Brague, Rémi. 2003. *The Wisdom of the World: The Human Experience of the Universe in Western Thought*. Chicago: University of Chicago Press.

Brett, Annabel S. 2011. *Changes of State: Nature and the Limits of the City in Early Modern Natural Law*. Princeton, NJ: Princeton University Press.

Brunner, Emil, and Karl Barth. 2002. *Natural Theology: Comprising 'Nature and Grace' by Professor Dr. Emil Brunner and the Reply 'No!' by Dr. Karl Barth*. Trans. Peter Fraenkel. Eugene: Wipf and Stock.

Brutus, Junius. 1579. *Vindiciae, contra tyrannos: sive, de Principis in Populum, Populique in Principem, legitima potestate*. Edimburgi: Thomas Gaurin.

Brutus, Junius. 1648. *Vindiciae contra Tyrannos: A Defence of Liberty against Tyrants*. London: Matthew Simmons and Robert Wilson.

Brydon, Michael. 2006. *The Evolving Reputation of Richard Hooker: An Examination of Responses*. Oxford: Oxford University Press.

Bull, George. 1932. 'What Did Locke Borrow from Hooker?' *Thought* 7 (1): 122–35.

Burns, J. H., ed. 1988. *The Cambridge History of Medieval Political Thought, c. 350 – c. 1450*. Cambridge: Cambridge University Press.

Burns, J. H., and Mark Goldie, eds. 1991. *The Cambridge History of Political Thought, 1450–1700*. Cambridge: Cambridge University Press.

Canning, J. P. 1988. 'Introduction: Politics, Institutions, Ideas.' In *Cambridge History of Medieval Political Thought, c.350 – c. 1450*, ed. J. H. Burns, 341–66. Cambridge: Cambridge University Press.

Cargill Thompson, W. D. J. 1980. 'The Philosopher of the "Politic Society": Richard Hooker as a Political Thinker'. In W. D. J. Cargill Thompson, *Studies in the Reformation: Luther to Hooker*, 131–191. London: Athlone Press.

Carney, Frederick S. 1960. 'The Associational Theory of Johannes Althusius: A Study in Calvinist Constitutionalism'. PhD dissertation, University of Chicago.

Carney, Frederick S. 1995. 'Translator's Introduction'. In Johannes Althusius, *Politica: an abridged translation of Politics Methodically Set Forth and Illustrated with Sacred and Profane Examples*, trans. Frederick S. Carney, ix–xxxiv. Indianapolis: Liberty Fund.

Carroll, Anthony J. 2009. 'The Importance of Protestantism in Max Weber's Theory of Secularisation'. *European Journal of Sociology* 50 (1): 61–95.

Cavanaugh, William. 2006. 'From One City to Two: Christian Reimagining of Political Space'. *Political Theology* 7 (3): 299–321.

Cavanaugh, William. 2018. 'The Fall of the Fall in Early Modern Political Theory'. *Political Theology* 18 (6): 475–94.

Chadwick, Henry. 1964. *The Reformation*. Harmondsworth: Penguin.

Clark, R. S. 1998. 'Calvin on the *Lex Naturalis*'. *Stulos Theological Journal* 6 (1–2): 1–22.

Coates, Wendell. 2000. *Oakeshott and His Contemporaries*. Selinsgrove, PA: Susquehanna University Press.

Collingwood, R. G. 1970. *The Idea of History*. Oxford: Oxford University Press.

Collins, Jeffrey R. 2005. *The Allegiance of Thomas Hobbes*. Oxford: Oxford University Press.

Collins, Jeffrey R. 2009. 'Interpreting Thomas Hobbes in Competing Contexts'. *Journal of the History of Ideas* 70 (1): 165–80.

Collinson, Patrick. 1990. *The Elizabethan Puritan Movement*. Oxford: Oxford University Press.

Condren, Conal. 2000. *Thomas Hobbes*. New York: Twayne.

Cromartie, Alan. 2000. 'Theology and Politics in Richard Hooker's Thought'. *History of Political Thought* 21 (1): 41–66.

Curthoys, Jean. 1998. 'Thomas Hobbes, the Taylor Thesis and Alasdair Macintyre'. *British Journal for the History of Philosophy* 6 (1): 1–24.

Cuttica, Cesare. 2011. 'Sir Robert Filmer (1588–1653) and the Condescension of Posterity: Historiographical Interpretations'. *Intellectual History Review* 21 (2): 195–208.

Cuttica, Cesare. 2012. *Sir Robert Filmer (1588–1653) and the Patriotic Monarch: Patriarchalism in Seventeenth-Century Political Thought*. Manchester: Manchester University Press.

Daly, James. 1983. 'Some Problems in the Authorship of Sir Robert Filmer's Works'. *The English Historical Review* 98 (389): 737–62.

Damrosch Jr., Leopold. 1979. 'Hobbes as Reformation Theologian: Implications of the Free-Will Controversy'. *Journal of the History of Ideas* 40 (3): 339–52.

Davison Hunter, James. 2017. 'Liberal Democracy and the Unraveling of the Enlightenment Project'. *The Hedgehog Review* 19 (3): 22–37.

De Benoist, Alain. 2000. 'The First Federalist: Johannes Althusius'. *Telos* 118: 25–58.

Deneen, Patrick J. 2018. *Why Liberalism Failed*. New Haven: Yale University Press.

d'Entrèves, Alessandro P. 1959. *The Medieval Contribution to Political Thought: Thomas Aquinas, Marsilius of Padua, Richard Hooker*. New York: Humanities Press.

Dominiak, Paul. 2017. 'Hooker, Scholasticism, Thomism, and Reformed Orthodoxy'. In *Richard Hooker and Reformed Orthodoxy*, ed. W. Bradford Littlejohn and Scott N. Kindred-Barnes, 101–26. Göttingen: Vandenhoeck & Ruprecht.

Dominiak, Paul. 2020. *Richard Hooker: The Architecture of Participation*. London: T&T Clark.

Dowey, Edward A. 1994. *The Knowledge of God in Calvin's Theology*. Grand Rapids, MI: Eerdmans.

Duke, George. 2014. 'Hobbes on Political Authority, Practical Reason and Truth'. *Law and Philosophy* 33: 605–27.

Duke, George, and Robert P. George, eds. 2017. *The Cambridge Companion to Natural Law Jurisprudence*. Cambridge: Cambridge University Press.

Dunn, John. 1969. *The Political Thought of John Locke*. Cambridge: Cambridge University Press.

Dunn, John. 1984. *Locke*. Oxford: Oxford University Press.

Eccleshall, Robert. 1978. *Order and Reason in Politics: Theories of Absolute and Limited Monarchy in Early Modern England*. Oxford: Oxford University Press.

Eisenach, Eldon J. 1982. 'Hobbes on Church, State and Religion'. *History of Political Thought* 3 (2): 215–43.

Elazar, Daniel J. 1991. 'The Multi-faceted Covenant: The Biblical Approach to the Problem of Organizations, Constitutions, and Liberty as Reflected in the Thought of Johannes Althusius'. *Constitutional Political Economy* 2 (2): 187–208.

Elazar, Daniel J. 1995. 'Althusius' Grand Design for a Federal Commonwealth'. In Johannes Althusius, *Politica: an abridged translation of Politics Methodically Set Forth and Illustrated with Sacred and Profane Examples*, trans. Frederick S. Carney, xxxv–xlvi. Indianapolis: Liberty Fund.

Eppley, Daniel. 2007. *Defending Royal Supremacy and Discerning God's Will in Tudor England*. Aldershot: Ashgate.

Forde, Steven. 2001. 'Natural Law, Theology, and Morality in Locke'. *American Journal of Political Science* 45 (2): 396–409.

Freddoso, Alfred J. 1991. 'God's General Concurrence with Secondary Causes: Why Conservation is Not Enough'. *Philosophical Perspectives* 5 (Philosophy of Religion): 553–85.

Friedeburg, Robert V. 1998. 'From Collective Representation to the Right of Individual Defence: James Steuart's *Ius Populi Vindicatum* and the Use of Johannes *Althusius' Politica* in Restoration Scotland'. *History of European Ideas* 24 (1): 19–42.

Friedeburg, Robert von. 2006. '*Persona* and Office: Althusius on the Formation of Magistrates and Councillors'. In *The Philosopher in Early Modern Europe: The Nature of a Contested Identity*, ed. Conal Condren, Stephen Gaukroger and Ian Hunter, 160–81. Cambridge: Cambridge University Press.

Friedrich, Carl J. 1932. 'Introduction'. In Johannes Althusius, *Politica methodice digesta of Johannes Althusius (Althaus) reprinted from the third edition of 1614*, ed. Carl J. Friedrich, xiii–xcix. Cambridge, MA: Harvard University Press.

Friedrich, Carl J. 1964. 'Preface'. In Johannes Althusius, *The Politics of Johannes Althusius*, trans. Frederick S. Carney, vii–xii. Boston, MA: Beacon Press.

Fulford, Andrew. 2014. 'Participating in Political Providence: The Theological Foundations of Resistance in Calvin'. In *For the Healing of the Nations: Essays on Creation, Redemption and Neo-Calvinism*, ed. Peter Escalante and W. Bradford Littlejohn, 105–38. Charleston: Davenant Press.

Ganoczy, Alexandre. 1987. *The Young Calvin*. Trans. David Foxgrover and Wade Provo. Philadelphia, PA: Westminster Press.

Ganoczy, Alexandre. 2004. 'Calvin's Life'. In *The Cambridge Companion to John Calvin*, ed. Donald K. McKim, 3–24. Cambridge: Cambridge University Press.

Gentles, Ian. 2007. *The English Revolution and the Wars in the Three Kingdoms 1638–1652*. Harlow: Pearson Longman.

Gert, Bernard. 1988. 'The Law of Nature as the Moral Law'. *Hobbes Studies* 1: 26–44.

Gibbs, Lee W. 2002. 'Richard Hooker: Prophet of Anglicanism or English Magisterial Reformer?' *Anglican Theological Review* 84 (4): 943–60.

Gibbs, Lee W. 2002. 'Richard Hooker's *Via Media* Doctrine of Scripture and Tradition'. *Harvard Theological Review* 95 (2): 227–35.

Gibbs, Lee W. 2008. 'Life of Hooker'. In *A Companion to Richard Hooker*, ed. W. J. Torrance Kirby, 1–25. Leiden: Brill.

Gierke, Otto von. 1957. *Natural Law and the Theory of Society, 1500–1800*. Trans. Ernst Barker. Boston, MA: Beacon Press.

Gierke, Otto von. 1958. *Political Theories of the Middle Age*. Boston, MA: Beacon Press.

Gierke, Otto von. 1966. *The Development of Political Theory*. Trans. Bernard Freyd. New York: Howard Fertig.

Gillespie, Michael Allen. 2008. *The Theological Origins of Modernity*. Chicago: University of Chicago Press.

Glover, Willis B. 1960. 'God and Thomas Hobbes'. *Church History* 29 (3): 275–97.

Goldie, Mark. 1983. 'John Locke and Anglican Royalism'. *Political Studies* 31: 61–85.

Goldie, Mark. 2018. 'John Locke, the Early Lockeans, and Priestcraft.' *Intellectual History Review* 28 (1): 125–44.

Goldsmith, M. M. 1966. *Hobbes's Science of Politics*. New York: Columbia University Press.

Gordon, Bruce. 2002. *The Swiss Reformation*. Manchester: University of Manchester Press.

Gordon, Bruce. 2009. *Calvin*. New Haven, CT: Yale University Press.

Gordon, Peter E. 2013. 'Between Christian Democracy and Critical Theory: Habermas, Böckenförde, and the Dialectics of Secularization in Postwar Germany'. *Social Research: An International Quarterly* 80 (1): 173–202.

Gordon, Peter E. 2016. 'The Idea of Secularisation in Intellectual History'. In *A Companion to Intellectual History*, ed. Richard Whatmore and Brian Young, 230–46. Chichester: Wiley-Blackwell.

Gough, J. W. 1973. *John Locke's Political Philosophy*. Oxford: Clarendon Press.

Grabill, Stephen J. 2006. *Rediscovering the Natural Law in Reformed Theological Ethics*. Grand Rapids, MI: Eerdmans.

Grabill, Stephen J. 2013. 'Althusius in Context: A Biographical and Historical Introduction.' In Johannes Althusius, *On Law and Power*, trans. Jeffrey J. Veenstra, xix–xlvii. Grand Rapids, MI: CLP Academic.

Gregory, Brad S. 2012. *The Unintended Reformation: How a Religious Revolution Secularized Society*. Cambridge, MA: Harvard University Press.

Grislis, Egil. 1971. 'Calvin's Use of Cicero in the *Institutes* I:1–5: A Case Study in Theological Method'. *Archiv für Reformationsgeschichte* 62: 5–37.

Grislis, Egil. 2002. 'The Role of Sin in the Theology of Richard Hooker'. *Anglican Theological Review* 84 (4): 881–96.

Haakonssen, Knud. 1996. *Natural Law and Moral Philosophy*. Cambridge: Cambridge University Press.

Haakonssen, Knud. 2017. 'Early Modern Natural Law Theories'. In *The Cambridge Companion to Natural Law Jurisprudence*, ed. George Duke and Robert P. George, 76–102. Cambridge: Cambridge University Press.

Haakonssen, Knud, and Michael J. Seidler. 2016. 'Natural Law: Law, Rights and Duties'. In *A Companion to Intellectual History*, ed. Richard Whatmore and Brian Young, 377–401. Chichester: Wiley-Blackwell.

Haas, Gene. 2012. 'Calvin, Natural Law, and the Two Kingdoms'. In *Kingdoms Apart: Engaging the Two Kingdoms Perspective*, ed. Ryan G. McIlhenny, 33–47. Phillipsburg, NJ: Presbyterian and Reformed Publishing.

Hamilton, Sidney G. 1903. *Hertford College*. London: F. E. Robinson & Co.

Hampsher-Monk, Iain. 1992. *A History of Modern Political Thought: Major Political Thinkers from Hobbes to Marx*. Oxford: Blackwell.

Hancey, James O. 1976. 'Locke and the Law of Nature'. *Political Theory* 4 (4): 439–54.

Harris, Ian. 1994. *The Mind of John Locke: A Study of Political Theory in Its Intellectual Setting*. Cambridge: Cambridge University Press.

Harrison, Peter. 2007. *The Fall of Man and the Foundations of Science*. Cambridge: Cambridge University Press.

Haude, Sigrun. 2002. 'Anabaptism'. In *The Reformation World*, ed. Andrew Pettegree, 237–56. London: Routledge.

Heal, Felicity. 2005. *The Reformation in Britain and Ireland*. Oxford: Oxford University Press.

Helm, Paul. 2004. *John Calvin's Ideas*. Oxford: Oxford University Press.

Herdt, Jennifer A. 2014. 'Calvin's Legacy for Contemporary Reformed Natural Law'. *Scottish Journal of Theology* 67 (4): 414–35.

Hill, Christopher. 1985. 'Covenant Theology and the Concept of "A Public Person"'. In Christopher Hill, *The Collected Essays of Christopher Hill*, vol. 3: *People and Ideas in 17th Century England*, 300–24. Amherst: University of Massachusetts Press.

Hill, W. Speed. 2008. 'Works and Editions II'. In *A Companion to Richard Hooker*, 41–4. Leiden: Brill.

Hochstrasser, T. J. 1993. 'Conscience and Reason: The Natural Law Theory of Jean Barbeyrac'. *The Historical Journal* 36 (2): 289–308.

Hochstrasser, T. J. 1995. 'The Claims of Conscience: Natural Law Theory, Obligation, and Resistance in the Huguenot Diaspora'. In *New Essays on the Political Thought of the Huguenots of the Refuge*, ed. John Christian Laursen, 15–52. Leiden: Brill.

Hochstrasser, T. J. 2000. *Natural Law Theories in the Early Enlightenment*. Cambridge: Cambridge University Press.

Hochstrasser, T. J., and P. Schröeder, eds. 2003. *Early Modern Natural Law Theories: Context and Strategies in the Early Enlightenment*. Dordrecht: Springer.

Hoekstra, Kinch. 2007. 'Hobbes on the Natural Condition of Mankind'. In *The Cambridge Companion to Hobbes's Leviathan*, ed. Patricia Springborg, 109–27. Cambridge: Cambridge University Press.

Höpfl, Harro. 1982. *The Christian Polity of John Calvin*. Cambridge: Cambridge University Press.

Höpfl, Harro, and Martyn P. Thompson. 1979. 'The History of Contract as a Motif in Political Thought'. *American Historical Review* 84 (4): 919–44.

Horwitz, Robert. 1992. 'Locke's *Questions Concerning the Law of Nature: A Commentary*'. *Interpretation* 19 (3): 251–306.

Hotson, Howard. 2000. *Johann Heinrich Alsted 1588–1638: Between Renaissance, Reformation, and Universal Reform*. Oxford: Oxford University Press.

Hotson, Howard. 2002. 'The Conservative Face of Contractual Theory: The *Monarchomach* Servants of the Count of Nassau-Dillenburg'. In *Politische Begriffe und historisches Umfeld in der* Politica methodice digesta *des Johannes Althusius*, ed. Emilio Bonfatti, Giuseppe Duso and Merio Scattola, 251–90. Wiesbaden: Harrassowitz Verlag.

Hotson, Howard. 2007. *Commonplace Learning: Ramism and Its German Ramifications 1543–1630*. Oxford: Oxford University Press.

Hueglin, Thomas. 1979. 'Johannes Althusius: Medieval Constitutionalist or Modern Federalist?' *Publius: The Journal of Federalism* 4 (1): 9–42.

Hueglin, Thomas O. 1999. *Early Modern Concepts for a Late Modern World: Althusius on Community and Federalism*. Waterloo: Wilfred Laurier University Press.

Hunter, Ian. 2001. *Rival Enlightenments: Civil and Metaphysical Philosophy in Early Modern Germany*. Cambridge: Cambridge University Press.

Hunter, Ian. 2006. 'The University Philosopher in Early Modern Germany'. In *The Philosopher in Early Modern Europe: The Nature of a Contested Identity*, ed. Conal Condren, Stephen Gaukroger and Ian Hunter, 35–65. Cambridge: Cambridge University Press.

Hunter, Ian. 2007. *The Secularisation of the Confessional State: The Political Thought of Christian Thomasius*. Cambridge: Cambridge University Press.

Hunter, Ian. 2011. 'Natural Law as Political Philosophy'. In *The Oxford Handbook of Philosophy in Early Modern Europe*, ed. Desmond M. Clarke and Catherine Wilson, 475–99. Oxford: Oxford University Press.

Hunter, Ian, and David Saunders, eds. 2002. *Natural Law and Civil Sovereignty: Moral Right and State Authority in Early Modern Political Thought*. London: Palgrave Macmillan.

Hunter, Ian, and David Saunders. 2003. 'Introduction'. In Samuel Pufendorf, *The Whole Duty of Man According to the Law of Nature*, ix–xvii. Indianapolis: Liberty Fund.

Ingalls, Ranall. 2008. 'Sin and Grace'. In *A Companion to Richard Hooker*, ed. W. J. Torrance Kirby, 151–83. Leiden: Brill.

Inwood, Brad, and Fred D. Miller, Jr. 2015. 'Law in Roman Philosophy'. In *A Treatise of Legal Philosophy and General Jurisprudence*, vol. 6: *A History of the Philosophy of Law from the Ancient Greeks to the Scholastics*, ed. F. Miller, Jr and C. Biondi, 133–65. Dordrecht: Springer.

Kauffmann, Thomas. 2006. *Konfession und Kultur: Lutherischer Protestantismus in der zweiten Halfte des Reformationjahrhunderts*. Tübingen: Mohr Siebeck.

Kempa, William. 2001. 'Calvin on Natural Law'. In *John Calvin and the Church: A Prism of Reform*, ed. Timothy George, 70–97. Louisville, KY: Westminster/John Knox Press.

Kennedy, Simon P. 2016. 'Was there a Calvinist Resistance Theory?' *Ad Fontes* 1 (3): 7–8.

Kennedy, Simon P. 2019. 'Richard Hooker as Political Naturalist'. *The Historical Journal* 62 (2): 331–48. doi:10.1017/S0018246X18000080.

Kennedy, Simon P. 2019. 'Rethinking *consociatio* in Althusius's *Politica*'. *Journal of Markets and Morality* 22 (2): 305–16.

King, Peter. 1829. *The Life of John Locke: With Extracts from His Correspondence, Journals, and Common-place Books*. London: H. Colburn.

Kirby, Torrance. 2004. '"Relics of the Amorites" or "Things Indifferent"? Peter Martyr Vermigli's Authority and the Threat of Schism in the Elizabethan Vestiarian Controversy'. *Reformation & Renaissance Review* 6 (3): 313–26.

Kirby, W. J. Torrance. 1990. *Richard Hooker's Doctrine of the Royal Supremacy*. Leiden: Brill.

Kirby, W. J. Torrance. 1999. 'Richard Hooker's Theory of Natural Law in the Context of Reformation Theology'. *Sixteenth Century Journal* 30 (3): 681–703.

Kirby, W. J. Torrance, ed. 2008. *A Companion to Richard Hooker*. Leiden: Brill.

Kirby, W. J. Torrance, 2011. 'From "Generall Meditations" to "Particular Decisions": The Augustinian Coherence of Richard Hooker's Political Theology'. In *Sovereignty and Law in the Middle Ages and Renaissance*, ed. Robert Sturges, 43–65. Turnhout: Brepols.

Künkler, Mirjam, and Tine Stein. 2017. 'State, Law, and Constitution'. In Ernst-Wolfgang Böckenförde, *Constitutional Political Theory: Selected Writings*, ed. Mirjam Künkler and Tine Stein, 1–35. Oxford: Oxford University Press.

Lang, August. 1909. 'The Reformation and Natural Law'. In *Calvin and the Reformation*, ed. William Park Armstrong, 56–98. New York: Fleming H. Revell.

Laslett, Peter. 1948. 'Sir Robert Filmer: The Man versus the Whig Myth'. *The William and Mary Quarterly* 5 (4): 523–46.

Legutko, Ryszard. 2016. *The Demon in Democracy: Totalitarian Temptations in Free Societies*. New York: Encounter Books.

Leith, John H. 1989. *John Calvin's Doctrine of the Christian Life*. Louisville, KY: Westminster/John Knox Press.

Leithart, Peter J. 1990. 'That Eminent Pagan: Calvin's Use of Cicero in *Institutes* 1.1–5'. *Westminster Theological Journal* 52 (1): 1–12.

Leithart, Peter J. 1993. 'Stoic Elements in Calvin's Doctrine of the Christian Life, Part I: Original Corruption, Natural Law, and the Order of the Soul'. *Westminster Theological Journal* 55 (1): 31–54.

Leithart, Peter J. 1993. 'Stoic Elements in Calvin's Doctrine of the Christian Life, Part II: Mortification'. *Westminster Theological Journal* 55 (2): 191–208.

Leithart, Peter J. 1994. 'Stoic Elements in Calvin's Doctrine of the Christian Life, Part III: Christian Moderation'. *Westminster Theological Journal* 56 (1): 59–85.

Lessay, Franck. 2007. 'Hobbes's Covenant Theology and Its Political Implications'. In *The Cambridge Companion to Hobbes's Leviathan*, ed. Patricia Springborg, 243–70. Cambridge: Cambridge University Press.

Letham, Robert. 2009. *The Westminster Assembly: Reading Its Theology in Historical Context*. Phillipsburg: P & R.

Levin, Yuval. 2014. Interview with Bill Kristol. Accessed at http://conversationswithbillkristol.org/transcript/yuval-levin-transcript/ (7 November 2017).

Leyden, Wolfgang von. 1956. 'John Locke and Natural Law'. *Philosophy* 31 (116): 23–35.

Lindberg, Carter. 2010. *The European Reformations*. Malden, MA: Wiley-Blackwell.

Littlejohn, W. Bradford. 2013. '"More than a swineherd": Hooker, Vermigli, and an Aristotelian Defence of the Royal Supremacy'. *Reformation & Renaissance Review* 15 (1): 68–83.

Littlejohn, W. Bradford. 2015. *Richard Hooker: A Companion to His Life and Work*. Eugene: Wipf & Stock.

Littlejohn, Bradford. 2017. 'Cutting Through the Fog in the Channel: Hooker, Junius, and a Reformed Theology of Law'. In *Richard Hooker and Reformed Orthodoxy*, ed. W. Bradford Littlejohn and Scott N. Kindred-Barnes, 221–40. Göttingen: Vandenhoeck & Ruprecht.

Littlejohn, W. Bradford. 2017. *The Peril and Promise of Christian Liberty: Richard Hooker, the Puritans, and Protestant Political Theology*. Grand Rapids, MI: Eerdmans.

Littlejohn, W. Bradford, and Scott N. Kindred-Barnes, eds. 2017. *Richard Hooker and Reformed Orthodoxy*. Göttingen: Vandenhoeck & Ruprecht.

Lobban, Michael. 2007. *A History of the Philosophy of Law in the Common Law World, 1600–1900*. Dordrecht: Springer.

Löwith, Karl. 1949. *Meaning in History*. Chicago: Chicago University Press.

Luce, Edward. 2017. *The Retreat of Western Liberalism*. London: Little, Brown.

Luther, Martin. 1955–. *Luther's Works*, ed. Jaroslav Pelikan, trans. Jaroslav Pelikan et. al. 54 vols. St Louis, MO: Concordia Publishing House.

Macaulay, Thomas Babington. 1899. *The History of England from the accession of James the Second*. New York: Longmans, Green, and Co.

Malcolm, Noel. 2002. *Aspects of Hobbes*. Oxford: Clarendon Press.

Markus, R. A. 1970. *Saeculum: History and Society in the Theology of St Augustine*. Cambridge: Cambridge University Press.

Markus, R. A. 1988. 'The Latin Fathers'. In *The Cambridge History of Medieval Political Thought c. 350 – c. 1450*, ed. J. H. Burns, 92–122. Cambridge: Cambridge University Press.

Martinich, A. P. 1992. *The Two Gods of* Leviathan: *Thomas Hobbes on Religion and Politics*. Cambridge: Cambridge University Press.

Martinich, A. P. 1999. *Hobbes: A Biography*. Cambridge: Cambridge University Press.

Martinich, Aloysius. 2005. *Hobbes*. New York: Routledge.

McCullock, Matt. 2006. 'Johannes Althusius' *Politica*: The Culmination of Calvin's Right of Resistance'. *The European Legacy* 11 (5): 485–99.

McGrade, A. S. 1989. 'Introduction.' In Richard Hooker, *Of the Laws of Ecclesiastical Polity*, ed. A. S. McGrade, 11–40. Cambridge: Cambridge University Press.

McGrath, Alister E. 1986. 'John Calvin and Late Mediaeval Thought: A Study in Late Mediaeval Influences on Calvin's Theological Development'. *Archiv für Reformationsgeschichte* 58–78.

McGrath, Alister E. 1990. *A Life of John Calvin: A Study in the Shaping of Western Culture*. Oxford: Blackwell.

McGrath, Alister E. 2004. *The Intellectual Origins of the European Reformation*. London: Blackwell.

McLaughlin, R. E. 2007. 'The Radical Reformation'. In *Cambridge History of Christianity*, vol. 6: *Reform and Expansion 1500–1660*, ed. R. Po-chia Hsia, 37–55. Cambridge: Cambridge University Press.

McNeill, John T. 1946. 'Natural Law in the Teaching of Reformers'. *The Journal of Religion* 26 (3): 168–82.

McNeilly, F. S. 1968. *The Anatomy of Leviathan*. London: Macmillan.

Milbank, John, and Adrian Pabst. 2016. *The Politics of Virtue: Post-Liberalism and the Human Future*. Lanham, MD: Rowman & Littlefield.

Miller, Fred D. 2000. 'Naturalism'. In *The Cambridge History of Greek and Roman Political Thought*, ed. Christopher Rowe and Malcolm Schofield, 321–43. Cambridge: Cambridge University Press.

Miller, Patrick Lee. 2017. 'The Implosion of Western Liberalism'. *Quillette*. Accessed at https://quillette.com/2017/11/05/implosion-western-liberalism/ (8 November 2017).

Mintz, Samuel I. 1970. *The Hunting of Leviathan: Seventeenth-Century Reactions to the Materialism and Moral Philosophy of Thomas Hobbes*. Cambridge: Cambridge University Press.

Morgan, Edmund S. 1988. *Inventing the People: The Rise of Popular Sovereignty in England and America*. New York: W. W. Norton.

Müller, Jan-Werner. 2018. 'What the Dictum Really Meant – And What It Could Mean for Us'. *Constellations* 25 (2): 196–206.

Muller, Richard A. 2003. *Post-Reformation Reformed Dogmatics: The Rise and Development of Reformed Orthodoxy, ca. 1520 to 1725*. Grand Rapids, MI: Baker Academic.

Muller, Richard A. 2012. *Calvin and the Reformed Tradition*. Grand Rapids, MI: Baker Academic.

Munz, Peter. 1952. *The Place of Hooker in the History of Thought*. London: Routledge & Kegan Paul.

Nederman, Cary J. 1988. 'Nature, Sin and the Origins of Society: The Ciceronian Tradition in Medieval Political Thought'. *Journal of the History of Ideas* 49 (1): 3–26.

Nederman, Cary J. 2009. *Lineages of European Political Thought: Explorations Along the Medieval/Modern Divide from John of Salisbury to Hegel*. Washington, DC: The Catholic University of America Press.

Neisel, Wilhelm. 1980. *The Theology of Calvin*. Grand Rapids, MI: Baker Book House.

Neuser, Wilhelm H. 2009. 'Stations – France and Basel'. In *The Calvin Handbook*, ed. Herman Selderhuis, 23–30. Grand Rapids, MI: Eerdmans.

New, John F. 1968. 'The Whitgift–Cartwright Controversy'. *Archiv für Reformationsgeschichte* 59: 203–12.

Noberto, Bobbio. 1993. *Thomas Hobbes and the Natural Law Tradition*. Trans. Daniela Gobetti. Chicago: University of Chicago Press.

Noll, Mark A., ed. 1991. *Confessions and Catechisms of the Reformation*. Leicester: Apollos.

Oakeshott, Michael. 1999. *On History and Other Essays*. Indianapolis: Liberty Fund.

Oakeshott, Michael. 2004. 'Political Thought as a Subject of Historical Inquiry'. In Michael Oakeshott, *What is History? and Other Essays*, ed. Luke O'Sullivan, 403–42. Exeter: Imprint Academic.

Oakeshott, Michael. 2006. *Lectures in the History of Political Thought*. Ed. Terry Nardin and Luke O'Sullivan. Exeter: Imprint Academic.

Oakley, Francis. 1961. 'Medieval Theories of Natural Law: William of Ockham and the Significance of the Voluntarist Tradition'. *Natural Law Forum* 6: 65–83.

Oakley, Francis. 1997. 'Locke, Natural Law, and God – Again'. *History of Political Thought* 18 (4): 624–51.

Oakley, Francis. 1999. *Politics and Eternity: Studies in the History of Medieval and Early-Modern Political Thought*. Leiden: Brill.

Oakley, Francis. 2005. *Natural Law, Laws of Nature, Natural Rights*. New York: Continuum.

Oakley, Francis. 2006. 'In Praise of Prolepsis: Meaning, Significance and the Medieval Contribution to Political Thought'. *History of Political Thought* 27 (3): 407–22.

Oakley, Francis. 2010. *Empty Bottles of Gentilism: Kingship and the Divine in Late Antiquity and the Early Middle Ages (to 1050)*. New Haven, CT: Yale University Press.

Oakley, Francis. 2012. *The Mortgage of the Past: Reshaping the Ancient Political Inheritance (1050–1300)*. New Haven, CT: Yale University Press.

Oakley, Francis. 2015. *The Watershed of Modern Politics: Law, Virtue, Kingship and Consent (1300–1650)*. New Haven, CT: Yale University Press.

Oakley, Francis, and Elliot W. Urdang. 1966. 'Locke, Natural Law, and God'. *Natural Law Forum* 11: 92–109.

O'Donovan, Joan Lockwood. 1991. *Theology of Law and Authority in the English Reformation*. Grand Rapids, MI: Eerdmans.

O'Donovan, Oliver. 1996. *The Desire of the Nations: Rediscovering the Roots of Political Theology*. Cambridge: Cambridge University Press.

O'Donovan, Oliver. 1999. 'Government as Judgement'. *First Things* (April): 36–44.

O'Donovan, Oliver, and Joan Lockwood O'Donovan, eds. 1999. *From Irenaeus to Grotius: A Sourcebook in Christian Political Thought*. Grand Rapids, MI: Eerdmans.

Palmer, Ada. 2014. *Reading Lucretius in the Renaissance*. Cambridge, MA: Harvard University Press.

Pangle, Thomas L. 1990. *The Spirit of Modern Republicanism: The Moral Vision of the American Founders and the Philosophy of Locke*. Chicago: Chicago University Press.

Parker, Kim Ian. 2004. *The Biblical Politics of John Locke*. Waterloo: Wilfred Laurier University Press.

Parker, T. H. L. 1995. *Calvin: An Introduction to His Thought*. Louisville, KY: Westminster/John Knox Press.

Parker, T. H. L. 2012. *Portrait of Calvin*. Minneapolis: Desiring God.

Parkin, Jon. 2003. 'Taming the Leviathan: Reading Hobbes in Seventeenth-Century Europe'. In *Early Modern Natural Law Theories: Contexts and Strategies in the Early Enlightenment*, 31–52. Dordrecht: Springer.

Parry, Stanley. 1953. 'The Political Science of Johannes Althusius'. PhD dissertation, Yale University.

Partee, Charles. 1977. *Calvin and Classical Philosophy*. Leiden: Brill.

Perrott, M. E. 1998. 'Richard Hooker and the Problem of Authority in the Elizabethan Church'. *Journal of Ecclesiastical History* 49 (1): 29–60.

Pocock, J. G. A. 1971. 'Time, History, and Eschatology in the Thought of Thomas Hobbes'. In *Politics, Language and Time: Essays on Political Thought and History*, by J. G. A. Pocock, 148–201. New York: Atheneum.

Pocock, J. G. A. 1987. *The Ancient Constitution and the Feudal Law: A Study of English Historical Thought in the Seventeenth Century*. Cambridge: Cambridge University Press.

Pye, Tom. 2016. 'Property, Space and Sacred History in John Locke's *Two Treatises of Government*'. *Modern Intellectual History* 1–26. doi:10.1017/S1479244316000299.

Rabieh, Michael S. 1991. 'The Reasonableness of John Locke and the Questionableness of Christianity'. *The Journal of Politics* 53 (4): 933–57.

Rawls, John. 2005. *Political Liberalism: Expanded Edition*. New York: Cambridge University Press.

Reik, Miriam M. 1977. *The Golden Lands of Thomas Hobbes*. Detroit, MI: Wayne State University Press.

Rickless, Samuel C. 2014. *Locke*. Chichester: Wiley-Blackwell.

Riley, Patrick. 1973. 'How Coherent is the Social Contract Tradition?' *Journal of the History of Ideas* 34 (4): 543–62.

Rorty, Richard. 1988. *Contingency, Irony, and Solidarity*. Cambridge: Cambridge University Press.

Rosenthal, Alexander S. 2008. *Crown under Law: Richard Hooker, John Locke, and the Ascent of Modern Constitutionalism*. Plymouth: Lexington Books.

Runia, David T. 1986. *Philo of Alexandria and the Timaeus of Plato*. Leiden: Brill.

Ryan, Alan. 2012. *The Making of Modern Liberalism*. Princeton, NJ: Princeton University Press.

Scattola, Merio. 2003. 'Before and After Natural Law: Models of Natural Law in Ancient and Modern Times'. In *Early Modern Natural Law Theories: Context and Strategies in the Early Enlightenment*, ed. T. J. Hochstrasser and P. Schröeder, 1–30. Dordrecht: Springer.

Schilling, Heinz. 1992. *Religion, Political Culture and the Emergence of Early Modern Society: Essays in German and Dutch History*. Leiden: Brill.

Schochet, Gordon J. 1969. 'The Family and the Origins of the State in Locke's Political Philosophy'. In *John Locke: Problems and Perspectives*, ed. John W. Yolton, 81–98. Cambridge: Cambridge University Press.

Schochet, Gordon J. 1971. 'Sir Robert Filmer: Some New Bibliographical Discoveries'. *The Library* 26 (2): 135–60.

Schochet, Gordon J. 1975. *Patriarchalism in Political Thought: The Authoritarian Family and Political Speculation and Attitudes Especially in Seventeenth-Century England*. Oxford: Basil Blackwell.

Schochet, Gordon J. 1996. 'Why Should History Matter? Political Theory and the History of Discourse'. In *The Varieties of British Political Thought, 1500–1800*, ed. J. G. A. Pocock, Gordon J. Schochet and Lois Schwoerer, 321–57. Cambridge: Cambridge University Press.

Schreiner, Susan E. 2001. *The Theatre of His Glory: Nature and the Natural Order in the Thought of John Calvin*. Grand Rapids, MI: Eerdmans.

Seagrave, S. Adam. 2015. 'Locke on the Law of Nature and Natural Rights'. In *A Companion to Locke*, ed. Matthew Stuart, 373–93. Chichester: Wiley-Blackwell.

Seligman, Adam B. 1992. *The Idea of Civil Society*. New York: Free Press.

Sheehan, Jonathan. 2016. 'Thomas Hobbes, D.D.: Theology, Orthodoxy, and History'. *The Journal of Modern History* 88 (2): 249–74.

Siedentop, Larry. 2014. *Inventing the Individual: The Origins of Western Liberalism*. Cambridge, MA: Belknap Press.

Simmons, A. John. 1992. *The Lockean Theory of Rights*. Princeton, NJ: Princeton University Press.

Skinner, Quentin. 1964. 'Hobbes's "Leviathan"'. *The Historical Journal* 7 (2): 321–32.

Skinner, Quentin. 1969. 'Meaning and Understanding in the History of Ideas'. *History and Theory* 8 (1): 3–53.

Skinner, Quentin. 1978. *The Foundations of Modern Political Thought.* 2 vols. Cambridge: Cambridge University Press.

Skinner, Quentin. 1996. *Reason and Rhetoric in the Philosophy of Hobbes.* Cambridge: Cambridge University Press.

Skinner, Quentin. 2002. *Visions of Politics,* vol. 1: *Regarding Method.* Cambridge: Cambridge University Press.

Skinner, Quentin. 2002. 'The Context for Hobbes's Theory of Obligation'. In Quentin Skinner, *Visions of Politics,* vol. 3: *Hobbes and Civil Science,* 264–86. Cambridge: Cambridge University Press.

Skinner, Quentin. 2002. 'Hobbes and the Purely Artificial Person of the State.' In Quentin Skinner, *Visions of Politics,* vol. 3: *Hobbes and Civil Science,* 177–208. Cambridge: Cambridge University Press.

Skinner, Quentin. 2005. 'Hobbes on Representation'. *European Journal of Philosophy* 13 (2): 155–83.

Smith, James K. A. 2017. *Awaiting the King: Reforming Public Theology.* Grand Rapids, MI: Baker Academic.

Sommerville, J. P. 1982. 'From Suarez to Filmer: A Reappraisal'. *The Historical Journal* 25 (3): 525–40.

Sommerville, J. P. 1983. 'Richard Hooker, Hadrian Saravia, and the Advent of the Divine Right of Kings'. *History of Political Thought* 4 (2): 229–45.

Sommerville, J. P. 1991. 'Absolutism and Royalism in the Seventeenth Century'. In *Cambridge History of Political Thought, 1450–1700,* ed. J. H. Burns and Mark Goldie, 347–73. Cambridge: Cambridge University Press.

Sommerville, J. P. 1992. *Thomas Hobbes: Political Ideas in Historical Context.* London: Macmillan.

Sorrell, Tom. 1991. *Hobbes.* London: Routledge.

Sorrell, Tom. 2007. 'Hobbes's Moral Philosophy'. In *The Cambridge Companion to Hobbes's Leviathan,* ed. Patricia Springborg, 128–53. Cambridge: Cambridge University Press.

Spellman, W. M. 1988. *John Locke and the Problem of Depravity.* Oxford: Clarendon Press.

Spragens, Thomas A. 1973. *The Politics of Motion: The World of Thomas Hobbes.* London: Croom Helm.

Stanton, Timothy. 2008. 'Hobbes and Locke on Natural Law and Jesus Christ'. *History of Political Thought* 29 (1): 65–88.

Stanton, Timothy. 2011. 'Authority and Freedom in the Interpretation of Locke's Political Theory'. *Political Theory* 39 (1): 6–30.

Stanton, Timothy. 2012. 'On (Mis)interpreting Locke: A Reply to Tate'. *Political Theory* 40 (2): 229–36.

Stanwood, P. G. 2008. 'Works and Editions I'. In *A Companion to Richard Hooker*, ed. W. J. Torrance Kirby, 27–39. Leiden: Brill.

Stein, Tine. 2018. 'The Böckenförde Dictum – On the Topicality of a Liberal Formula'. *Oxford Journal of Law and Religion* 7 (1): 97–108.

Stevenson Jr, William R. 2004. 'Calvin and Political Issues'. In *The Cambridge Companion to John Calvin*, ed. Donald K. McKim, 173–87. Cambridge: Cambridge University Press.

Stonebraker, Johnathan, and Sarah Irving. 2015. 'Natural Law and Protestantism: A Historical Reassessment and its Contemporary Significance'. *Oxford Journal of Law and Religion* 4 (3): 421–41.

Strauss, Leo. 1953. *Natural Right and History*. Chicago: Chicago University Press.

Strauss, Leo. 1958. 'Locke's Doctrine of Natural Law'. *The American Political Science Review* 52 (2): 490–501.

Strauss, Leo. 1959. 'On the Basis of Hobbes's Political Philosophy'. In Leo Strauss, *What is Political Philosophy?: And Other Studies*, 170–96. Westport, CT: Greenwood Press.

Strauss, Leo. 1963. *The Political Philosophy of Hobbes*. Chicago: University of Chicago Press.

Strauss, Leo, and Joseph Cropsey, eds. 1969. *History of Political Philosophy*. Chicago: Rand McNally & Company.

Systma, David S. 2014. 'Sir Matthew Hale (1609–1676) and Natural Law in the Seventeenth Century'. *Journal of Markets and Morality* 17 (1): 205–56.

Tate, John William. 2012. 'Locke, God and Civil Society: Response to Stanton'. *Political Theory* 40 (2): 222–28.

Tate, John William. 2013. 'Dividing Locke from God: The Limits of Theology in Locke's Political Philosophy'. *Philosophy and Social Criticism* 39 (2): 133–64.

Taylor, A. E. 1938. 'The Ethical Doctrine of Hobbes'. *Philosophy* 13 (52): 406–24.

Taylor, Charles. 2007. *A Secular Age*. Cambridge, MA: Belknap Press.

The Holy Bible. 2007. Wheaton: Crossway.

Thompson, Anthony B. 1998. 'Licensing the Press: The Career of G. R. Weckerlin during the Personal Rule of Charles I'. *The Historical Journal* 41 (3): 653–78.

Thompson, Martyn P. 2012. 'The Logic of the History of Ideas: Mark Bevir and Michael Oakeshott'. *Journal of the History of Ideas* 73 (4): 593–607.

Thornton, Helen. 2005. *State of Nature or Eden?: Thomas Hobbes and His Contemporaries on the Natural Condition of Human Beings*. Rochester, NY: University of Rochester Press.

Tollefsen, Christopher. 2017. 'Natural Law, Basic Goods and Practical Reason'. In *The Cambridge Companion to Natural Law Jurisprudence*, ed. George Duke and Robert P. George, 133–58. Cambridge: Cambridge University Press.

Torrance, T. F. 1988. 'Interpreting the Word by the Light of Christ or the Light of Nature? Calvin, Calvinism, and Barth'. In *Calviniana: Ideas and Influence of Jean Calvin*, ed. R. V. Schnucker, 255–67. Kirksville, MO: Sixteenth Century Journal Publishers.

Troeltsch, Ernst. 1992. *The Social Teaching of the Christian Churches*. Louisville, KY: Westminster/John Knox Press.

Trueman, Carl R. 2002. 'Luther and the Reformation in Germany'. In *The Reformation World*, ed. Andrew Pettegree, 73–96. Abingdon: Routledge.

Tuck, Richard. 1979. *Natural Rights Theories: Their Origin and Development*. Cambridge: Cambridge University Press.

Tuck, Richard. 1986. 'A New Date for Filmer's *Patriarcha*'. *The Historical Journal* 29 (1): 183–6.

Tuck, Richard. 1992. 'The Christian Atheism of Thomas Hobbes'. In *Atheism from the Reformation to the Enlightenment*, ed. Michael Hunter and David Wootton, 111–30. Oxford: Clarendon Press.

Tuck, Richard. 1996. 'Hobbes's Moral Philosophy'. In *The Cambridge Companion to Hobbes*, ed. Tom Sorrell, 175–207. Cambridge: Cambridge University Press.

Tuckness, Alex. 1999. 'The Coherence of a Mind: John Locke and the Law of Nature'. *Journal of the History of Philosophy* 37 (1): 73–90.

Tuininga, Matthew J. 2017. *Calvin's Political Theology and the Public Engagement of the Church: Christ's Two Kingdoms*. Cambridge: Cambridge University Press.

Tully, James. 1980. *A Discourse on Property: John Locke and his adversaries*. New York: Cambridge University Press.

VanDrunen, David. 2006. 'Medieval Natural Law and the Reformation: A Comparison of Aquinas and Calvin'. *American Catholic Philosophical Quarterly* 80 (1): 77–98.

VanDrunen, David. 2010. *Natural Law and the Two Kingdoms: A Study in the Development of Reformed Social Thought*. Grand Rapids, MI: Eerdmans.

Vogt, Katja. 2016. 'Seneca'. In *The Stanford Encyclopedia of Philosophy*, ed. Edward N. Zalta. Accessed at https://plato.stanford.edu/archives/win2016/entries/seneca/.

Vorster, Nico. 2015. 'Symbiotic Anthropology and Politics in a Postmodern Age: Rethinking the Political Philosophy of Johannes Althusius'. *Renaissance and Reformation* 38 (2): 27–52.

Vorster, Nico. 2016. '"United but not Confused": Calvin's Anthropology as Hermeneutical Key to Understanding his Societal Doctrine'. *Journal of Church and State* 58 (1): 117–41.

Waldron, Jeremy. 2002. *God, Locke, and Equality*. Cambridge: Cambridge University Press.

Wallace, John M. 1980. 'The Date of Robert Filmer's *Patriarcha*'. *The Historical Journal* 23 (1): 155–65.

Wallace, Ronald S. 1959. *Calvin's Doctrine of the Christian Life*. Edinburgh: Oliver and Boyd.

Walzer, Michael. 1966. *The Revolution of the Saints: A Study in the Origins of Radical Politics*. London: Weidenfeld & Nicolson.

Warrender, Howard. 1970. *The Political Philosophy of Hobbes: His Theory of Obligation*. Oxford: Clarendon Press.

Watkins, J. N. W. 1973. *Hobbes's System of Ideas: A Study in the Political Significance of Philosophical Theories*. London: Hutchinson University Library Press.

Weber, Max. 2001. *The Protestant Ethic and the Spirit of Capitalism*. Trans. Talcott Parsons. Abingdon: Routledge.

Weithman, Paul. 2014. 'Augustine's Political Philosophy'. In *The Cambridge Companion to Augustine*, 234–52. Cambridge: Cambridge University Press.

Wendel, François. 1963. *Calvin: The Origins and Development of His Thought*. London: Collins.

West, Thomas G. 2012. 'The Ground of Locke's Law of Nature'. *Social Philosophy and Policy* 29 (2): 1–50.

Whaley, Joachim. 2011. *Germany and the Holy Roman Empire*, vol. 1: *Maximilian I to the Peace of Westphalia*. Oxford: Oxford University Press.

Witte, John. 2007. *The Reformation of Rights: Law, Religion and Human Rights in Early Modern Calvinism*. Cambridge: Cambridge University Press.

Witte, John. 2009. 'A Demonstrative Theory of Natural Law: Johannes Althusius and the Rise of Calvinist Jurisprudence'. *Ecclesiastical Law Journal* 11 (3): 248–65.

Witte, John. 2018. 'The Universal Rule of Natural Law and Written Constitutions in the Thought of Johannes Althusius'. In *Morality and Responsibility of Rulers: European and Chinese Origins of a Rule of Law as Justice for World Order*, ed. Anthony Carty and Janne Nijman, 167–86. Oxford: Oxford University Press.

Wood, Neal. 1983. *The Politics of Locke's Philosophy: A Social Study of 'An Essay Concerning Human Understanding'*. Berkeley: University of California Press.

Yolton, John W. 1958. 'Locke on the Law of Nature'. *The Philosophical Review* 67 (4): 477–98.

Yolton, John W., ed. 1969. *John Locke: Problems and Perspectives*. Cambridge: Cambridge University Press.

Zagorin, Perez. 2009. *Hobbes and the Law of Nature*. Princeton, NJ: Princeton University Press.

Zuckert, Michael P., and Catherine H. Zuckert. 2014. *Leo Strauss and the Problem of Political Philosophy*. Chicago: Chicago University Press.

# Index

EU representative:
Easy Access System Europe
Mustamäe tee 50, 10621 Tallinn, Estonia
Gpsr.requests@easproject.com